DURKHEIM IN DIALOGUE

Methodology and History in Anthropology

General Editors: David Parkin, Fellow of All Souls College, University of Oxford
David Gellner, Fellow of All Souls College, University of Oxford

DURKHEIM IN DIALOGUE

A Centenary Celebration of
The Elementary Forms of Religious Life

Edited by
Sondra L. Hausner

berghahn
NEW YORK · OXFORD
www.berghahnbooks.com

First published in 2013 by

Berghahn Books

www.berghahnbooks.com

© 2013, 2017 Sondra L. Hausner
First paperback edition published in 2017

Library of Congress Cataloging-in-Publication Data

Durkheim in dialogue : a centenary celebration of the elementary forms
of religious life / edited by Sondra L. Hausner.
    pages cm. — (Methodology and history in anthropology)
    Includes bibliographical references and index.
    ISBN 978-1-78238-021-4 (hardback) — ISBN 978-1-78533-345-3
(paperback) — ISBN 978-1-78238-022-1 (ebook)
    1. Durkheim, Émile, 1858–1917. Formes élémentaires de la vie
religieuse. English 2. Religion. 3. Totemism. 4. Cults. 5. Rites and
ceremonies. I. Hausner, Sondra L.
    GN470.D8D87 2013
    306.6—dc23

                                                              2013015470

British Library Cataloguing in Publication Data

A catalogue record for this book is available from the British Library

ISBN 978-1-78238-021-4 (hardback)
ISBN 978-1-78533-345-3 (paperback)
ISBN 978-1-78238-022-1 (ebook)

For my father, Bernard Hausner (1934–2012), with love

CONTENTS

ILLUSTRATIONS

Figures

Tables

ACKNOWLEDGEMENTS

The planning for this collection began at the Institute of Social and Cultural Anthropology at Oxford in 2011, just prior to the 2012 centenary of the text in whose honour it was written. I am grateful to Nick Allen, David Gellner and Wendy James for including me in their thinking at that time, and for their subsequent efforts corralling the very best thinkers in these fields to contribute. With characteristic and tireless graciousness, W.S.J. (Bill) Pickering made us feel that the publication was a worthwhile endeavour, in line with the work of the British Centre for Durkheimian Studies, and that our efforts might be useful to Durkheimians for many generations to come.

No publication can come to fruition without the support and logistical help of many people. My colleagues in the Faculty of Theology and Religion at Oxford, especially Mark Edwards and Johannes Zachhuber, were excited about the book and the unanticipated merging of the humanities and the social sciences that it might speak to. Alison Wiblin at St. Peter's College effortlessly submitted the first and the last drafts of the manuscript to Berghahn at a moment's notice, and Kate Atherton at the Institute of Social and Cultural Anthropology offered critical help with coordination. Anita Murdoch provided an excellent index. Most especially, the authors of the chapters in the book were patient with their editor's erratic deadlines and detailed demands. I hope they will feel that the final publication reflects the best of their superlative thinking.

Three special sets of thanks are due to people without whom this book would never have come about. First, David Parkin supported the manuscript in full, and his comments have immeasurably helped the final draft; his encouragement for this volume and elsewhere has made it possible for me to be at Oxford. Second, Marion Berghahn at Berghahn Books was generous in her willingness to think about how we could get a publication to press in a short time period, Ann Przyzycki DeVita was an unwavering voice of encouragement, Lauren Weiss and Jaime Taber were always helpful, and Adam Capitanio and Elizabeth Berg were models of support and patience. And finally, I must acknowledge my intellectual debts to my ancestors. A. Thomas Kirsch introduced me to the wonders of Durkheimian sociology at Cornell University's Department of Anthropology in the late 1990s. Melvin Hausner, mathematician and uncle extraordinaire, taught me set theory when I was very young. The book is dedicated to my father, Bernard Hausner, who knew the great potential – and the limits – of knowledge in the social sciences, and also that all such knowledge pales in the pursuit of wisdom.

DURKHEIM IN DISCIPLINARY DIALOGUE

Sondra L. Hausner

Emile Durkheim's claim to being the father of sociology lies in his insistence that a model developed on the basis of one set of data may then be applied to many – ideally all – others. From the time Durkheim's most mature work, *The Elementary Forms of Religious Life* (*Les Formes Élémentaires de la Vie Religieuse*), was published in 1912, this premise has been the basis of social science. Even though we are not 'pure' scientists, social theorists posit hypotheses that must be tested in the face of emerging empirical evidence. These models either stand the test of time, as it were, proving themselves resilient and useful in the interpretation of new data, or they crumble in the face of evidence that shows they simply cannot explain the world as we thought they might. By taking up the premises of Durkheimian sociology a century on, we prod the social sciences of religion as far as we can.

The chapters in this book take up Durkheim's central premise in the sociology of religion – that religion is a social form that will continue to define a mode of human communication and connectedness – and continue to test it, in multiple contexts, with different bodies of evidence and from the vantage point of numerous theoretical and historical critiques. The volume was designed as an effort to commemorate the centenary anniversary of the publication of *The Elementary Forms of Religious Life*, which remains one of the core textbooks in sociology and has become a key source for understanding the study of religion (Durkheim 1995 [1912]). This collection brings together scholars from a range of disciplines to explore just how widely

Durkheim's legacy is felt in the natural, social and cultural sciences, present and past, and to consider the extent to which his description of religion as a social form may still be productively used. Sociology has come a long way in its first century and may, as in this volume, be seen alongside and even as the foundation of work on religion in anthropology and cognitive science, in addition to the core disciplines that Durkheim built upon in his time, namely archaeology, ethnology and political philosophy. Our findings, approaches, priorities and objects of study have changed a great deal over the last hundred years, but the methods and theories that Durkheim set out in 1912 remain quietly central, though often unacknowledged, in our contemporary multidisciplinary investigations.

In 2012, much substantive and methodological work (in not only the social sciences but also the psychological or cognitive sciences and even the humanities) can be traced, explicitly or implicitly, to *The Elementary Forms of Religious Life.* A philosopher by training, Durkheim based his model of the twinned nature of religion and society upon then recently released ethnographic accounts of Aboriginal life. His 1912 text set forth new innovations in both method, in that he was determined that society could be studied scientifically with a careful understanding of ethnographic material that could provide useful data, and theory, in that he had become convinced that at the heart of any social group were its shared categories, or sets of symbols, that also formed the essence of religious thought. From there, the world of social theory opened up, such that we may investigate every aspect of the person and every arena of socio-religious life, including ideology, cognition and experience.

These subtle interpretations of Durkheim's work are not always reflected in the contemporary teaching of *Elementary Forms.* Although discussions of sacred and profane are everywhere in contemporary public life and the terms are instantly recognizable, they are rarely attributed. This famous Durkheimian polarity may not, perhaps, reflect a perfect binary division in all cases, but it remains a seminal distinction in understanding the categorical dualisms that came to underpin French structuralism, feminist theory and linguistic, discursive and praxis-based models of social worlds and human realities. As a global category of identity, religion is arguably more important, not less, than it was a century ago, and yet definitions of the sacred are no further advanced (Pickering 2002: 32f.). If we wish to understand why this is so, we might well return to Durkheim's classic text, which reminds us that it is the category, not the content, of the sacred that matters so consistently to human populations across the ages.

Although we claim the discussion here is interdisciplinary, what follows is largely constituted by the various sub-disciplines of anthropology. Sociology is our progenitor, in the father figure of Durkheim; from this disciplinary starting point, we move outward to discuss the dynamics of ritual, the structures of mind, theories and histories of warfare and the tenets of human evolution. While social anthropology is at the heart of the volume, we draw on and contribute to cultural studies, history and archaeology in our conversations with the multiple theoretical fields that place religion at the core of their analyses. Sociological narratives are set alongside philosophical queries, so that anthropology – the analysis of particular cultural forms with an eye to the human condition more broadly – acts as an empirical and theoretical mediator, as Durkheim would have wanted.

Religion

The chapters in this volume argue that Durkheim's theoretical model of and for religion is still good to think with, even though a century has passed since he offered it, and the world has changed in multiple ways. What might surprise us, as scholars of religion and theorists of the social form at large, is that Durkheim's model is as good or better than it ever was, insofar as he can help us explain new modes of religion, or ways of being religious (or social), that he never encountered and that no one would have conceived of a century ago. Nationalist fronts, new religious movements and modern and postmodern forms of group formation – including cults, group associations, humanists, atheists, secularists and artists who claim to be anti-religious (never mind football clubs, rock concerts and Facebook) – need only look to *Elementary Forms* to understand the social dynamics at work, whether or not we (or they) call it religion. The capacity of a theory of religion to explain forms of collective life whose members refuse to call themselves religious presents us with a paradox of definition that is part and parcel of Durkheim's intention: to what extent may religion be considered a core feature of human collectivity? What is called a religion by whom? This secondary question (different from the one Durkheim set out to solve but no less salient today), grounded in contemporary cultural politics, emerges from a growing global consciousness about the potency of the human bonds on which we all depend. These are the social emotions that Durkheim placed at the centre of his work.

We might conceive of Durkheim's core problematic as one of set theory: how much individual cognition – or the sense of identity that attaches to it – is shared by the collective to which a person belongs? The problem is one of categorization, and it grows out of the central question of cognitive classification in *Elementary Forms*. How is a social group defined or delimited, that is, where does the group boundary end, and who draws it in the symbolic sand? To what extent are rules of social and conceptual logic shared between the most so-called primitive human societies and the most seemingly advanced, in the form of the French Republic? This is set theory as applied to human sociology: Durkheim asks us first to establish the formative relations between the individual and his or her collective, and then to scale up the model such that each collective may also be understood as an individual or holistic entity in relation to the whole of human society.

Religion is both the core of the analysis and a tool for thinking about human collectivity in general. Religiosity and sociality (and spirituality, too, which is no different) are equally significant in the theoretical framework Durkheim gives us. This equivalence has been the cause of some consternation on both sides: from the theological perspective, religion is seen as 'reduced' to a social set of meanings; from the sociological perspective, religion is seen as insufficient as a base explanation or definition of many social phenomena, including (and perhaps especially) secularism. These equations misconstrue what Durkheim intends to show: that religion is primary, and perhaps universal, because it is the mechanism that enables collectives to bind together. Theological premises are not undone by such a position: what is rather offered is the possibility that theologies – in all their human variety – share a use value; they need not be posited against each other but understood as viable means for social health. Nor is sociological work in fields other than religion maligned; instead, religion is shown to be a human activity that grounds other spheres of social life insofar as it is understood as the very capacity of the human mind to distinguish between orders of experience.

Theologians may worry that explaining the mechanisms of something called religion somehow undoes or undermines it, or that understanding how religion serves a social purpose (and why it is as effective as it is) will somehow expose belief as an edifice or falsity, like the Wizard of Oz standing small and meek behind his curtain. But this logic does not do justice to Durkheim – or to the human beings he seeks to describe. We give of ourselves to the totem, or to God, and in so doing, we create collectivities, of ourselves and for ourselves; from our beliefs and the gods that we pray to, we become people. To understand this process is not to undermine it: in the Durkheimian reading, people do not see or believe in a deity that is not there; they see and feel a force that *is*. That human societies create – and feel bonded by – their God or their gods might be taken as the core of human experience, including moments of extraordinary spiritual effervescence. Durkheim not only explains how religion and religious institutions serve as the glue of human societies but also, possibly, gives us a clue as to the source of individual (as well as collective) mystical experience. No theologian or sociologist could disagree that we gain strength from knowing who we belong to, whether we draw from totemic, divine or human realms.

Durkheim famously argues that all religions are true. He must argue from this intellectual position because his work is premised on the insistence that all peoples are capable of working from the basic structures of human logic. If his intention were to undermine the weight of religion in the world, we would expect the oft-heard opposite assertion that all religions are false. Durkheim argues that religions cannot be false: they work, as they are meant to (and there is nothing duplicitous about their function). What he seeks is a model whereby any cultural form can emerge as logically coherent, encoded in its premises of belief. This position requires a true ecumenism – the acknowledgement that another religion is as true to its members as the theologian's is to him.

Political or social scientists interested in alternative social formations may worry about the opposite pole, namely that Durkheim does not allow for the secularist position that seems all too apparent in the world today. Again, this critique misconstrues the central problematic of *Elementary Forms*: collectivity *is* religion, even, ironically, in the form of secularism. Such an equation undermines neither society nor religiosity (although scholars who care more about one pole or the other fear it unbalances their side, failing to see the strength that accrues to both sides through their linkage). Durkheim thus explains the primacy and endurance of religion in the modern world (even or especially when secularism forms part of a global political discourse) as that which enables our social selves.

Is this position tautological? If religion is that which keeps society going, are we obliged to see religion where we see society? If an avowedly secularist society is considered religious in the Durkheimian rendering, is there room for sociality outside of religion? Certainly, for Durkheim, such a construction is not theoretically possible, as he locates the sticky bonds of social life in religious thought, those shared categories that he considers central to the emergence of both society and religion. It is in these structures of thought that Durkheim locates the central dynamic of human life (which must be collective): it is both religion and society. To equate society with religion is not a tautology, then, but a transitive relation. We cannot be social without being religious, insofar as we draw our sense of ourselves from common meaning, and we cannot be religious without being social, even if some of the most intense religious practices may be undertaken in isolation. Beliefs and practices alike are drawn from a collective pool.

Durkheim is interested in how human minds work, and his answer, in brief, is through a set of categories or matrix for seeing the world. Religion is thus a phenomenon that must be traced to human minds (in opposition to doctrine, but not, significantly, in opposition to God). Far from negating religious experience, Durkheim appears to take effervescent, mystical and otherworldly experiences and accounts at face value. The human psyche is capable of transcendent life not because of institutions, but despite them – as evidenced by the primitive society he uses as his test case. Far from insisting that such experiences are the purview of particular or unusual individuals, he goes further to suggest that such experiences may emerge precisely through the influence and effects of collective life. God is not denigrated in this equation: He is simply refracted into the many bodies that make up society, like the proverbial multiple drops of humanity that together form the Hindu oceanic divine.

Method and Theory

Durkheim's methods have been and remain the subject of much critique, including by some of the authors of the chapters in this volume. Students today are wont to call him a 'reductionist' or, critically, an 'armchair anthropologist', although he wrote *Elementary Forms* a decade before anthropology became a discipline of actual fieldwork upon Malinowski's unwitting but perhaps fortuitous stranding in the Pacific. Many worry that Durkheim did not correctly read his sources (the ethnographic diaries of Spencer and Gillen), or that he drew his own inferences from them without acknowledging the diversity of practices in Aboriginal societies. Even staunch Durkheimians question him on some of these points. In this volume, for example, Watts Miller suggests the material he used from the ethnographic record was selectively drawn to prove his theoretical point, and Chau exposes what he calls Durkheim's 'conceptual sleight of hand' in that he allowed the data from a particular society to stand in or become the model for a universal form of society.

Ironically, these critiques lie at the very heart of the science that Durkheim wished to develop and apply to social life: he would be proud of his protégés. Developing a general model of society, derived from the empirical evidence of life in a particular society, that might work as a lens through which to analyse other societies (analogous to a model of religion that might equally be drawn from and used as a way of understanding the multiplicity of religions) is the challenge he set himself. If he has come up with a theory that stands the test of further empirical evidence, more power to it. If new data emerges to bend it out of shape, the model will have to adjust. Data from a particular case becomes theory that might – or might not – be generalizable, with an acknowledgement that moving from the particular to the general may alter the terms.

This dialogue or dialectic, intrinsic to the methods of *Elementary Forms*, is what grounds the social sciences today, making data useful and theories dynamic. If a previously generalizable theory is shown to fail or falter in light of new evidence, the theory must be modified. Here lies the power of data, which is otherwise meaningless beyond the nugget of information it contributes to the encyclopaedia of human ephemera. Yet a theory that is promoted with no evidence is nothing beyond a thought experiment. Concrete data and conceptual theory must exist in conversation with each other, each refining the other: theory gives meaning to the interpretation of data; data grounds the details of theory. Ultimately, this social scientific project is what Durkheim wished to establish with the publication of *Elementary Forms* (see Allen, Pickering and Watts Miller 1998).

By pursuing the methods of advanced knowledge, we may come to understand the bases of human thought, from which we have built ourselves up and will continue to develop into the future, for our cognitive capacity has no end. But this is not a call for science to trump religion: if religion can be identified through a scientific process of investigation (even the sort that depends on only one experiment), we need not conclude that God is false. On the contrary: *Elementary Forms* testifies to not only the presence of religion, but also the presence of God. Religion *exists*, and God *exists*, everywhere, among human beings. Indeed, human beings cannot live without a god, or God, or the gods. We are the god we worship, as every church in history has proclaimed.

Perhaps even more significant for the Western philosophical tradition is that religion in *Elementary Forms* gives us reason. In this volume, Fields reminds us that '[w]hen human beings learned to sophisticate perception with conception, however bizarre the result, they gained the intuition that internal relations may exist between externally disparate things. Durkheim claimed that religion thus made philosophy and science possible.' Science and religion implicate each other in *Elementary Forms*, each giving rise to the other. The chapters in this volume take Durkheim's methodological dialectics to their full expression in a contemporary world, drawn from cases as far-flung as China and Africa, and applied to contexts as varied as Star Trek and rebel insurgencies. Each case aims to push or pull or deploy or debate the core conceptual frameworks set forth in *Elementary Forms* (and the authors sometimes disagree as to how successful those frames are). There is no single disciplinary method used by the contributors to this book. But each piece takes on the basic, critical dialogue between data – whether it be ethnographic narrative, television script, historical archive or human bone – and theory, to come to a potentially universal conclusion about the human race and its relation to religion. This dialectical construction lies at the heart of Durkheimian social science because, he intimates, it reflects the mechanism of the human mind, just as religion does.

What follows applies Durkheimian theory to the exigencies of war, in the case of ethnographic work in Sierra Leone (Richards) or the historical archives of colonial Sudan (Baumann). Durkheim himself is set into his own historical time by the intellectual genealogies of a moral social order (Ji), mental representations (Stedman Jones) and the potential links between religion and society writ large (Watts Miller). The uses of *Elementary Forms'* theoretical framework are expanded outward in time, to see if they might apply to contemporary popular culture (Child) or archaeological deep history (Gamble). And the model itself is probed further (Allen), in dialogue with other major theorists of the twentieth century (Hausner) or in possible parallel with other sociological categories, such as race (Fields).

The book is divided into five parts, including an opening and a closing chapter, and three substantive sections that reflect Durkheim's main theoretical contributions. The first of these, *Social Forms* (Part II), focuses on the classic collectives in three rather non-classical forms. Together, discussions of the role of religion in the post-communist Chinese state, the solidarity that emerges from ritual initiations into African youth militia and the interrogation of television as a cultural form investigate the various ways collectives may be understood in contemporary contexts.

The next section of the book, *Collective Minds* (Part III), takes up the possibility that Durkheim gives more weight to individual members of society – or at least their mental capacities – than is commonly understood (see also Watts Miller 1996). As Durkheim argues, society as an abstract form cannot exist anywhere but in the minds of individual people; his great innovation was to enquire whether that abstract form might be collectively produced, as a reflection and also enabler of the social form itself. At stake here is whether the sacred/profane dichotomy lies at the base of the human mind – or whether that binary distinction may ground complex systems of classification. If the human mind may be cognitively mapped, does it follow that we might trace it back in human history to the origins of the species itself? Is the mind the root of human sociality?

The last section, *Effervescence* (Part IV), looks at the ritual dynamics that Durkheim places at the core of the interaction between any individual and his or her collective. What is that mechanism, and might we look to Freud to help us understand it? And what of agency: must effervescence imply the continuity of a social form, or might it enable historical change in its liminal, transformative capacity? Finally, is it enough to consider human beings in ritual – or might we claim that, in a different cultural context or festival form, we need to hear the voices of all the beings present in order to understand fully the effervescent emotions that produce collective life? Here, in this final set of essays, effervescence is offered up as the mode (totemic, narrative, festive) through which collective minds become social forms.

Chapters of the Book

Karen Fields, the translator of a recent English edition of *Elementary Forms*, opened Durkheim up to a new generation of anglophone scholars that would read his dynamic assertions about perennial tensions – between the particular and the general, the part and the whole, the case and the model, the cultural and the universal – in her evocative, sensitive language. Are the Arunta the same as the French, or not? Fields brings her own voice to this volume, where she explores soul as a universal referent for Durkheim. If soul is present in every society, 'so, too, is blood', Fields reminds us. Soul may be the way Durkheim knows that religion is everywhere, for it is both the evidence and the result of religion. And blood – the blood of a person, the blood of a race – may be understood as both that which binds and that which demands social action. In Fields's account, blood becomes a symbolic stand-in for science in the politics of race segregation histories in the United States, pushing us to reconsider what, actually, determines the contours of a socially defined group, and the extent to which

Durkheim's famous answer – religion – might be seen as precisely traversing the divide between nature and culture.

The next chapter, which opens the group of essays in Part II, investigates a different location, but it is impelled by the same passionate determination to consider the constitution of society with a clear – and a just – eye. Recalling the potential of the Durkheimian collective, Ji Zhe calls on his readers to be vigilant about the make-up and rule of a social order, using the case of China as a state where, in some historical instances, solidarity has been imposed rather than emerging organically, a state of affairs that will never be satisfactory. Ji uses Durkheim's own comparative method to bring the political philosophy of Rousseau (as interpreted by Durkheim, and then by American sociologist Robert Bellah) together with that of China, both in its 'traditional' guise (although tradition can be invoked in many ways and for many reasons) and in the form of contemporary Chinese politics. Those who claim Confucianism is a kind of Chinese contemporary civil religion must do so in the spirit of a just and voluntary polity, not as a patriotic statement that demands a singular set of morals to underscore the state's regime.

State and rebel politics also ground Paul Richards's consideration of the mechanisms of warfare in Sierra Leone in the third chapter of the volume. Rather than political philosophy, however, Richards uses the work of cognitive scientists studying sound and dance to indicate how unity may arise from shared sense experiences. Richards considers how social formations of even the most violent or terrifying variety – the initiation of child soldiers – may draw precisely on Durkheimian notions of solidarity. He reopens the question of the piacular rite and reminds us of the possibility that violence or trauma may, ironically, serve the same purpose of social cohesion that joyous effervescence is usually thought to.

Louise Child's essay stays in the realm of blood sacrifice, though not in the literal sense. Child draws our attention to the relationships between blood and solidarity as popularly represented tropes in the American television serial *The Sopranos*. Her analysis also shows how collective perceptions of time may be what unify a social group – on this planet or in outer space, as represented in the television series *Deep Space Nine*. Sacred time, as experienced by a character who departs from his regular social milieu, is precisely 'without differentiation'. The collective experience of shared temporality can be the ground of mystical transformation, whereby the individual finds the collective within himself. By exploring both literal and metaphorical or psychological cases, the television dramas that are the focus of

Child's analysis are able to deliver her Durkheimian interpretations of the moral tensions inherent in a social order that requires solidarity to survive but also uses mechanisms such as therapy to cultivate individual wholeness.

Part III begins with N.J. Allen's piece, which distils the essence of the Durkheimian contribution to thinking about the human mind. Even if we acknowledge that the sacred/profane dichotomy is not always or purely an operative distinction (the River Ganges is both the holiest body of water and a good place to wash), the opposition gives us a binary with which to cognize. *Elementary Forms* contains the very roots of structuralism in social theory (de Saussure had written his famous lectures on linguistics eight years before its publication). In this volume, Allen identifies Durkheim's distinction between the sacred and the profane – the logic of oppositional thinking – as a fundamental contribution to the way the human sciences understand the functioning of human societies. From this logic springs an understanding of the way kinship works (taken to its logical conclusion by Lévi-Strauss), as well as the possibility that social structure may be correlated to the structures of the human mind.

Clive Gamble asks whether such social insights might have helped us understand deep human time as well as the depth of the human mind. But the history of archaeology has, until recently, pre-empted the Durkheimian model: 'the suggestion that religion would be familiar not because it was Christian but because it was social countered the very impulse that justified the search.' Although the human capacity for symbolic representation – and indeed, totemism itself – were all the rage in archaeology at the turn of the twentieth century, Durkheim was largely ignored as an interpretative scholar, although he might well have furthered our analysis of these principles. Gamble attempts to right this historical oversight, suggesting that Durkheimian theory might have advanced archaeological thinking about early human religious practice and social configuration. Even in a field where it has been largely overlooked, *Elementary Forms* still has contributions to make.

Susan Stedman Jones takes us back to the era of the text's publication, looking at reviews published in 1913. She wonders, a century later, whether *Elementary Forms* was misunderstood, even by some of anthropology's luminaries, who did not quite intuit the structuralist inklings of the work. The delicate balance of theory and ethnography was the focus of most of the reception of the book at the time, such that the philosophical force of the ideas encoded therein were in a sense delayed in coming in to their full intellectual potential (arguably until Lévi-Strauss recovered them in a reclaiming of cognitive binary thinking half a century later). Early anthropologists, though heavily influenced by the notion of collective solidarity, seemed to misread the text, emphasizing weakly interpreted ethnographic data. For example, Malinowski, an innovator in the field, critiques him but does not seem up to the task of using the theoretical or conceptual advancements that Durkheim offers in methodological stead. Representations – the categories – as the basis of religion are fully explored here.

Stedman Jones reminds us that categories of cultural meaning are both projected outward into public domains and interpreted inwardly by the humans that inhabit them. Durkheim was deeply concerned with the inner (*le dedans*) and its relation with the outer (*le dehors*): to assume that only the collective form interested him wilfully misunderstands his intention to describe the complete social process at work. Both Gamble and Stedman Jones regard Durkheim's work as pioneering in its ability to understand the way human beings relate to each other through lenses of representation, and even symbolic imaginaries. What they hint at is how Durkheim lays the groundwork for the social science of the future, which would become primarily concerned with questions of identity, in terms of how people see themselves as individuals, groups or both, and also how they project or represent those selves to others (Barth 1969). These kinds of self-projections, or practices (or performances, in some renderings), are multilayered. They are aspects of the mind that are inextricably connected to the way people act or behave in the world: representation is not – and cannot be – separate from action. The essays in this section point to how cognitive mechanisms, far from being ignored by the text, are at the heart of Durkheim's analysis.

Here we emerge with possibilities for the future of cognitive science in the history and heart of sociology: how do human minds work, individually and in collectivity? There is a psychological dimension to the way we function, especially in the capacity of creative effervescence. Durkheim has been critiqued for giving insufficient attention to the individual in his weighting of the collective, but the authors here suggest that individual minds – cognitive processes – are also considered in *Elementary Forms* if we care to look for them. In Part IV, Sondra Hausner continues by interrogating where, in the cycle of collective to individual to collective, we find the possibility of agency. Against the frequent critique that Durkheim prioritizes the collective over the individual, she reclaims the role of the individual in his analysis. The collective cannot exist but for the minds of individuals: as Durkheim famously argues, it is the interaction between the individual and the collective that makes the whole system work. Lest we forget, 'Man is double.'

Any detailed ethnographic case will tell the story of individuals. Gerd Baumann acts as both an ethnographer and a historian in his case history of the Sudan, a story that continues today. In the unfolding of any event, or the description of any set of collective actions, individual choices are made and individual actions are conducted. These decisions and acts may defer to collective ideologies or defy them; they may be demonstrations of allegiance or aggression. Whether they are experienced or interpreted as such depends on the exigencies of the situation and the context, as well as the collective set of representations on which the culture of the particular group depends. The Durkheimian method of generality does not foreclose particularity; on the contrary, the capacity to generalize depends precisely upon the availability of material with which to assert the model, much as the events of history depend upon the individuals who live it, be they colonial administrators, rebels or historical archivists.

If particularity is all, Adam Chau pulls our appreciation of Durkheim into the festival arena of modern Taiwan. Chau insists that in describing the kind of event that is sure to inspire human effervescence, we must recall all the elements of such a collective gathering, including the food, animals, winds and smells of a particular space-time. An effervescent event cannot be adequately represented without these sensory overloads, he intimates, nor are humans the only species to consider in our analyses of ritual: collective effervescence, it turns out, is a ritual experience on much more than the human level. From the kind of ethnography that he describes as 'red hot', Chau gives us a sense (literally) of all the living (and dead) beings present at the Righteous Martyrs Festival in Xinpu, Taiwan. His descriptions evoke a sense of being there at the festival, such that we develop a subjective intuition of how it is that collective effervescence works at all: the heat, the liquid, the pulsations and the dynamism all play a part in producing the social event that Durkheim and his legacy point to. Chau worries that the ethnographic voice has been subordinated to the theoretical or philosophical work of *Elementary Forms*, and he wishes to bring it – or rather, the occasions that inspire it – right back up to the surface. The feeling of the festival is evoked through the narratives of a giant pig, a crocodile (both of whom are killed during the ritual event, but whose narratives need not be cut short by virtue of moving between the worlds), a betel nut, an iron frame (used to hold the pig once it is on display), a ghost and, finally, the collective advocate of the group of martyrs in whose honour the entire event is performed and experienced.

Effervescence was not always a productive force for Durkheim. In the final chapter of this volume, W. Watts Miller carefully takes us through the evolution of Durkheim's concern with effervescence, which slowly evolved in his own thinking to become a positive force for the stability of society. Watts Miller plays with Durkheim's temporalities: we learn how, by changing location from ancient Israel to Australia, Durkheim moves backward in evolutionary time to find the essence of the theory. He can also move forward in evolutionary time to the French Republic: to his great and enduring credit, he deliberately draws out the parallels between the ideologies of Republican secularism and clan-based or totemic life. They stretch into an evolutionary timeline of humanity's past, present and future, reflecting his confidence in the universal capacity of the human mind. Collective mind is remarkably stable in this evolutionary historical model; what changes through time is its chosen expression.

In situating Durkheim historically, Watts Miller leaves us with a reminder that the theoretical innovation in *Elementary Forms* is itself indebted to anthropologists of religion of its own time, particularly James Frazer. Durkheim criticizes Frazer, of course, for assuming a difference between science and religion (if not between magic and religion). But Watts Miller indicates that it is Frazer's insistence that religion and society are two sides of the same coin that makes its way into the heart of *Elementary Forms* as a theory of the 'indivisibility of social and religious life'. Frazer leaves the insight untouched, letting it take hold in Durkheim's intellectual and methodological imagination. Frazer has taken his rightful place in the history of anthropological thinking on religion as a great cataloguer of religious and symbolic practices, but it is Durkheim who has left us with a theory – a philosophical attempt – to consider the place of human beings in the religions they create.

A philosopher eminently concerned with historical and ultimately social situatedness, Durkheim did not, as is often wrongly assumed, ignore the specificity of temporal location, or the way things change over time. The accusations of fixity, stasis or synchrony may not adequately allow for the deep changes that are inherent in his evolutionary (or even historical) view. But more importantly, they may not adequately consider Durkheim's awareness of the dynamism within social structure. Effervescence may keep social forms alive and constant, in one sense, but it also implies flow and fluidity, change and shift, as fundamental principles of human life, even when they are meant to keep things recognizably themselves.

Durkheim for the Next Century

Minds can be individual, or collective, or both. The possibility of historical shift that Durkheim hints at is more readily understood at the level of deep time, and the repeated cognitive processes that, taken together, explain the evolution of the human race. These are the layers and layers of representations that Stedman Jones equates with the categories, the shared bases of *a conscience collective*, which must, by definition, be in flux as an interactive product of the individual minds that together constitute the collective one. For Durkheim, the main difference between primitive and modern societies might be thought of as one of layering: the basic structures of mind might be the same, but the more modern the society, the more self-conscious its members become – and the more layers of representation emerge to account for its complexity.

As a whole, this book pushes Durkheimian theory to its current ethnographic and theoretical limits. Chau's evocation of sense in a Chinese festival – what it is like to be the crocodile getting gutted, or the betel nut being chewed – reminds us once again that an event is in the eye (or the gut) of the beholder. Data, whatever its form, must be digested through an interpreter, whoever that may be. Whether we perceive a social fact correctly depends precisely on our capacity to distinguish mystification (when we convince ourselves to take the representation for the referent) from mysticism (when we have understood the category in all its layers, or where there is no deeper place to go, for we have understood its essence). Durkheim's unique brilliance is his insistence that there is both a universal truth and manifold possible representations of it. Multiple forms of social life, both elementary and elemental, are no less correct when removed in time or in space (as was he from his own data). The primitive aspect, not limited to so-called primitive societies, is to be caught up in the categories themselves, or to be unwilling or unable to see their very malleability or refractive capacity.

Composition is a theme that emerges repeatedly in these chapters, as the process of producing a social form from symbolic representations demands it. For Chau, 'compositional assemblage' is the way to understand the festival dynamics that underscore effervescence. For Richards, 'compositional resources' are a way to understand the energy, produced by effervescent events, that collectivities want and need to harness, insofar as it can be redirected in all kinds of ways depending on who the 'group' is understood to include. In both contexts, we are reminded that although we tend to think of agency as individualistic, it may equally be thought of as collective action, in the form of ritual. How and by whom collectives are determined or defined – as far as which kinds of humans or other beings count in a social universe – are the variable terms of the equation. The particular ways groups are confirmed in their compositions, or to what end they are cultivated by their respective rituals, will be the subject of much future work in the social sciences and the humanities.

This volume is a different kind of composition. Each of the authors has studied Durkheim on his or her own terms, using his or her own favourite edition or translation. These essays reveal the kinds of intellectual debates that contemporary Durkheimians are grappling with in their own disciplinary fields and fieldwork locations. Working with a group of scholars as talented as these, in dialogue with one of the great theorists of the twentieth century, has been an honour indeed. My hope is that the discussions that take place between the voices in these pages will bring studies of the collective and of ritual to new levels, claiming a single source of shared intellectual inspiration. We have found dynamism in what has been critiqued as static, explanatory value in what is thought of as descriptive, occasions of mourning and also of joy in the way we relate to one another as human beings. Ours is another layer of thought on Durkheim himself, and on his text. We have tried to place Durkheim in context, reconfiguring the theoretical achievements of *The Elementary Forms of Religious Life* as an enduring, vibrant way to consider social orders, mental processes and effervescent times in an ever-changing world.

References

Allen, N.J., W.S.F. Pickering and W. Watts Miller. 1998. *On Durkheim's* Elementary Forms of Religious Life. London and New York: Routledge.

Barth, F. 1969. *Ethnic Groups and Boundaries: The Social Organization of Culture Difference.* London: Allen & Unwin.

Durkheim, E. 1995 [1912]. *The Elementary Forms of Religious Life,* trans. K.E. Fields. New York: Free Press.

Pickering, W.S.F. (ed.) 2002. *Durkheim Today.* New York and Oxford: Berghahn Books.

Watts Miller, W. 1996. *Durkheim, Morals and Modernity.* London: UCL Press.

PART I

Commencement

Chapter 1

THE NOTION OF SOUL AND *SCIENCE POSITIVE*

A RETRIEVAL OF DURKHEIM'S METHOD

Karen E. Fields

> Human blood is only an organic liquid.
> —Emile Durkheim, *The Elementary Forms of Religious Life*

> Blood is the soul itself seen from outside.
> —Emile Durkheim, *The Elementary Forms of Religious Life*

I begin with a puzzle. In August 2010, the Atlanta Red Cross appealed to potential donors among students at the Atlanta University Center, a consortium of historically black colleges, in these words:

> African American donors provide the best chance of survival for pa-
> tients of color with rare blood types or those who must have repeated
> transfusions for sickle cell anemia, heart disease, kidney disease or
> trauma. Blood from a donor with a similar ethnic background to that of
> the patient is less likely to be rejected or cause complications or illness.[1]

Were those statements true? Had up to date research proved that races possess distinguishing bloods, a notion discredited at the end of World War II? 'Yes' would mean that science has upheld belief, an uncom-mon occurrence. I wrote immediately to inquire about the science. The Red Cross replied promptly and enclosed two eye-opening sci-entific articles – eye-opening in that they owe less to science than to religion in Durkheim's sense: 'a system of ideas by which individuals imagine the society of which they are members and the obscure, yet intimate, relations they have with it' (1995 [1912]: 227). I propose to study that reply with the help of Durkheim's argument in Book II, Chapter 8 (hereafter II.8), of *The Elementary Forms of Religious Life*, 'The Notion of Soul.' There, he says – twice – that blood is 'the soul seen from outside' (1995 [1912]: 246, 262).

Durkheim inferred this relationship of blood to soul from his analysis of totemic rites conducted in Australia. Among those peoples, he wrote, there was 'no religious ceremony in which blood has no role to play' (1995 [1912]: 137). Only through such ceremonies did they acquire the totemic identities they shared not just with animals and plants, but first and foremost with each other. Although fascinated by those exotic doings, most European observers saw nothing like them in their own midst. Durkheim looked more closely. At the very beginning of *Elementary Forms*, he declared that he was not studying an 'archaic' religion as an end in itself, but rather as a step towards comprehending 'a fundamental and permanent and aspect of humanity'. One way to honour the centenary of Durkheim's masterpiece is to retrieve and re-examine the methodological claim that he accordingly made: 'Some will object that a single religion ... is a narrow basis for such an induction. But it is no less true that when a law has been proved by a single well-made experiment, this proof may be generalized' (1995 [1912]: 418).

Today, such talk by a sociologist would court offhand dismissal. It epitomizes the old-fashioned aspirations of *science positive*. Long ago, Talcott Parsons influentially diagnosed Durkheim's borrowing from the natural sciences as mistaken in principle, and well nigh perfectly ill suited to the study of religion. For him, religion is intrinsically a matter of subjective meaning. The objects that 'constitute the symbolic reference' of religious ideas 'do not meet the criteria of scientific methodology' (Parsons 1968 [1937]: 411–41). They are '*non*empirical' (Parsons 1968 [1937]: 420–29, esp. 422). That unsettling term faithfully renders his intuition that religious life, by its very nature, commands a hermeneutic approach to its study.[2]

Durkheim's intuition was certainly not that. To him, the invisible objects of religious life are objective phenomena, 'social facts'. 'Nonempirical'? Nothing of the sort. For a social fact to exist objectively, it need not exist materially; and if it exists objectively, it stands open to empirical study; thereafter, the problem is one of adequate method. Natural science offered analogies – for instance, the spectacular work of Pierre and Marie Curie, who were isolating new elements. Might not religion consist of 'a certain number' of fundamental ideas and practices that 'have the same objective meaning everywhere?' (Durkheim

1995 [1912]: 4, 6). If it did, then it should be possible to 'isolate' (his term) them from their various ethnographic 'compounds' (my term). I have borrowed that idea. In what follows, I will show that soul persists today in the 'elemental form'[3] Durkheim found in Australian ethnography, and that his method suited his experiment.

Retrieving Durkheim's Method

Elementary Forms studies the artifices and collective mechanics by means of which human beings fashion the ties that bind them, a question of both theoretical and practical import. In the 1890s, when Durkheim began the investigations that culminated in *Elementary Forms*, France was roiling in a general crisis that gave practical urgency to the effort to grasp the 'how' of those artifices and mechanisms. His work reflects that crisis, beginning with his doctoral thesis, *The Division of Labour in Society* (1893). In 1894, the anti-Semitic railroading of Captain Alfred Dreyfus revealed with ominous clarity what was at stake. If sociology could produce fundamental science about 'the religious nature of man' (Fournier 2007: 33–34; 382; 275–82),[4] the time to attempt that science had come.

For 'reasons of method', Durkheim sought to isolate 'the constituent elements' of religious life from 'simple' cases (Durkheim 1995 [1912]: 5–6). More controversially, then as now, he assumed the continuity of nature. In his view, society was not an empire within an empire, situated in nature but exempt from nature's orderliness. Those who held the contrary harboured 'an idea of causality that is extraordinarily reminiscent of the one on which magic was based for so long' (1995 [1912]: 373n30). To such thinkers, who retained 'the mind-set of primitives', 'true miracles' seemed possible (1995 [1912]: 25–26). But rigorous empirical science was indispensable. Just as a systematically empirical physics made it possible to build reliable bridges across mighty waters, so might a similarly equipped sociology help to build the new moral bridges required by the scope and complexity of modern societies.

In drawing 'simple' cases from homogeneous societies, Durkheim had methodological, not prescriptive, intent. To be sure, some students of ancient myths and bygone institutions sought to promote crude homogenizing nationalisms (allegedly) rooted in tribal pasts (Forti 2006: 12). Durkheim's own goal was to work out how to make room for the dignity of the human individual 'as such', and to build cohesion suited to the diversity of modern social life (see Fields 2002). Perhaps a special attraction of *science positive* was that the 'magical' mode of laws and proclamations had been tried in 1789, with the *Declaration of the Rights of Man and Citizen*. At the turn of the twentieth century, that grand achievement was all but unintelligible to many in France.

When Durkheim spoke of studying an 'archaic' religion in order to comprehend 'present-day man', he added, 'for there is none other that we have a greater interest in knowing well' (1995 [1912]: 1). The stakes were high for all the French, but particularly for French Jews, who had acquired citizenship after the grand *Declaration* of the century before. In Bordeaux, where Durkheim taught, the crisis boiled into the streets as violent *effervescences collectives:* 'Thousands of people demonstrated with the cries "Death to the Jews", "Death to Zola", "Death to Dreyfus"'. Rocks smashed windows. Anti-Semitic posters shouted from public benches (Fournier 2007: 365). Murder was done (Fournier 2007: 241). Durkheim feared a 'reaction against the principles we thought were settled' (Fournier 2007: 367). In 1898, he co-founded the Bordeaux section of the *League for the Defence of the Rights of Man and Citizen,* and served as its secretary. In the same year, his academic collaborator Célestin Bouglé presented, and speedily published, a series of lectures on salient issues of the day. Bouglé signaled the danger of ideas such as 'nation-ness (*nationalité*), race, and class', and warned that the 'philosophy of races' might become 'a weapon in the hands of the leaders of anti-Semitism' (Fournier 2007: 381).

As any reader of *Suicide: A Study in Sociology* learns, Durkheim had reservations about the race science that was developing at the same time as sociology, but he nonetheless read it with care.[5] By contrast, most readers of *Elementary Forms* do not notice that the totemic clans he studied are analogous to races (though without hierarchy and antagonism). Like Europe's races, totemic groups claimed similar appearance derived from common descent. Unlike their European counterparts, who by the nineteenth century had a science of biology to reckon with (however rickety its empirical foundations), the clans overcame phenotypic dissimilarity by painting on what was needed and acting it out. In Europe, the would-be science often resorted to descriptive measurement and diagrams – lettered equivalents of painting on and acting out physical resemblance.[6] In that case, the ancient formula of creating and expressing sameness and difference could serve as well to hone long blades. In Europe, therefore, the elemental repertoire – ritual, myth, costume, décor, soul and sacredness – had the same power it had in Australia, but found much more to do with that power.

Considered as an 'element' of religious life, soul may be compared to carbon in nature. It may be thought of as present in compounds as different from one another as olive oil and TNT. The totemic clans of *Elementary Forms* are race-like, as different from one another as kangaroos are from emus, but like olive oil, they are stable compounds. Others explode. In 1870, Durkheim (then twelve years old) witnessed the birth of a nasty French 'nation-ness' in an anti-Jewish *effervescence collective* that followed the German victory (Fournier 2007: 32). Many years later, his riveting, disturbing account of a night-time, fire-lit totemic celebration showed people creating and expressing several things at once: their shared sacredness; their shared descent from a giant snake, Wollunqua; and each individual's frenzied participation in the sharing of a collective soul (Durkheim 1995 [1912]: 218–20). There, he displayed soul as a human artefact that is at once domestic and wild.

In her analysis of soul, as certain Nazi philosophers developed the concept, Simona Forti begins by asking how it is that 'the idea of racism is so effective in exalting differences and conflict, on one hand, and in nailing the individual to his collective identity on the other' (2006: 12). Forti pinpoints these philosophers' intent rereading of Plato, which enabled them to abandon quasi-biological race, with its troublesome empirical loose ends, and to elaborate instead a methodically adapted 'metaphysics of form', a theory, she says, that 'owes much more to Plato than to the laws of genetics' (2006: 12). In that fashion, they weaponized the idea of soul as visible race. In Forti's terms, 'Race thus [became] a phenomenon perceived by our senses as an expression of the soul that, according to the words of the *Phaedo,* is related to what is "divine, immortal, rational, indissoluble and always identical to itself"' (2006: 17–18, 17n28). Inspired, Alfred Rosenberg reasoned that 'if "the soul is race seen from inside", then race is the soul seen from outside' (Forti 2006: 14). For him, the mind's eye and that of the body might be enlisted interchangeably, and at will. As an idea that appealed to a racist philosopher such as he, soul demands attention.

Durkheim gives it a chapter of its own. II.8, 'The Notion of Soul', is rarely commented upon, perhaps because, for some readers, its ethnographic density registers as 'mere' ethnography. In fact, the Australian ethnography offered Durkheim a laboratory in which to isolate soul, the element, from the blur of activity by which soul is made real. To discount it is therefore to discount evidence that can be found nowhere else – in effect, to leave the lab. Systematic method in that lab required a means of identifying soul by '*external* signs', as Durkheim might have said. To this task, he brought two sets of intellectual tools, one from his upbringing in the household of a rabbi, and the other from his philosophical education. In his Jewish upbringing he had encountered his own soul, from early childhood, as soon as he learned to thank God for its daily return, the first thing each morning even before washing (Fields 1995: xxix). He thus encountered soul as objective fact far too early in life to be persuaded later on that it was usefully thought of as 'nonempirical'. In his public education, he encountered the idea of soul through various settings of classical problems inherited in the West from ancient Greece. Without such tools, he might easily have overlooked something real that lies hidden in plain sight. Soul has properties by which it can be recognized.

It is recognizable in collective solutions to a basic problem of social life, individual identity. II.8 depicts people of different Australian tribes working out, one way and another, who a newborn is, of what ancestor the baby is an 'avatar' and who every individual is at different moments in life. Their theory of procreation transcends the biology of physical appearance, possesses a folk genetics that extends the span of each individual life backward and forward in time, and operates with an ontology that links both of the foregoing back again, to individual personhood and, simultaneously, to the named collectivity concerned (Durkheim 1995 [1912]: 272–75). A woman provides genetic information when she recalls where she was when she felt the first signs of pregnancy. Divination reveals which ancestor impregnated her as she passed near a tree associated with a particular totem. A celebrant hands to a young Kangaroo man undergoing initiation a sacred object made of incised stone, saying, 'Here is the body of a Kangaroo.' In the rite, that object serves as 'the body of the ancestor, the actual individual, and the totemic animal, all at once' – three beings that form 'an indissoluble unity', 'whose shared essence is the totemic principle', soul (Durkheim 1995 [1912]: 259–64, 267). The notion of soul thus provides a framework for an indefinite number of things.

The Singularity of Soul

Soul binds. It is *essentially* an essentialist idea. There is no non-essentialist way to express it. Its singularity is its ability to encompass the individual and the collective in a single concept that is abstract yet potent. When 'soul' is conceived individually, 'the' or 'a' modifies it.[7] When soul is conceived collectively, it is 'a kind of generic essence that becomes individualized only secondarily and superficially'

(Durkheim 1995 [1912]: 268). In Durkheim's account, the idea of soul is 'coterminous with humanity', and all of its basic features have been present since the beginning (1995 [1912]: 242). That idea provides for a continuous individual personhood that emerges through relationships with others, within a community that has continuous personhood of its own. Durkheim's rearing within a close-knit Jewish community provides an example. Naming is crucial. The individual name marks an internally integrated 'who', and the collective name an internally integrated 'what'. The basic property, exhibited by both, may be thought of as an 'identity programme' of soul with the logical features set forth by Plato – rational, indissoluble, always identical to itself, and so on. It then activates sub-programmes in accordance with that logic. When soul is present in complex social compounds, as an 'element' of religious life, it can be identified by that logic.

While naming launches the identity programme, specialized in the individual 'who' and the collective 'what', action incarnates soul in the visible world and emits into that world a stream of evidence for soul's objective reality. Even though soul is ideal, like Berkeley's tree that crashes down unheard in the forest, it is perfectly well equipped to weigh, unbidden, on conscious awareness. First and perhaps above all, that ideal yet objective *thing* regularly contradicts appearance. Durkheim recounts an exchange that the ethnographers Baldwin Spencer and Francis Gillen had with a man of the Kangaroo totem. Apparently the informant has been struggling to make them 'see' that he and the animal are the same, for they say: 'He responded by showing us a photograph we had just taken of him: "Look who is exactly the same thing as I. Well! It is the same with the kangaroo." The Kangaroo was his totem.' (1995 [1912]: 134). The man could not have expressed, or even have possessed, his matrilineal descent without his seemingly 'nonempirical' statement. Notice that, although membership of the Kangaroo clan bound him, it did not confer on him useful attributes, such as a kangaroo's speed. The objective reality of his kangaroo-ness unforgettably establishes two further points: Soul is not directly utilitarian, and soul has direct bearing on obligation.

The idea of soul enables human beings not only to impose ideal sameness on material difference, but also to impose ideal difference on material sameness. The identity programme transfigures what is *merely* visible. Its routines can be captured at work in twentieth-century America, far beyond Australia's world of totemic clans. Thus, when Walter White, a Negro with blond hair and blue eyes, infiltrated the Ku Klux Klan to expose lynching, he ran the risk of being lynched for pretending to be a white man (White 1948). White's Negro identity, like the Kangaroo identity of the Australian human, owed nothing to his outward appearance. Neither does the Red Cross's category 'African American', with which I began. These examples bring out a paradox of reason itself. When human beings learned to sophisticate perception with conception, however bizarre the result, they gained the intuition that internal relations may exist between externally disparate things. Durkheim claimed that religion thus made philosophy and science possible (1995 [1912]: 239–40).

Dominique Merllié has reminded us how sharply Durkheim criticized Lucien Lévy-Bruhl, who conceived of the difference between religious and scientific thought as an abrupt discontinuity, and drew a parallel contrast between primitive and modern mentalities (Merllié 1998). Durkheim argued the opposite. The stunning last lines of II.7 are specifically directed against Lévy-Bruhl: 'There is no gulf [*solution de continuité*] between the logic of religious thought and the logic of scientific thought.... [Religious thought] employs logical mechanisms with a certain gaucheness, but none of them are unknown to it' (Durkheim 1995 [1912]: 240n61, 241). Even if Durkheim is right, though, it does not follow that movement along his continuum is necessarily a march in only one direction. In fact, religion and science (hence primitive and modern mentalities) can govern thought simultaneously, or in quick and unnoticed succession. I will return to that point.

If a religion is, as Durkheim said, 'a system of ideas by means of which individuals imagine the society of which they are members, and the obscure yet intimate relations they have with it' (1995 [1912]: 227), science can never fully emancipate itself from religion. As social beings, scientists participate in that collective imagining, even as the conscientious ones work hard to bracket it. From that standpoint, Descartes's path to radical individualism snaps into focus, and his special self-discipline loses some of its power to offend virtue. When he connected his *res cogitans*, 'thinking thing', to a first-person singular Latin verb, *cogito*, he marked his recognition that scientific discipline is devilishly hard to achieve, precisely because human beings have and inhabit a world they collectively imagine (1992 [1979]: 57). Not giving that very difficulty its due, Lévy-Bruhl simplistically paired modern with scientific mentalities. In consequence, his long-delayed reply to Durkheim's criticism, to which Merllié properly draws attention, could not solve the problem he created for himself by thinking with polar opposites. Instead, his proposed solution – to 'understand' or at least not to '*mis*understand' (Merllié 1998: 33, 36, 36n3) the primitive or the religious human – makes the problem easier to see. If the

'A' of one is the 'not-A' of the other, and vice versa, 'understanding' is helpless to elaborate either term. The A/not-A system can say nothing about real-world mixtures, and it entails no rational method of distinguishing one from the other. In contrast, Durkheim's identification of soul, by external traits, offers a method of detecting this religious idea in ethnographic particulars of concrete activity, even in the midst of activity intended as science.

A while ago, the Kangaroo man who instructed his ethnographers brought out the key element of the identity programme. Shared name is shared essence. As a name-essence, soul is 'qualitatively invariable' and always 'identical to itself' (Durkheim 1995 [1912]: 260–61, 272). Naming makes continuous individual personhood thinkable as *the same* over the life course, often beyond. It does the same work for the clan (nation, people, race), which joins individuals across time and space. In the letter with which I began, the name 'African American' corresponds to blood imagined by the Red Cross as shared by all who bear the name, and at the same time appears to indicate a consequential biological reality: 'the best chance of survival'. There is more. When a 'qualitatively invariable' thing is subdivided, it remains equal to itself in all its parts, as in the alchemist's formula *Totum ex parte* (Durkheim 1995 [1912]: 230, 268). Just as 'a fragment of a relic has the same virtues as the whole relic', the 'smallest drop of blood contains the same active principle as all the blood' (1995 [1912]: 231; 231n44). And what it touches, it transforms. Thus, when the Virginia legislature built this property of soul into the 'one drop rule' of its 'Preservation of Racial Integrity Act of 1924' against interracial marriage, it followed the alchemists' principle to the letter. Finally, soul is the bearer and transmitter of moral as well as physical attributes, and those attributes may be communicated to living beings and inanimate objects. Procedures based on contiguity and (postulated) similarity can enable this communication routinely, or preclude it absolutely.

When the Australian informants describe the traits by which they recognize soul, they emphasize its immateriality [*spiritualité*] in various ways: 'invisible to ordinary people'; 'vague and variable'; 'unstable and indefinite'; 'changeable from one moment to the next'; 'rarefied and subtle'; 'ethereal, comparable to shadow or wind'. Sometimes they bring out a related property of soul, its exemption from material causality: Soul 'does not affect the senses as bodies do'. Or as the poetic saying of the Tully River tribes has it, '[The soul] has no bones' (1995 [1912]: 244). Causality as pertinent to hunting, and to profane activities generally, differs absolutely from that of rites performed to ensure the reproduction of hunted species. In those rites, workaday cause and effect are suspended; and when workaday causality is suspended, magical principles take over: 'Like produces like' and 'the part evokes the whole'.[8] Invisibility and suspended causality are properties of ideal things. Thus, the witch's flying broomstick is not even imagined to have moving parts; nothing about it requires a mechanical principle. Sometimes the absence of moving parts can serve as a telltale sign that an ideal thing – for instance, the notion of soul – is governing a seemingly scientific explanation, even if the scientist concerned is unaware of having shifted to its characteristic logical programme.

Ideal things acquire an objective existence through human action. Only by that means can things acquire sacredness or soul, which Durkheim brings together by calling soul 'a particular application of the beliefs relative to sacred things' (1995 [1912]: 265). Neither soul nor sacredness is inherent in physical objects. To exist, both must be added to objects, and both come into being through a definite process. Durkheim's famous definition of religion contains both a process and its product:

> A religion is a unified system of beliefs and rites relative to sacred things, that is to say, things set apart and forbidden – beliefs and practices which unite into one single moral community called a Church, all those who adhere to them. (1995 [1912]: 44)

At the beginning of III.1, 'The Negative Cult and Its Functions', Durkheim makes explicit the sequence that is implicit in the definition: 'What distinguishes [sacred things] is a discontinuity between them and profane things. ... A whole complex of rites *seeks to bring about that separation, which is essential*' (1995 [1912]: 303; my emphasis).

Through the same ritual processes by which physical objects acquire sacredness, soul acquires physical 'substrates' (1995 [1912]): 245–46) that serve as its 'residences'. Durkheim lists common ones: 'the heart, the breath, the placenta, the blood, the shadow, the liver, the fat of the liver, and the kidneys', but above all the blood. When Emu men open their veins and allow their shared Emu blood to mingle on the sanctuary rock of their clan, their shared blood becomes Emu soul. Emu soul is made manifest by that very act, and is made distinct from other kinds of soul by the very same act (Jay 1992: 6–7). The result is visible to all as 'the soul seen from outside' – not only to the Emu participants, but also to Spencer and Gillen, who photographed Emu soul for the monograph in which Durkheim saw it (Spencer and Gillen 1904), or more precisely, 'saw' it. Soul, itself, is invisible. Furthermore, it takes up no space. Like sacredness, it is *inétendu*. With teacherly repetition, Durkheim periodically reminds his reader not to imagine that physical objects can make known their sacredness without first having been made sacred themselves. Here is an example:

> Nothing comes out of nothing. The sensations the world evokes in us cannot, by definition, contain anything that goes beyond that world. From something tangible, one can only make something tangible; from extended substance [*étendu*] one cannot make unextended substance [*inétendu*]. (1995 [1912]: 226)[9]

I am now convinced that he did not have in mind the eleven-syllable mouthful 'extended substance/unextended substance', but that in fact he meant to express abrupt discontinuity, *abruptly.* In English, the body/soul pair would have accomplished that. In 1995, however, as I struggled to translate that passage, I failed to consult the 1880 *Littré* (the French counterpart of the Oxford English Dictionary).[10] The *Littré* quotes Voltaire ('an immaterial being [*inétendu*] governing a material being [*étendu*]'), then Buffon ('of the two, one is [*inétendu*], immaterial and immortal') and finally Catholic teaching ('In theology, the body of Jesus is said to be *inétendu* in the Eucharist'). The fact that the theological usage accommodates the sacred/profane contrast clinches the point. This new clarity, in turn, exposes another mistake. I conflated Descartes's pair *res extensa/res cogitans* with the far older pair *étendu /inétendu* (and meanwhile imagined for him a Latin pair *res extensa/res inextensa*). Neither the French pair nor my spurious Latin translation of it belonged to his project.[11] The pair *res cogitans/res extensa* served him, precisely, as a means of extracting his mind from religion – once again in Durkheim's sense of 'imagining the society...'. Precisely because it is both activated and maintained collectively, the sacred/profane contrast that transfigures reality cannot prosper on the solitary, silent, and denuded expanse of Descartes' *Second Meditation* (1992 [1979]: 91). One last point: Giving the body/soul pair its due unshrouds the literary bridge with which Durkheim connected the Warramungas' noisy effervescence of II.7 to the quiet, immaterial invisibility of soul with which II.8 begins.

The Duality of Blood

'Man is double', as Durkheim often says. So, too, is blood. On one hand, 'human blood is only an organic liquid' (Durkheim 1995 [1912]: 228). It is the red liquid that circulates in the arteries and veins, carrying oxygen and carbon dioxide to and from the tissues. On the other, blood has a social life. Its social life comes into view whenever blood functions as the substrate of soul. Natural blood has 'moving parts' associated with its biological functioning. As soul, by contrast, blood has no moving parts of its own, but acquires them from human action and imagination. Thus equipped, blood can consecrate and purify, it can profane and pollute, and it can create and enforce the boundaries of human groups. Furthermore, when blood assumes the name of a group, it bears the group's soul (Kangaroo-ness, Emu-ness, and, for that matter, Bouglé's disturbing 'nation-ness'), as well as collective moral and physical attributes. Natural blood has no such assignments, and no biological equipment with which to carry them out. When they are in fact carried out, it is by human beings who do so on natural blood's behalf.

Two early twentieth-century studies of classification bring out the duality of blood. In 1903, Durkheim and Marcel Mauss published *Primitive Classification*, which explored the conceptual underpinning of social organization based on clans (1963 [1903]). In that world, blood could exist in as many 'types' as there were named groups. In 1900–1901, Karl Landsteiner proposed a scientific classification of natural blood types independent of self-naming groups. In an elegant series of experiments, he demonstrated that blood can be classified according to the presence or absence of certain antigens (at first, types A and B) (*Journal of the National Medical Association* 1960: 280). His study of nature's blood types helped to explain why transfusions at times healed patients and at others killed them. Before that work, people believed that the blood of close kin was best, a potentially fatal error. Blood as soul has no part in saving lives. Biological blood has no part in delimiting kin groups. That duality of blood established a complex twentieth-century career for the ancient conception of blood as soul.[12]

In 1902, David Starr Jordan, then the president of Stanford University, bestrode the two understandings. Here, he speaks of blood according to the science of his day:

> We know that the actual blood in the actual veins plays no part in heredity, that the transfusion of blood means no more than the transportation of food, and that the physical basis of the phenomena of inheritance is found in the structure of the germ cell and its contained germ-plasm.

Here, by contrast, he speaks of blood as soul, equally at home in modern America and in stone- tool–using Australia:

> The blood which is 'thicker than water' is the symbol of race unity. In this sense, the blood of the people concerned is at once the cause and

the result of the deeds recorded in their history. ... Wherever an Englishman goes, he carries with him the elements of English history. It is a
British deed which he does, British history that he makes. Thus, too, a
Jew is a Jew in all ages and climes, and his deeds everywhere bear the
stamp of Jewish individuality. A Greek is a Greek; a Chinaman remains
a Chinaman. In like fashion, the race traits color all history made by
Tartars, or Negroes, or Malays. (Lederer 2008: 111)

Notice that, as the substrate of soul, blood has taken on soul's property of qualitative invariance. According to Starr, there is one blood
to a group, a group's blood is the same in all its parts, and all who
share that blood also share certain attributes – in his apt phrase, its
'individuality'.

In 1895, a writer for the *New York Times* faced an American consequence of blood's qualitative invariance when it is in service as soul.
Assigned the obituary of Frederick Douglass, the celebrated son of
a slave and a slave owner, the writer set aside custom. Rather than
compose a stately sequence of declarative sentences, he composed a
zigzagging sequence of questions that explored the anomaly of a man
with two souls:

> It might not be unreasonable, perhaps, to intimate that his white blood
> may have something to do with the remarkable energy he displayed
> and the superior intelligence he manifested. Indeed, it might not be
> altogether unreasonable to ask whether, with more white blood, he
> would not have been an even better and greater man than he was, and
> whether the fact that he had black blood may not have cost the world
> a genius, and be, in consequence, a cause for lamentation instead of a
> source of lyrical enthusiasm over African possibilities. It is always more
> or less foolish to credit or discredit a race with the doings, good or bad,
> of a particular member of that race, but if it must be done, plain justice
> should see to it that the right race gets the glory or the humiliation.
> (Tucker 1994: 35)

Here again, the properties of soul are present and accounted for: one
to a group, shared attributes to match, found in all parts of the group
in question. Here, too, causality is suspended. In so far as Douglass's
'white' blood 'explains' his exceptional qualities, his father's lesser
qualities must go unexplained.

In his novel *Light in August*, written a generation later, William
Faulkner combined blood as soul with the strange cause and effect
to which blood in its ideal form is subject. Faulkner's protagonist, Joe
Christmas, who in appearance is white, has a black essence that remains invisible until he is lynched. But when the lynch mob castrated
the 'white nigger' Joe Christmas, 'the pent black blood seemed ... to
rush out of his pale body like the rush of sparks from a rising rocket;

upon that black blast the man seemed to be soaring into [the towns-people's] memories forever and ever.' 'Black' blood can exist only as metaphor, however. It was Faulkner's genius not to invent new meta-phors, but instead to write realistically and ethnographically. He thus represented a world where there can exist such a thing as a 'negro cabin', a wooden structure with a race.[13] And, as Durkheim does at II.7.3 (1995 [1912]: 219–21), he allowed the frenzy of the efferves-cent ritual to subside into the quiet power of reinforcing memory. The mob sees and recalls physical evidence that appears to corroborate what, in fact, it can only have witnessed with the mind's eye. In the heat of the moment, the mob's actions create evidence, not of Joe Christmas's individual ancestry (which is never ascertained) but of the collective soul in which his individuality participated.

> The black blood drove him first to the negro cabin. And then the white blood drove him out of there, as it was the black blood which snatched up the pistol and the white blood would not let him fire it.... It was the black blood which swept him by his own desire beyond the aid of any man, swept him up into that ecstasy out of a black jungle where life has already ceased before the heart stops and death is desire and fulfilment. And then the black blood failed him again. (Faulkner 1992 [1932]: 424–25).

Blood as Race 'Seen' from Inside

It goes without saying that Landsteiner's modern and scientific classi-fication had few repercussions in the real-world models of Faulkner's fictional Mississippi circa 1932. But to assign such a locale to Lévy-Bruhl's 'primitive' and 'religious' category is to illuminate nothing about it unless 'religious' receives adequate definition. ('Primitive' I leave aside as hopelessly imprecise other than as an epithet.) In Faulkner's town, religion no doubt thrived in the denominational form it takes in secular society, where individuals may choose which church to attend. But religion also thrived there in Durkheim's sense, as a way of imagining the society of which individuals are members, and who is who within it. No one can freely join or leave such a reli-gion. No such thing as a secular alternative exists. Just as individual Australians were not free to choose a clan, so individual Mississip-pians were not free to choose a race; nor could they opt out of the reigning religion. The Oxford English Dictionary suggests two possible Latin sources of the word 'religion' as used today: *relegere* and *relig-are* – roughly, 'reading' and 'binding'. In general, Landsteiner's blood classification had no immediate import for 'reading religion', so to speak. 'Binding religion' was another matter.

As knowledge of Landsteiner's classification spread, researchers noticed the misfit between blood's science and its binding religion. Syncretism is a common response to the ill-fitting forms of an alien faith, and the objective classification of blood was indeed alien in its implication that all human blood was fundamentally the same. That sameness could not underwrite the required, and seemingly self-evident, difference. Scientific syncretism thus appeared as though on cue. Researchers began to look for blood-borne racial differences that might resolve into the native classification. To succeed, they of necessity thought with soul, and thus with its logic of qualitative invariance within the groups classified. In 1907, for example, a German doctor claimed to have developed a test that could distinguish reliably between the serum of an Arab, a Caucasian, a Negro, a Malayan, and a Chinese person (Lederer 2008: 108). In the 1920s, *Hygeia,* a magazine produced for the lay public by the American Medical Association, periodically reported on tests with which biologists proposed to demonstrate the 'striking difference' between Gentile and Jewish blood (Lederer 2008: 108). While some searched for markers and tests for them, others sought to redeem the old racial classification by studying the statistical distribution of the blood types within the old categories (Starr 2002: 44–77). Nazi scientists would eventually conceive of type B blood (found somewhat more frequently among Eastern Europeans and Jews than among non-Jewish Germans) as a 'marker' of the 'darker, Asiatic races' (Starr 2002: 134). Because soul is immaterial to start with, blood conceived as soul could (and always can) accommodate any and every statistical distribution so conceived.

Methodical syncretism did not preclude frantic collision. In September 1935, soon after the Nuremberg Blood Law took effect, natural blood met its social counterpart on the Nazis' howling heath of modernity. When the law forbade blood mixing, it envisaged procreation and marriage – but said nothing about transfusion (Jewish Virtual Library 2011 [1935]). An unsettling practical question rushed into that silence. Was the 'racial character' of an Aryan patient 'altered' when a Jewish doctor, Hans Serelman, saved the patient's life with a transfusion of his own 'Jewish' blood? On 19 October, a certain Professor Leffler, highly placed in the racial-political bureau of the National Socialist Party, issued a ruling. He dismissed the public unease as 'sheer nonsense', the product of 'mental confusion due purely to the figurative use of the word "blood" in the sense of heredity' (*New York Times* 1935).

But the law spoke of 'defilement' – that is, profanation. Practical thinking about defilement was not 'mental confusion' but terrible ritual clarity of the sort that makes the sacred/profane dichotomy absolute (Durkheim 1995 [1912]: 303–13). Blood, as soul, was indifferent to the biological properties of its substrate. In consequence, the Jewish doctor's donation of natural blood did indeed save an Aryan's life, but it was by no means obvious that the Jewish doctor's 'figurative' blood had saved the Aryan as such. Dr. Serelman's conviction and imprisonment left the issue burning. The Aryan lived on, but as what? When the ruling came, the *New York Times* headlined the key point: 'Says Transfusion Can't Alter Race' (1935). Leffler's ruling, based on the current science, met sustained opposition. Wartime blood donors were compelled to prove their Aryan ancestry (Lederer 2008: 50). In 1942, some researchers claimed to have developed a blood test for 'non-Aryanism' (Lederer 2008: 118).

By then, Americans were experiencing a public collision of their own on identical terrain. The year before, as two doctors, Charles R. Drew and John C. Scudder, developed the Red Cross Blood Bank, the War Department promoted blood donation as a citizen's duty. When black American citizens stepped forward to donate, however, they met determined opposition. Rather than repeat a story told elsewhere, I note only that blood was drafted into its ancient ritual function of delimiting community (Fields and Fields 2012: 59–60). As the United States readied for war and the Red Cross Blood Bank's preparations became more urgent, the War Department appeased the opposition. It allowed black people to donate, but ordered segregation of the blood: in its words, 'for reasons not biologically convincing', but 'commonly recognized [as] psychologically important in America'.[14] Drew called that ruling 'indefensible from any point of view' (Love 1997: 49). He returned to his post at Howard University and participated in black Americans' fight to reverse the policy. The sane, and the insane, logistics of the programme then fell to Scudder.

When the War Department promoted blood donation as a citizen's duty, black Americans claimed it as every citizen's right. No American, black or white, missed the point. As of old, admission to a communal sacrifice indicated who stood within the community and who outside it.[15] The campaigners won, but their victory provoked insulting ritual elaboration: separate days to keep donors separate, separate refrigerators (or shelves therein) to keep the collected blood separate, special batching procedures for processing blood plasma separately, a 'do you mind?' sign-off for transfusion patients and blood labelling by race. Some collectors simplified by accepting blood from black donors but quietly discarding it (Lederer 2008: 118). Here, then, was a textbook example of Durkheim's belief-creating rites and rite-expressing beliefs that publicly created, day in and day out, two opposed blood 'types', one sacred and one profane.

When the wartime blood banks discarded the blood of black donors, they discarded what scientists knew about natural blood. In 1946, Ashley Montagu wrote that 'the sooner the facts concerning blood are made known the better' (1952 [1946]: 217). In 1950, William C. Boyd, a distinguished immunochemist, underlined the fact that blood is no respecter of families, let alone races:

> There is no evidence that the results of transfusion depend upon race. If you need a transfusion, the blood of a healthy Negro or Chinese, if he is of the same blood group as you, will be of the same clinical value as the blood of a 'Caucasian,' and the blood of your brother or sister, if of the wrong group, may kill you. (*Journal of the National Medical Association* 1960: 280)[16]

In the same year, the Red Cross announced that it had ceased its practice of blood segregation (Lederer 2008: 122). As the 1950s advanced, however, the wartime struggle for civil rights entered a new phase, and Southern legislatures began to enact blood segregation into law. To them, as to the Red Cross and the War Department earlier, it made no difference that the case for such a law was 'not biologically convincing'. In the meantime, some communities were rearing future zealots. A Louisiana legislator of the next generation opposed repeal of his state's blood segregation law with the passion reserved for the utmost commitments of the South's old-time religion: 'I would see my family die and go to eternity before I would see them have a drop of nigger blood in them' (Lederer 2008: 134). He seemed ready for such a consequence. Others preferred to revisit the science.

In 1959, Dr. Scudder, Dr. Drew's erstwhile colleague, offered a 'new philosophy' that bore the tag line 'Unto each his own.' He presented it in a short talk at the annual convention of the American Association of Blood Banks – usually a quiet affair, but he had won a large audience by giving advance interviews to the press. His talk stirred a controversy to which a *New York Times* headline added spice: 'Blood Expert Says Transfusion between Races May Be Perilous' (Kenny 2006: 459).[17]

Conscious that the lay public might assume that Scudder's 'new philosophy' represented new science, Dr. W. Montague Cobb of the National Medical Association[18] invited him to publish his findings. In a symposium organized by the association's journal, Scudder might present before peers 'a concise statement of his premises and evidence', a step he had until then skipped. Having heard and read accounts of the oral presentation, Cobb suspected that his ideas were based not 'upon controlled studies under his direction, but upon an ambiguous synthesis of material from various areas in which he became interested as an admittedly amateur geneticist' (*Journal of the National Medical Association* 1960: 281). In due course, Scudder submitted his paper, and the responses of an expert panel were published alongside it. The symposium appeared in the July 1960 issue of the *Journal of the National Medical Association*. By invitation later that year, Scudder republished it in *Mankind Quarterly*, the journal of the International Association for the Advancement of Ethnology and Eugenics (Kenny 2002: 277).

Scudder's paper illustrates logical procedures by which soul, an elemental form of religious life, may enter unannounced into work meant to be scientific. If Scudder had been free to operate according to the ancient logic of blood as soul, 'black' and 'white' blood would have been incompatible by definition, and would have raised no question of material causation. To address scientists, however, he needed an account of cause and effect. Accordingly, he offered tables to show that certain blood antigens occurred with different frequency among the black and white people tested. (Recall the effort, mentioned earlier, to interpret type B blood as a 'marker' of the 'Asiatic'.) He then built his argument principally on two cases (Scudder and Wigle 1960: 107). In the first, a white male veteran, transfused during preparation for heart surgery, had displayed an 'atypical' antibody against an antigen found to occur with greater frequency among black people (93 per cent) than white (77 per cent). In the second, a black Canadian woman who had sickle cell anaemia displayed an antibody against an antigen found to occur with greater frequency among white people (74 per cent) than black (26 per cent). For him, the tables showed that both patients had been sensitized by transfusion with racially alien blood – more precisely, racially alien antigens.

One of the commentators pointed out what would have been obvious to anyone who read the tables directly. They revealed that Scudder's white American had stood at least 7 chances in ten of receiving mismatched blood from a white donor (supposedly 'matched' by race), and that his black Canadian had stood about 1 chance in 4 of experiencing the same mishap. The tables showed that, in fact, nature had provided only moderate variation between Scudder's designated races – but his core conception required categorical difference. His attempt at scientific demonstration thus betrayed the elemental form of religious life that lay embedded within it: soul.

Fundamentally, therefore, Scudder's thought exhibited reason, but not in its scientific form. At the same time, his tables exhibited scientific form, but did not govern his reasoning. He attempted to apply the material cause and effect of antigens, moving parts of natural blood, to the ideal blood that emerges from ritual activity – for instance, the wartime practices of the Red Cross described above. Blood in its ideal form, as soul, is readily recognized. Unlike natural blood, it is 'qualitatively invariant' (Durkheim 1995 [1912]: 271) within the group held to possess it, and to possess it in distinction from other groups with other bloods. To find that the cause of the two patients' adverse reactions was their transfusion with *racially* incompatible blood, he assumed the qualitative invariance of racially exclusive bloods with corresponding antigens. His own evidence belied that assumption. Only in ideal form can 'black' and 'white' blood be said to exist. The moving parts of natural blood have no ideal equivalents, and ideal blood has no moving parts of its own. Still, an ideal thing can be set in motion verbally – and so it turned out. Scudder's campaigning through interviews proved more efficacious than his scientific paper proved convincing. Cobb ended the remarks previously quoted by observing that, 'in giving the advance story to the press, which he stated he did, [he has] caused a great deal of trouble, the long-term effects of which cannot be determined.'

Fifty years later (and sixty years after announcing the end of blood labelling by race), the Red Cross mailed the donor appeal with which I began. What sort of science was it that, in 2010, supported the Red Cross's claim that blood supposedly 'matched' by race gave black transfusion patients their 'best chance of survival'? With the reply came two articles: a 1990 report on research by Elliott Vichinsky et al. titled 'Alloimmunization in Sickle Cell Anemia and Transfusion of Racially Unmatched Blood', published in the *New England Journal of Medicine*; and a 2008 review of current research by Beth Shaz et al., published in *Transfusion Reviews* under the title 'Blood Donation and Blood Transfusion: Special Considerations for African Americans'.

In the article by Vichinsky et al., the phrase 'racially unmatched blood' discloses its Scudderian descent, yet differs from its antecedent in an important respect. It contains no evidence that, for the authors, blood and race had the same subjective meaning they had for Scudder, that their intentions replicated his, or that they inclined toward his eugenical values. Scudder freely interwove his evidence and argument with his favourite opinions about arranged marriage and caste endogamy in India, and about the breeding of great racehorses (*Journal of the National Medical Association* 1960: 282). Writing thirty years later,

Vichinsky et al., promoted no such opinions but, instead, a utilitarian agenda:

> Our study illustrates the problem of participation of black persons in an urban blood-banking program. ... The screening of white donors to obtain compatible blood for alloimmunized patients with sickle cell anemia would result in a ten-fold increase in the costs of blood-banking. (1990: 1621)

The authors' kinship with Scudder is therefore not their subjective cast of mind but the objective structure of their logic. In both papers, blood emerges in elemental form, as soul; the identity programme activates itself; and the principle of material causation blinks off and on.

To summarize briefly: Vichinsky et al. compared two groups of children at their hospital, in Oakland, California. All were receiving transfusions as treatment for anaemia. The groups were designated (in a deployment of the A/not-A system) as 'black' and 'nonblack' (1990: 1618). Of the 107 black children, all of whom had sickle-cell anaemia, 30 per cent suffered immune reactions after transfusion. Of the 19 non-black children, all of whom had chronic anaemias other than sickle cell, 5 per cent had that experience. The donors were assumed to be white. The researchers' question was this: What explained the higher alloimmunization rate of the black sickle-cell patients? Their answer: 77 per cent of the antibodies produced by the sickle-cell patients who suffered the reactions were against four proteins differently distributed in the black and white populations tested, but found 'predominantly in white populations'. Now, their conclusion: 'Alloimmunization is a common, clinically serious problem in sickle cell anemia that it is *partly* due to racial differences between the blood donor and recipient populations.' (1990. Vichinski et al. 1617; my emphasis.) Notice the qualifier 'partly'. At the time of publication, the authors did not escape forceful rebuttal, on both methodological and clinical grounds, through letters published in the New England Journal of Medicine (Pereira et al. 1990; Bordin 1990).[19]

They were not rebutted but amplified in a New York Times article provocatively headlined 'Uneasy Doctors Add Race-Consciousness to Diagnostic Tools'. In that article, which aggrandized the research report, the 30 per cent who suffered the reaction rose to 'about one-third' (Leary 1990: C1). Be that as it may. The supposedly racial cause of 'one-third' of the outcomes failed to explain the remaining two-thirds. That fortunate majority had no place in the analysis, and silently disappeared. In the authors 'partly racial' explanation, race, as a cause, stood suspended most of the time – thus exhibiting a tolerance for mystery that is familiar in religion but strange in science. If ideal blood is in question, there is no mystery. Under the alchemist's principle *Totum ex parte*, the part stands for the whole. But for material blood, and under scientific principles, the authors' qualifying the word 'racial' with 'partly' cannot repair the oddity of an 'explanation' that does not account for most of the data. This twenty-year-old paper came to me as the scientific basis of Red Cross blood policy in 2010.

The 2008 article by Shaz et al. provides an overview of recent research about blood donation and transfusion, with the unifying subtitle 'Special Considerations for African Americans'. The topics range from the alarming, such as the reasons why first-time African American donors often do not return (2008: 204–5), to the terrifying, a statistically derived rationale for using only black blood donors in the treatment of black sickle-cell patients, based on a model that predicts they will share a suite of blood factors 93 per cent of the time (2008: 207).[20] Ponder the implications of such a model (which, when Shaz et al. reported, had not yet undergone clinical trials). Ponder, too, what the authors treat as a regrettable lacuna in research to date: 'Little is known about blood utilization by race or ethnicity' (2008: 211). They observe, however, that such work is under way. There has already been a study of 'transfusion rates based on race and ethnicity, that used Medicare billing to tabulate the different rates of elderly black, white, and Hispanic patients' (2008: 210). And so on in this vein. Here, then, is an ethnographic hive of embodied activity in which men and women simultaneously assume and discover that races have distinguishing bloods and corresponding 'special considerations' in matters of blood transfusion. From that hive comes an endless supply of fresh input for the identity programme of soul – that is, for blood as race, or, again, as soul seen from the outside.

The authors carefully define their subject, but the definition is useless if the subject is natural blood:

> We use the term 'African American' to represent people of African descent living within the United States, thus encompassing not only those who identify with African American culture but also those who identify with other cultural groups such as English-speaking Caribbean and African immigrants. We use the term 'white' to represent white or Caucasian non-Hispanic individuals (2008: 202).

The centuries-long mixing that constitutes 'African descent' in the New World is news to almost no one, but apparently is either unknown to the authors or incompatible with the logic that they apply to blood. The immense genetic diversity of Africa's populations is well documented, but has no place within that logic (Achenbach 2009).[21] Language and culture are independent of biological ancestry, but in the authors' world, it seems, both are, like totemic clans, internally unified and externally distinguished by differing bloods. In sum, the ancient correspondence of collective identity with blood persists where few would expect to find it. The fact that 'African American' has now acquired a place in the scientific classification of blood testifies to that persistence. 'African American' is a name. The name evokes an essence. That essence is soul. Soul haunts science.

I speculated that positivism attracted Durkheim as a method of applying disciplined reason to problems set in an era of madness. I then applied the method he developed in *Elementary Forms* to the madness of our own day. That method brings out the centrality of rites – observable doing – in a resolutely empirical project for the sociological study of collective identifications. Talcott Parsons scolded Durkheim posthumously for having ignored the 'nonempirical' and 'subjective' aspects of religion in his book about what he called (advisedly, I think) 'religious life', not 'religion' tout court. What do those dissatisfactions amount to? I conclude by imagining how Durkheim might have answered.

Parsons complained, above all, that Durkheim 'never explicitly or in any way consciously abandoned his materialistic position' – a 'carryover from earlier stages' that stood 'in need of correction' (1968 [1937]: 413). But the subject and method of *Elementary Forms* require no such move. There, soul emerges from ethnography as something that is ideal yet actual and that, besides, often takes the entirely observable form of blood. Perhaps more crucially for Parsons, though, Durkheim's materialistic position allowed 'no status whatever to ... elements *not susceptible of empirical treatment* from the points of view both of the observer and of the actor' (1968 [1937]: 426; my emphasis). That worry would amaze Durkheim. Are God, the supernatural and the miraculous to receive a 'status' in an *empirical* science of sociology, even though they are unavailable to most people's observation (even the believers') most of the time? What sort of 'status' might that be? Durkheim's method 'eliminates' everything but social reality, Parsons goes on to say (1968 [1937]: 420). Once again, though, what eliminated reality is available to be put back in? Durkheim might simply have replied with another question: Isn't empirical reality challenging enough? When Descartes stepped out on his lonely road, confident that a merciful God would not allow an evil demon to confound his perception permanently, he toiled to learn *how* to learn about empirical reality.

Parsons might then shift ground to fire his biggest gun, the centrality of subjective meaning to sociological method: 'The full methodological import of his theory is not clear until one turns to the subjective aspect, which he did not do in any way – else the remaining positive elements of his thought must have collapsed under the strain' (1968 [1937]: 427). What strain? Well before the work of theorizing, strain comes with every effort to extract from individual informants the reasons, or the meaning, of this or that rite. Strain comes, too, with the often dizzying opacity of available replies – for example, the reason given at Joshua 5:4–7 for a great multitude of circumcisions done at a place called the hill of the foreskins – because the young men were uncircumcised (Jay 1992: 8–9). Durkheim insisted that rites first, foremost and above all are things periodically *done*, creating collective realities that otherwise can neither come into being nor persist. The Australian ethnography reveals kinds of ritual doing that exhibit the same logic when found in disparate places far from Australia – indeed, so disparate and so far from the Australian clans Durkheim studied that the only thing they have in common is the presence of human beings.

Finally, given my encounter with a certain sort of science, I find one criticism, framed by Parsons as a rhetorical question, more intriguing than all the rest: 'If the reality underlying religion is an empirical reality, why should religious ideas take symbolic form in a way in which scientific ideas do not?' Don't they?

Notes

I thank Ayala Emmett for many discussions, Sondra Hausner for sharp-witted querying when it counted and Maïmouna F. Bagate for technical readings.

1. Cynthia A. Smith, Regional Manager, Minority Recruitment and Diversity Outreach, American Red Cross, 19 August 2010, in author's possession.
2. See specifically Parsons (1968 [1937]: 427).
3. See my discussion of 'elemental' (for *élémentaire*) in 'Religion as an Eminently Social Thing', in Durkheim (1995 [1912]: lix–lxi).
4. My translations. This rich study has just appeared in English (Fournier 2012).
5. See Durkheim (1966 [1897]: 82–103, esp. 83).
6. Nell Irvin Painter has demonstrated the use of photography and diagrams to establish the objective reality of (so-called) racial 'types' (2010: 212–45).

7. When Joseph Ward Swain translated the title of II.8 as 'The Notion of *the* Soul' to render Durkheim's title, *La Notion d'âme*, he used one 'the' too many. *La Notion de l'âme* is not the same thing. See Fields (1996).
8. This is the fascinating subject of III.3, 'Mimetic Rites and the Principle of Causality'; see Durkheim (1995 [1912]: 360–61, 366).
9. Cf. Durkheim (1995 [1912]: 349n55).
10. See my comparison of the four English translations in Fields (2005).
11. Another retranslation has appropriated this error. See Durkheim (2001 [1912]: 348n170) and Fields (2004: 200).
12. M. F. Ashley-Montagu's (1952 [1946], esp. chap. 3) dissection of the ancient blood mystique, in its twentieth-century racist manifestation, still rewards the reader. For a judicious reappraisal, see Hazard (2011).
13. Compare Durkheim (1995 [1912]: 151), where animate and inanimate beings classified together 'are only modalities of the totemic being'.
14. Quoted in Robyn Mahone-Lonesome (1990: 77) and Lederer (2008: 117).
15. Nancy Jay (1992: 44) describes an ancient Greek lawsuit that turned on this point.
16. William C. Boyd, *Genetics and the Races of Man: An Introduction to Modern Physical Anthropology* (Oxford: Blackwell, 1950), 151. Quoted by W. Montagu Cobb.
17. Kenny quotes A. C. Wehrein's *New York Times* article (7 November 1959), A2, A3.
18. The National Medical Association was founded in 1895. Seventy-four years later, the American Medical Association opened to African American doctors. Within the NMA, Dr. Cobb led a long fight against the policies of the AMA. See Washington (2008).
19. A physician told of transfusions delayed even though blood from a racially different donor was available. (See Bordin. 1990: 1420 and Fields and Fields (2012: 64–66).
20. They add, as if all else were settled in science, that 'the social and ethical implications of racially labeling blood must be carefully considered, even if the use is limited to the care of sickle cell patients' (Shaz et al. 2008: 207).
21. Achenbach reports on Sarah A. Tischkoff et al., 'The Genetic Structures and History of Africans and African Americans', *Science* 324(5930, 22 May 2009): 1035–44.

References

Achenbach, J. 2009. 'Africans Have World's Highest Genetic Diversity, Study Finds', *Washington Post*, 1 May, Met 2 Edition, p. A4.

Bordin, G. M. Correspondence, *The New England Journal of Medicine* 323(15): 1420.

Descartes, R. 1992 [1979]. *Méditations métaphysiques*, with an Introduction by Michelle Beyssade and Jean-Marie Beyssade. Paris: Garnier-Flammarion.

Durkheim, E. 1966 [1897]. *Suicide: A Study in Sociology*, trans. J.A. Spaulding and G. Simpson, ed. George Simpson. New York: Free Press.

———. 1995 [1912]. *The Elementary Forms of Religious Life*, trans. K.E. Fields. New York: The Free Press.

———. 2001 [1912]. *The Elementary Forms of Religious Life*, ed. M.S. Cladis and C. Cosman. New York: Oxford University Press.

———, and M. Mauss. 1963 [1903]. *Primitive Classification*, trans. R. Needham. Chicago: University of Chicago Press.

Faulkner, W. 1992 [1932]. *Light in August*. Norwalk, CT: Easton Press.

Fields, K.E. 1995. 'Religion as an Eminently Social Thing', in E. Durkheim, *The Elementary Forms of Religious Life*. New York: Free Press.

———. 1996. 'Durkheim and the Idea of Soul', *Theory and Society* 25: 193–203.

———. 2002. 'Individualism and the Intellectuals: An Imaginary Conversation between Emile Durkheim and W. E. B. Du Bois', in C. Lérat and N. Ollier (eds), *Expansions/Espansionismes dans le monde transatlantique, Actes du colloque international, Bordeaux, 25–27 janvier 2001*, Bordeaux, Maison des Sciences de l'Homme d'Aquitaine, and in a somewhat different version, *Theory and Society* 31(4): 435–62.

———. 2004. 'The Scholarly Translator's Work', *The Journal of the Historical Society* 4(2): 189–202.

———. 2005. 'Translating Durkheim on Religion', in T.F. Godlove (ed.), *Teaching Durkheim*. New York: Oxford, pp. 53–86.

Fields, B.J. and K.E. Fields. 2012. *Racecraft: The Soul of Inequality in American Life*. New York: Verso Books.

Forti, S. 2006. 'The Biopolitics of Souls: Racism, Nazism, and Plato', *Political Theory* 34(1): 9–32.

Fournier, M. 2007. *Emile Durkheim (1858–1917)*. Paris: Fayard.

———. 2012. *Émile Durkheim: A Biography*, trans. D. Macey. London: Polity Press.

Hazard, A.Q. 2011. 'A Racialized Deconstruction? Ashley Montagu and the 1950 UNESCO Statement on Race', *Transforming Anthropology* 19(2): 174–86.

Jay, N.B. 1992. *Throughout Your Generations Forever: Sacrifice, Religion, and Paternity*. Chicago: University of Chicago Press.

Jewish Virtual Library. 2011 [1935]. 'Law for the Protection of German Blood and German Honor (September 15, 1935)'. Retrieved 12 May 2011 from http://www.jewishvirtuallibrary.org/jsource/Holocaust/nurmlaw2.

Journal of the National Medical Association. 1960. Editorial: 'Blood Transfusion and Race' 52(4): 280–82.

Kenny, M.G. 2002. 'Towards a Racial Abyss: Eugenics, Wickliffe Draper, and the Origins of the Pioneer Fund [in 1937]', *Journal of the History of the Behavioral Sciences* 38(3): 259–83.

————. 2006. 'A Question of Blood, Race, and Politics', *Journal of the History of Medicine and Allied Sciences* 61(4): 457–91.

Leary, W.E. 1990. 'Uneasy Doctors Add Race-Consciousness to Diagnostic Tools', *New York Times*, 25 September, p. C1.

Lederer, S.E. 2008. *Flesh and Blood: Organ Transplantation and Blood Transfusion in Twentieth-Century America*. Oxford: Oxford University Press.

Love, S., with a Foreword by J. Hope Franklin. 1997. *One Blood: The Death and Resurrection of Charles R. Drew*. Chapel Hill: University of North Carolina Press.

Mahone-Lonesome, R. 1990. *Charles Drew*. New York: Chelsea House.

Merllié, D. 1998. 'Did Lucien Lévy-Bruhl Answer the Objections Made in *Les Formes élémentaires?*' In N.J. Allen, W.S.F. Pickering and W. Watts-Miller (eds), *On Durkheim's Elementary Forms of Religious Life*. London: Routledge, pp. 29–38.

Montagu, M.F.A. 1952 [1946]. *Man's Most Dangerous Myth: The Fallacy of Race, Third Edition*. New York: Harper & Bros.

New York Times. 1935. Wireless: 'Says Transfusion Can't Alter Race,' 20 October, p. 28.

Painter, N.I. 2010. *The History of White People*. New York: Norton.

Parsons, T. 1968 [1937]. *The Structure of Social Action, Vol. I*. New York: Free Press.

Pereira, A., R. Massara, and R. Castillo; and B.J. Wilson-Relyea. 1990. Correspondence, *The New England Journal of Medicine* 323(15): 1421–22.

Scudder, J.C. and W. Wigle. 1960. 'Safer Transfusions Through Appreciation of Variants in Blood Group Antigens in Negro and White Blood Donors, Including Two Case Reports Showing Development of Anti-jk(a); Jk(b); Anti-S and Anti-Fy(a) Iso-antibodies', *Journal of the National Medical Association* 52(2): 75–80.

Shaz, B.H., J.C. Zimring, D.G. Demmons, and C.D. Hillyer. 2008. 'Blood Donation and Blood Transfusion: Special Considerations for African Americans', *Transfusion Medicine Reviews* 22(3): 202–14.

Spencer, B. and F.J. Gillen. 1904. *The Native Tribes of Central Australia*. London: Macmillan.

Starr, D. 2002. *Blood: An Epic History of Medicine and Commerce*. New York: HarperCollins.

Tucker, W.H. 1994. *The Science and Politics of Racial Research*. Champagne: University of Illinois Press.

Vichinsky, E.P., MD, A. Earles, PNP, R.A. Johnson, MD, M.S. Hoag, MD, A. Williams, MT, and B. Lubin, MD. 1990. 'Alloimmunization in Sickle Cell Anemia and Transfusion of Racially Unmatched Blood', *New England Journal of Medicine* 322(23): 1617–21.

Washington, H.A. 2008. 'Apology Shines Light on Racial Schism in Medicine', *New York Times*, 29 July, p. F5.

White, W.F. 1948. *A Man Called White: The Autobiography of Walter White*. New York: Viking.

PART II

Social Forms

Chapter 2

RETURN TO DURKHEIM

CIVIL RELIGION AND THE MORAL
RECONSTRUCTION OF CHINA

Ji Zhe

Every concept has its destiny. In 1967, Robert N. Bellah published 'Civil Religion in America', which would strongly influence the contemporary sociology of religion. In this article, he took up anew the term 'civil religion', which had first appeared two hundred years earlier in Jean-Jacques Rousseau's *On the Social Contract,* and coined it as a new concept for bringing out the religious dimension of American political discourse and public life. In the following two decades, this concept led social scientists in the United States into heated debate over the origins, definitions and functions of civil religion (Gehrig 1981; Mathisen 1989). But these debates failed to reach any agreement and instead rendered the concept ideologically polysemous (see Richey and Jones 1974; Lüchau 2009), including 'civil religion' as a form of national self-worship. Feeling that this development was against his original intention, Bellah has tried to avoid using this concept since the 1980s. As he pointed out himself (Bellah 1989), even though the central theme of a subsequent work, *Habits of the Heart* (Bellah et al. 1985), is by nature still civil religion, he did not employ the term.[1]

Bellah's caution did not, however, diminish the enthusiasm about civil religion in the social sciences. Recently, the related research has become quite vigorous on both sides of the Atlantic. In Britain, homeland of the Puritanism that is often seen as a source of American civil religion, Grace Davie (2001) posited the possibility of a 'global civil religion' as a new perspective for the sociology of religion in the age of globalization. In France, where modern history has been deeply marked by Rousseau, the debates on civil religion between Jean Baubérot (2007, 2009) and Jean-Paul Willaime (2009) shed new light on the place of religion in public life and advanced the understanding of the reality and underlying principles of French secularism (*laïcité*). In the United States, Philip S. Gorski (2010, forthcoming) relocates civil religion in its ideational competition with religious nationalism and liberal secularism vis-à-vis the boundaries between religious and political communities in modern society; he argues that the political discourse of Barack Obama is a sign of the revival of American civil religion.

In the last few years, with the resumption of religious studies and the rise of cultural conservatism in China, the concept of civil religion has begun to attract the attention of Chinese scholars. Inspired by Bellah, Chen Ming (2007, 2009, 2012) argues that the notion of civil religion offers a new horizon for Chinese to find an appropriate place for Confucianism in contemporary and future China.[2] Confucianism, he asserts, could and should be rebuilt as a Chinese civil religion – that is, a universal symbolic reference for producing a moral consensus, expressed in both political conceptualization and folk rituals. He further points out the advantage of civil religion: it does not need an institutional apparatus, and so is quite suited to the weakly institutionalized situation of Confucianism in present-day China. Chen does acknowledge the paradox that would be inherent in establishing Confucianism as a state religion in the modern contexts,[3] and he distinguishes such a mandate from his proposition to rebuild Confucianism from the ground up, trying to conciliate cultural nationalism and constitutional democracy (Chen Yizhong 2012). Chen Ming's idea has evoked various responses, but most critics consider it to represent an open conservatism. Chen is certainly not the only advocate of a privileged political function of Confucianism in China: he and his *Yuandao* are at the centre of a group of scholars who are trying to combine cultural conservatism with a moderate claim for more political freedom.[4]

It is not surprising that the notion of civil religion has been linked to Confucianism, which was the dominant and universal religion in Chinese society for about two thousand years. At the beginning of the twentieth century, with the collapse of the imperial regime and especially the abolition in 1905 of the imperial system of civil service examinations, Confucianism lost its privileged status in both political and educational fields, and modern Chinese states excluded Confucianism from the new category of religion.[5] During the twentieth century, social movements seeking to revive Confucianism as a religion in China repeatedly appeared in various forms (Gan Chunsong 2006). In this context, the concept of civil religion provides a new discursive instrument for the intellectual imaginary of the status of Confucianism in post-1989 China, where the ideological vacuum is harsh.

But in the end, what is civil religion? Bellah's 'American civil religion' refers to the religious dimension of political institutions, and even of the whole social fabric of public life. This religious dimension is expressed in a set of beliefs, symbols and rituals that bestow a sacred and universal meaning to the concrete experiences of a particular nation-state. But what exactly are the relations between civil religion and those three elements that it brings together: religion, politics and society? If people have different ideas of what such relations are in reality and what they should be at a normative level, they have necessarily different and even opposite understandings and expectations of civil religion. In fact, these differences and divergences explain the controversy incited by the term civil religion. Therefore, I argue, an adequate interpretation of the relations between civil religion and religion, and politics and society, is the precondition for finding a good civil religion in the present-day Chinese context. My main purpose here is to attempt to reveal some fundamental positions contained in Bellah's concept of civil religion through a strategic return to Emile Durkheim (and Rousseau when necessary), by analysing the nature, function and constructive principles of a desirable civil religion.

Non-religious Sacredness

The term 'civil religion' is borrowed from Rousseau, but Bellah's ideas are directly derived from Durkheim. As Bellah claimed, despite misunderstandings about his use of the concept, his argument was clear, 'the sort of thing that any Durkheimian would have said' (1989: 147), and he has never recanted this position. While writing a series of articles on American civil religion, he concurrently edited and published *Emile Durkheim on Morality and Society* (Bellah 1973). In his Introduction to that work, Bellah declared admiringly that Durkheim was not only a sociologist, philosopher and moralist, but also 'a high priest and a theologian of the civil religion of the Third Republic and a prophet calling not only modern France but modern Western society generally to mend its ways in the face of a great social and moral crisis' (Bellah 1973: x). Bellah's view on Durkheim is shared by other scholars: Hans-Peter Müller (1988) argued that the concept of civil religion could help us understand how Durkheim in his later years searched for a solution to social integration in modern society by putting individual autonomy and collective conscience into the context of a democratic state and institutional differentiation. Recently, in the Introduction to the sixth edition of *Les formes élémentaires de la vie religieuse*, Jean-Paul Willaime (2008) also emphasized the importance of the theme of civil religion in Durkheim's studies.

Yet Durkheim never used the term civil religion except in his citation of Rousseau (Durkheim 1970 [1952]). How can one claim he had the idea of civil religion? Durkheim's sociology of religion, whose comprehensive expression is *Elementary Forms*, actually concerns 're-ligion' on two levels. When Durkheim argues that society is the ultimate source of moral authority and the mobilizing force of religion, he is talking about specific historical religions. When he argues for the necessity and the persistence of religion as a 'force *sui generis*' for humanity, his 'religion' refers in fact to the generic form of moral life that expresses the sacredness of society itself. These two facets are logically coherent, that is, they are dual aspects of the same fact. However, what is important here is that, in principle, the sacredness of society can be expressed in forms completely different from those of specific historical religions. According to Durkheim, as long as society exists in the history of human beings, religion in its general sense will not disappear. If a certain religion is not compatible with a new collective conscience, its function and status will be replaced by a new one. In modern society, facing the unprecedented rise of individual autonomy, division of labour and instrumental rationality, the old religions seem to have failed to provide a plausible moral foundation for the identity, action and intellectuality of modern people. In such a situation, in order to find a basic morality that can have universal resonance and guide the consciousness and practice of modern people, one should resort to secular rationality and leave behind the forms and contents of specific traditional religions. Thereby, even though Durkheim does not use the concept of civil religion directly, under the premise of the sacredness of society, his functionalist view of religion and rationalist theory of modernity open the door to civil religion. The former implies the possible presence of civil religion while the latter promises new form and content, distinguishing it from the religions of premodern society.

From this point of view, civil religion in a Durkheimian sense is the result of the dissociation of the sacredness of modern society from specific religions, and it can be seen as a secular substitute for traditionally dominant religions. Traditional society has no civil religion in its full meaning, since the expression of its sacredness is always through one or several specific religions. Only when the sacredness of society transcends the unalterable mystic dimension of specific religions can the possibility and necessity of civil religion emerge. Indeed, the word 'civil' has secular and non-religious connotations; to some extent, civil religion and secular beliefs are synonymous. Civil religion does not contradict secularization; the former is rather the necessary consequence of the latter.

In short, civil religion is common belief in the sacredness of a particular society, but it is not common religious belief. It is not a 'religion' as the term is usually understood, but a general horizon beyond the existent faiths, grown from the evolutive moral capacities of human beings. Durkheim explicitly points out the possible dissociation between new faiths and particularized religions in modern society in the Conclusion of *Elementary Forms:*

> There are no gospels which are immortal, but neither is there any reason for believing that humanity is incapable of inventing new ones. As to the question of what symbols this new faith will express itself with, whether they will resemble those of the past or not, and whether or not they will be more adequate for the reality which they seek to translate, that is something which surpasses the human faculty of foresight and which does not appertain to the principal question. (1964 [1912]: 428)

If Durkheim does not lay out his assumptions about the 'new faith' of humanity here, he does elaborate the relevant issues in *Professional Ethics and Civic Morals* (1958 [1950]). The civic morals he promotes are based not only on individual rights in civil institutions, but also on social associations such as 'corporations' that integrate professional and moral life. Meanwhile, moral education depends above all on rational secular education, especially in the human and social sciences (Durkheim 2002 [1925]).

In spite of his secularist vision of morality, Durkheim is aware that, in many cases, religious morals are just morals, neither more nor less: to simply eradicate religion from morals might destroy the latter. Hence, if the rationalization of morals means to 'discover the rational substitutes for those religious notions that for a long time have served as the vehicle for the most essential moral ideas' (2002 [1925]: 9), these substitutes do not exclude the resources provided by existing religions. At the same time, new morals might form their own symbols, saints and festivals, as happened during the French Revolution (Durkheim 1964 [1912]: 214). Thus, although the relations between civil religion and specific religions may be various, it is neither necessary nor appropriate for civil religion to become the 'avatar' of a specific religion.

Civil religion does not need the institutional form of common re-ligions, but neither is it the non-institutional expression of a specific religion. It is rather a set of diffuse collective sentiments that virtually express the general will of a society. As Bellah suggested more than once, civil religion resides mainly in habits, customs and public opin-ion as vehicles of simple but fundamental values (Bellah 1967; Bellah and Hammond 1980). By taking civil religion as a public expression of collective conscience, Bellah is faithful to both Durkheim and Rous-seau. In *On the Social Contract*, Rousseau regards morality, customs and public opinion as the most important kind of law:

> [It] is not graven on tablets of marble or brass, but on the hearts of the citizens. This forms the real constitution of the State, takes on every day new powers, when other laws decay or die out, restores them or takes their place, keeps a people in the ways in which it was meant to go, and insensibly replaces authority by the force of habit. I am speaking of morality, of custom, above all of public opinion ... (Rousseau 2003 [1762]: 36)

And Durkheim remarks that by morality, custom and public opinion Rousseau 'means the collective ways of thinking and acting which, without assuming an explicit and established form, determine the mentality and behaviour of human beings exactly as formal laws would do' (1970 [1952]: 122). Paradoxically, Rousseau writes that this formless law is not relevant to his study on government; indeed, the chapter on 'Civil Religion' was not included in the outline of the book but was written as a complement to the original manuscript and took the form of a sort of conclusion for the whole.[6] We might infer a certain correspondence between the chapter 'Civil Religion' and the informal 'law' implied in morality, custom and public opinion, since in the final analysis they are both concerned with collective moral feeling. According to Rousseau's assumptions, the articles of civil re-ligion should not be fixed exactly 'as religious dogmas, but as social sentiments without which a man cannot be a good citizen or a faithful subject' (2003 [1762]: 96). Moreover, 'the dogmas of civil religion ought to be few, simple, and exactly worded, without explanation or commentary' (2003 [1762]: 96). That is, they are somehow self-evident, arising as the expressions of moral humans.

For Republic

Interestingly, some of the dogmas Rousseau chose as iconic are explic-itly religious in nature, including 'the existence of a mighty, intelligent and beneficent Divinity, possessed of foresight and providence, the life to come, the happiness of the just, the punishment of the wicked', complemented by 'the sanctity of the social contract and the laws', and the rejection of 'intolerance' of some cults (2003 [1762]: 96). If freed from their context, these dogmas of Rousseau's civil religion could be seen as parallel to popular moral-religious teachings in China, such as 'There are Gods above one's head' (举头三尺有神明), 'Do right for the life to come if not for this one' (不修今世修来世), 'Good will be rewarded with good, and evil with evil' (善有善报, 恶有恶报), 'A righteous man does not fear officials and a good conscience is not afraid of ghosts' (理正不怕官, 心正不怕鬼), 'It exists if you believe it; and doesn't if you don't' (信则有, 不信则无).

However, Rousseau's civil religion seems much harsher than either these Chinese aphorisms or Bellah's interpretation of simple morality, custom and public opinion. For Rousseau, the dogmas of civil religion are fixed by the Sovereign. Although the Sovereign 'can compel no one to believe them, it can banish from the State whoever does not believe them' and even execute those who do not believe but pretend to believe in them:

> It can banish him, not for impiety, but as an anti-social being, incapable of truly loving the laws and justice, and of sacrificing, at need, his life to his duty. If anyone, after publicly recognising these dogmas, behaves as if he does not believe them, let him be punished by death: he has committed the worst of all crimes, that of lying before the law. (Rousseau 2003 [1762]: 96)

This passage is prone to misunderstanding, especially in the contemporary Chinese context, where 'rule by law' (法制) is not yet preconditioned by the 'rule of law' (法治).[7] If Rousseau's civil religion is only an ideological weapon of a state that employs law to rule the population, can there be something worse than that? To answer this question, we must understand 'the Sovereign' and 'the law', and learn why 'anti-social' is sinful. For Rousseau, not every political body is worthy of 'sovereignty', which is the abstract generalization of the active state of a political and moral union based on a social compact. Such a union can be nothing but a *Republic*; the 'social compact' can be summarized as one where '[e]ach of us puts his person and all his power in common under the supreme direction of the general will, and, in our corporate capacity, we receive each member as an indivisible part of the whole' (Rousseau 2003 [1762]: 9). Since every citizen in such a Republic forms part of the sovereignty, it obtains universal support and becomes then sacred and absolute. But exactly because of this social base, the sovereignty cannot surpass the limits set by the compact: if the Sovereign breaks the compact by treating its citizens unequally, violating the legal rights of each individual or transferring the sovereignty to any 'Master', then the sovereignty no longer represents the general will and thus is no longer legitimate.

As for citizens of the Republic who share the sovereignty, they should fulfil their obligations as subjects under the laws of the state, if their goal is to provide a sound public. To protect legal rights with active intent is also an obligation of the people: 'If ... the people promise simply to obey, by that very act it dissolves itself and loses what makes it a people' (Rousseau 2003 [1762]: 16). The sovereignty possesses authority, but it can be maintained only through law, which is the very expression of the general will. Since the social compact guarantees the unity between law and general will, to comply with law is also to comply with the general will, and to fulfil one's obligation becomes one with enjoying one's liberty. Thus, in Rousseau's arguments, if civil religion is set by the Sovereign and maintained by law, the condition is that this sovereignty is in the hands of the people and law is the expression of general will.

Once more, Rousseau's and Bellah's views on civil religion converge. Rousseau's launch of the concept of civil religion aimed to find a way out of the tensions between Christianity at the time and the new values incarnated by the Republic. Thus civil religion could be seen as the moral content of the social contract, or the sacred expression of general will, and the fundamental conscience of the Republic. Similarly, for Bellah, civil religion is the set of moral principles that grounds American public life; it cannot exist without the republican nature of the United States (cf. Bellah 1967, 1975). Bellah is against any self-worship by the state; he writes: 'at its best civil religion [is] realized in a situation where politics operates within a set of moral norms, and both politics and morality are open to transcendent judgment' (1974: 271). In fact, when Bellah brought forth the concept of civil religion, his real intention was to criticize U.S. politics during the Vietnam War period from a moral point of view.

Hence, contrary to some interpretations, the civil religion of Rousseau and Bellah does not aim to legitimize existing governments. To make good citizens for a democratic republic governed by law, civil religion needs to be alert to any violation of the general will by state power, holding the latter to the judgement of values rather than interests. Rousseau repeatedly asserts that if the Sovereign violates the rights of the citizens, it is no longer what it should be and people are not obliged to comply with it. Bellah (1967: 18) summarizes a citizen's rule by quoting Henry David Thoreau: 'If the law is of such a nature that it requires you to be an agent of injustice to another, then I say, break the law.'

Regrettably, in recent discussions of moral reconstruction in China some people have borrowed the term civil religion, explicitly or implicitly, without taking 'the sovereignty of the people' and 'civil rights' as its basic assumptions, as Rousseau and Bellah insisted upon. Some sophisticated scholarly works that tend to bind together the Chinese Communist regime – from Maoist revolution to post-Mao reform – and Chinese tradition, especially Confucianism (e.g., Chen Yun 2007; Gan Yang 2007; Liu 2007; Qi 2010; Ding 2011), exhibit symptoms of such a trend. Those demagogues advocating so-called 'Chinese values', 'the Chinese model' and 'the Chinese way' have never questioned the nature of the political regime in which they live, nor are they concerned with the enslaved state of Chinese citizens. Instead, they accept unconditionally the legitimacy of the current state: political slogans are upheld as the dogmas of Chinese civil religion; traditionalist rhetoric is used to legitimize the destruction of tradition; history is pushed into oblivion in the name of commemoration and the dead evil ones such as Mao Zedong are being brought back and re-envisioned as gods. The manipulations of these academic-visaged demagogues have had some effects, sometimes arousing sincere passions in the youth.

These developments are not good signs. They reflect the 'theological' crisis following the political crisis in contemporary China: if the construction of civil religion is not intended to pursue civil rights, to defend civil society – if it does not dare to make a moral critique of history and reality from the perspective of transcendental values – it can only be a double betrayal of both the 'civil' and 'religion'. Those who interpret civil religion as the legitimizing discourse of the existing power and try to manipulate it are blaspheming the sacred. Their witchcraft can distort the collective consciousness to a certain degree, but they cannot achieve their purpose of legitimizing a regime that violates the general will. Legitimacy can never be generated by the manipulation of discourse; by nature it depends on the moral choice of free citizens in public life. A true civil religion is precisely a set of basic rules that maintains a healthy public life, that is, republican values.

Defending Society

Probably the most complete and concise expression of republican values that mankind could conceive of is condensed in the national motto chosen by the French people of the Third Republic, during which Durkheim lived: 'Liberty, Equality, Fraternity'. These three terms can arouse one's conscience without further explication; they are the fundamental principles for constructing one of the most desirable societies that humanity could imagine. Few thinkers have deepened our understanding of society to the degree Durkheim has done. In his *Elementary Forms* (1964 [1912]; see also 1960 [1914]), the social is not only an intrinsic part of human nature, but also the eternal source of what comes to be construed as the sacredness of morals and values. Society transcends the banality of individual life and the volatility of political struggles; it is the root of civil religion.

Although Durkheim is not exactly a social contractist, he would undoubtedly agree that modern society should be based on a valid moral and legal consensus. Referring to Rousseau, Durkheim (1970 [1952]: 100–3) points out that with the social contract, people achieve the transition from a state of nature to the civil state; only then can the de facto order become a de jure order, from which civic morals emerge. In such a society, the collective transcends the individual and determines individual freedom; meanwhile, individual freedom is considered a sacred good and is translated into a right. Hence each person's freedom is no longer bounded by the strength of the individual but is drawn from his or her obligation, deriving from the fundamental contract, to respect the general will. It is the same for equality. Each member of the community gives to the public the property he or she possesses de facto; then society restores to citizens what it has thus received. The equal distribution of public property is moral and legitimate because it reflects the general will and is therefore just.

To a certain degree, the social contract resolves in theory the tensions between individual and society. Out of such a contract, society gains its nature as superior to that of individuals and at the same time preserves freedom and equality. In this situation, 'each personal will is absorbed into the collective will, for each person, "in giving himself to all, gives himself to nobody"' (Durkheim 1970 [1952]: 99). Inversely, only under a contract agreed upon by free citizens in equality can each individual and his or her partners bear in mind duty and law in all their interactions, acquiring the mutual recognition that constitutes society. For this reason, to defend society is above all to guarantee the equal rights and liberty of each of its members, so that both collectivity and individuality in human nature may be fully respected and united in a reasonable equilibrium.

Furthermore, defending society means the negation of the 'logic of force'. In Durkheimian sociology, a society worthy of the name is incompatible with the domination of violence: it can neither emerge out of violence nor be maintained by it. Humanity is precisely constituted by its capacity to liberate itself from the law of the jungle and by its 'goodwill' of 'gift-giving' to the weaker of its species. In other words, to defend society means to oppose 'the cult of power' or any kind of social Darwinism. Here, Durkheim again refers to Rousseau: if law is the keystone of the social system, its superiority must not be fictitious but rationally justifiable; 'even if the right of the stronger could be justified rationally, it would not provide a basis for society. A society is an organized body in which each part is dependent upon the whole and vice versa' (Durkheim 1970 [1952]: 97). As Rousseau intimates, only reasonable and just law can win voluntary submission and bring forth genuine harmony.

It is important to emphasize that 'harmony' is a natural outcome of social justice but is not itself a fundamental value. It is unacceptable to confuse harmony with justice, and worse still to replace justice with so-called harmony. Since the slogan of building a 'harmonious society' (和谐社会) was coined by the Chinese Communist Party (CCP) in 2005, both western scholars and media have widely considered it partial evidence of the onset of a new political incarnation of Confucianism. In reality, however, the discursive context of the CCP's 'harmony' is wholly unrelated to Confucianism; its actual meaning is nothing but 'stability' (稳定). Since the violent suppression of the 1989 Tiananmen protests, the CCP has been haunted by the sentiment that it is reaching the end of its destiny, and by an insurmountable fear of the impending eruption of civil resistance. Stability – the monopoly of political power by the CCP for as long as possible – has become the regime's foremost preoccupation. This stability does not rely upon the rule of law, the separation of power or any efficient institutional arrangements for social negotiation and equilibrium, but on a rigid negation of all dissidence or social mobilization for rights. In such a context, the CCP never hesitates to resort to violence to put down non-official social mobilizations; any political criticism or protest is liable to be censored or sanctioned in the name of the maintenance of 'harmony'. How could such an alienating, violent policy be compatible with Confucian virtues such as *ren* (仁, humanness) and *yi* (义, justice)?[8]

Indeed, Rousseau pointed out more than two centuries ago that the despot too can assure his subjects civil tranquillity:

> But what do they gain, if the very tranquillity they enjoy is one of their miseries? Tranquillity is found also in dungeons; but is that enough to make them desirable places to live in? The Greeks imprisoned in the

cave of the Cyclops lived there very tranquilly, while they were awaiting their turn to be devoured. (Rousseau 2003 [1762]: 5)

In other words, power and violence cannot establish a desirable order. The stability maintained by a dictatorship may last for a relatively long time, but this stability is itself a violent aggression. The logic of force revered by a dictatorship directly erodes the basis of society. Once the domination of the weak by the strong becomes the operational principle of a society, this society is no longer the material and spiritual shelter of its members, but an anonymous enemy. The recent series of tragic incidents in China[9] warn us that when marginalized or traumatized members try to take revenge on society through the same logic of force imposed by the dominating groups, the victims will often be the weakest members of that society.

China Cosmopolitan and the Religion of Humanity

If the goal of defending any given society is to maintain justice and solidarity, then these two principles must be held supreme, and the justice and solidarity of another society may not be violated, either. Only by combining the concrete experiences of a community with these universal values can individual societal orders obtain lasting moral righteousness. Hence, civil religion as the expression of the sacredness of society must also accommodate the relationships between different societies, and between individual societies and the whole of humanity. This is not to deny that each nation will have its particular collective conscience and thus its specific civil religion. But after all, civil religion is not national religion or ethnic religion: it aims at forming good citizens of a civilized society, rather than members of a national or ethnic community (though the two do not necessary contradict each other). At least in terms of the subject of civil religion, the differences caused by national cultures are much less problematic than the difficulties caused by political intervention. In so far as the Chinese government often uses a vulgar cultural particularism as a pretext for its abuse of human rights, anyone promoting civil religion in China should be vigilant to ensure that it not become the last refuge of 'patriotism'.

Bellah (1967: 18) quoted Thoreau's words to explain the principles of American civil religion: 'I would remind my countrymen that they are men first, and Americans at a late and convenient hour.' Contrary to some Chinese authors with nationalist spirit (for example Chen Yong 2007), this conception is not foreign to Chinese culture: a Chinese is first a human being and then a Chinese. 'China' (Zhongguo,

中国), the country at the 'centre', is a cosmopolitan concept in terms of civilization: it primarily means the centre of morals and values rather than the centre in terms of geography or power. Any society can be 'China' if it can fulfil human virtues to the maximum and provide a civilizational model for mankind. When the so-called country of China is disrespectful of human beings, or when it destroys justice, it loses its status as a civilizational centre and is no longer 'China' but a country of savages. This is precisely the view of 'China' expressed in the Confucian classics *Spring and Autumn* (春秋) edited by Confucius. Han Yu (韩愈, 768–824 CE), a famous man of letters of the Tang dynasty, summarizes it this way (1996: 2664): 'According to *Spring and Autumn* edited by Confucius, if vassals adopt the civilities of savages, they should be treated as savages; if they advance to adopt Chinese civilities, they should be treated as Chinese.' The modern scholar Yang Shuda (杨树达, 1885–1956 CE) further elaborates (1986: 67): 'The idea of *Spring and Autumn* is the following: if savages evolve to the level of China, consider them as Chinese. If China becomes savage, consider it as a country of savages.'

From this point of view, 'China' is a de-substantialized notion. In fact, in traditional Chinese thought, a distinction has long existed between *guo* (国, State) and *tianxia* (天下, All-Under-Heaven or World). *Guo* is a political entity with territory, integrated into the cyclic temporality of prosperity and decadence. In contrast, *tianxia*, defined in cultural and ethical terms, is an imaginary category reflecting a universal and eternal space where people living on the earth are unified by the rule of the highest and most sacred order: Heaven. Mencius (about 380–289 BCE), one of the greatest Confucian thinkers and the most important successor to Confucius, has emphasized that 'there are instances of individuals without *ren* ('benevolence' or 'humaneness') who have got possession of a *guo*, but there has been no instance of *tianxia* being controlled by one without *ren*'. In other words, only when a ruler follows the Way (*Dao*, 道) or 'the Heart of the People' (*minxin* 民心), can he have the dignity to reign over *tianxia*.

The concept of *tianxia* offers a wider horizon than that of regional power, and fundamental values rather than realpolitik. In this sense, Gu Yanwu (顾炎武, 1613–1682 CE), distinguished more clearly between *guo* and *tianxia*:

> There is the perishing of *guo*; there is also the perishing of *tianxia*. What is the difference between them? I say: the changing of names and titles [of dynasties] is the former, while blocking *ren* (humaneness) and *yi* (justice) even to the degree of 'leading on beasts to devour men, and men to devour one another', is the latter. (Gu 1984: 1014)

The saying 'leading on beasts to devour men, and men to devour one another' (率兽食人, 人将相食) comes from Mencius. It is used to describe the state of anomie and de-civilization created by an evil polity, while *tianxia* connotes the universal values and social orders of humanity and justice. When political power monopolizes or abuses resources so that humanity and justice cannot manifest, society disintegrates and 'China' loses its foundation. After distinguishing between *guo* and *tianxia*, Gu points out that politicians protect the state, but everyone protects *tianxia*.

This tradition seems to provide a good starting point for building a civil religion in today's China. It suggests that the legitimacy of the state does not come from force but from the transcendental values encoded in civilized social relations, implying thus the combination of national spirit and universal values. In this regard, Durkheim's moral sociology seems more inspiring than Rousseau's political philosophy. Rousseau's society is limited to the city republic, while Durkheim has examined the relationship between different societies and their corresponding moralities, and attempted to explain the unification of national objectives and human ideals. No doubt human ideals rank higher than national objectives.

In the line of Durkheimian sociology, morality can only come from within society. When mankind has not yet formed a unified human society with its proper consciousness and individuality, the respect of human morality is just empty words. Durkheim's proposed resolution is very instructive:

> The only way of resolving this difficulty, which troubles public thinking, is to seek the realization of the human ideal through the most highly developed groups that we know, through those closest to mankind as a whole, but without confusing the two – that is to say through the efforts of specific nations. To eliminate all such contradictions, thus satisfying the requirements of our moral consciousness, it suffices that the State commit itself as its main goal not to expanding, in a material sense, to the detriment of its neighbors, not to gaining greater strength than they, or to becoming richer than they; but to the goal of realizing among its own people the general interests of humanity – that is to say, committing itself to an access of justice, to a higher morality, to organizing itself in such a way that there is always a closer correspondence between the merit of its citizens and their condition of life with the end of reducing or preventing individual suffering. From this point of view, all rivalry between different countries disappears and, consequently, all contradiction between cosmopolitanism and patriotism. (Durkheim 2002 [1925]: 76–77)

In other words, it is by the return to man per se that one can find the way to combine national concern and higher, more universal human ideals. This is what Durkheim has called the 'religion of humanity' centred on the 'human person (*personne humaine*)':

> The human person, whose definition serves as the touchstone according to which good must be distinguished from evil, is considered as sacred. ... Whoever makes an attempt on a man's life, on a man's liberty, on a man's honour inspires us with a feeling of horror, in every way analogous to that which the believer experiences when he sees his idol profaned. Such a morality is therefore not simply a hygienic discipline or a wise principle of economy. It is a religion of which man is, at the same time, both believer and God. (Durkheim 1975a [1898]: 61–62)

This passage might be Durkheim's most explicit statement on modern civil religion, although he did not use the term directly. With this 'religion of humanity' Durkheim went beyond, to a certain degree, both the societist determinism of morality and the liberal version of individualism. On the one hand, as Bellah (1976: 158) has remarked, Durkheim did not see such a universal civil religion 'as some mere projection of the larger society, some making of the larger society into an object of ultimate concern', but focused it on 'a religious respect for "the human person" whose rights and dignity must not be violated by arbitrary corporate authority'. On the other hand, even though this religion is individualistic, it is by no means the 'egoistic cult of the self' advocated by utilitarian individualism, but the glorification of 'the individual in general': 'Its motive force is not egoism but sympathy for all that is human, a wider pity for all sufferings, for all human miseries, a more ardent desire to combat and alleviate them, a greater thirst for justice' (Durkheim 1975a [1898]: 64). Ruth Wallace (1977) called the individualism thus understood Durkheim's 'international civil religion', given its potential to combine defence of individual rights and the interests of society as a unified effort; respecting the rights of everyone in each country would be a way to realize the dignity of humanity as a whole.

Crisis and Prophet

Both Wallace and Bellah consider Durkheim a prophet of civil religion, or someone who calls the state to judgement, pointing out future directions in times of political and moral crisis. Bellah (1967) argues that the words of such prophets – Lincoln, Thoreau and Senator J. William Fulbright, who spoke out against the Vietnam War and appealed to the state to follow America's humane and democratic traditions – have salvaged the tradition of American civil religion. His respect and admiration for these prophets demonstrate once again that the mission of civil religion is to criticize the state from a moral stance rather than to defend the present power. It is this prophetic or critical element that distinguishes civil religion from the political use of religion or politics in religious guise (Lüchau 2009: 382).

The current political and social crisis in China calls for the appearance of prophets. Hasn't the crisis been serious enough? However, today's Chinese elite still evince cynical self-deception, nationalist arrogance and utilitarian selfishness. After 1989, the trust between the dominating class and the people was lost, and there is no valid ideology beyond the broad strokes of utilitarianism and nationalism. Some intellectuals oppose 'traditional culture' to universal values, simplify 'thoughts' by turning them into instruments of power and compete with each other to become the representatives of a fictitious China. As for religious figures, the double pressure from the market and the state has filled their discourse with philistine tactics of expediency. The majority have neither the intention to advocate the critical views that are beneficial to society nor the courage to publicly engage with them.

Honesty forces us to accept Weber's exhortation to modern intellectuals through Isaiah's oracles: many people despair, having received nothing after centuries of yearning for the coming of prophets and saviours (1922). Even though we may be shaken when we realize this, as Chinese, we have no choice: we must keep up our hopes for the reconstruction of the Chinese society and its values. Maybe reviewing the prophecy of Durkheim in his 'religious sentiments at the present time' can help us adjust our focus:

> We aspire to a higher justice than any of the existing formulae can express in a way that will satisfy us. These latent aspirations which disturb us will someday succeed in becoming more clearly conscious of themselves, in translating themselves into definite formulae which men can rally round and which will become a nucleus for the crystallization of the new beliefs. It is pointless to try to discern the content of these beliefs. Will they remain general and abstract, will they be linked with personal beings who will incarnate them and represent them? These are historical contingencies that one cannot foresee.
>
> The only thing that matters is to sense above the moral coldness which prevails on the surface of our collective life, the sources of warmth which our societies carry in themselves. One can go further and say with some precision that it is among the working classes in particular that these new forces are in the course of formation. (Durkheim 1975b [1919]: 186–87)

Thus may we keep our confidence high.

Notes

An earlier version of this chapter was published in Chinese in 社会学研究 [Sociological Studies] 2011(1): 118–32.

1. For the role of the concept of civil religion and its evolution in Bellah's sociology, see Bellah (2002) and Gorski (2010).
2. Before publishing his 'Rebuilding Confucianism as Civil Religion' (儒教的公民宗教说), Chen also published the Chinese translation of Bellah's 'Civil Religion in America' and related background and comments (Bellah 2007; Chen Yong 2007) in the famous cultural-conservative annual *Yuandao* (原道, *In Search of the Way*) that he edits.
3. Confucian fundamentalist projects have already been launched by Jiang Qing (2003, 2004) and Kang Xiaoguang (2004).
4. Some other intellectuals, who neither believe in democracy nor explicitly use the term 'civil religion', have also tried to reinterpret Confucianism as a potential or even real ideological and moral basis of contemporary China. For more details about Confucian revival and cultural conservatism with political concerns in contemporary China, see Billioud and Thoraval (2008, 2009).
5. The concept of 'religion' (*zongjiao* 宗教) is not a native Chinese category. Imported via Japan in the late nineteenth century, the western conception of 'religion' was progressively adopted by the early modern Chinese political and cultural elite (Chen Hsi-yuan 1999). A religion based on the Christian model, centred around a church, became the only legitimate form of religious organism (Goossaert 2008). Because of the abolition of imperial examination and ritual systems, Confucianism was deprived of its mechanism for the renewal of specialized 'priests' and was no longer considered a perfect embodiment of an institutionalized religion. Yu Yingshi (2004) vividly described this critical state of Confucianism in Modern China with his famous metaphor 'wandering spirit' or 'disembodied soul' (*youhun* 游魂).
6. 'Civil Religion' is Chapter VIII of the last part – Book IV – of *On the Social Contract*. Yet since Chapter IX, 'Conclusion', is composed of only several insignificant sentences, the Chapter 'Civil Religion' could be seen as the substantial conclusion.
7. In 'rule of law', the government serves the law and all legal principles are subject to certain supreme moral concerns, whereas in 'rule by law', the law is only an instrument of power. Without 'rule of law', 'rule by law' can be amoral and even evil, though it may be more predictable and thus in one sense better than 'rule without law'. For a discussion on this question in Chinese legalist tradition, see Winston (2005).
8. For a more complete analysis of the semantic, political and social meanings of the CCP's slogan of harmony, see Ji (forthcoming). Nakajima (2009) has remarked that in the contemporary Chinese intellectual discourse about Confucianism, justice is either absent or replaced by harmony.

9. In just the two months of March and April 2010, five attacks in Chinese
   schools and kindergartens wounded or killed more than fifty children
   and adults. In these and other terrifying incidents, the perpetrators of
   violence were often themselves victims of social injustice and exclusion,
   for whom the violence targeted at innocents was to 'retaliate against
   society'.

References

Baubérot, J. 2007. 'Exist-t-il une religion civile républicaine?' *French Politics,
     Culture & Society* 25(2): 3–17.

———. 2009. 'Pour une sociologie interculturelle et historique de la laïcité',
     Archives de Sciences Sociales des religions 146: 183–99.

Bellah, R.N. 1967. 'Civil Religion in America', *Daedalus* 96: 1–21. (Chinese
     translation: 罗伯特·贝拉. 2007. '美国的公民宗教', trans. Chen Yong
     陈勇, in 原道 13: 123–41.)

———. 1973. 'Introduction', in R.N. Bellah (ed.), *Emile Durkheim on Morality
     and Society.* Chicago: University of Chicago Press, pp. ix–lv.

———. 1974. 'American Civil Religion in the 1970's' (augmented version),
     in R.E. Richey and D.G. Jones (eds), *American Civil Religion.* New York:
     Harper & Row, pp. 255–72.

———. 1975. *The Broken Covenant: American Civil Religion in Time of Trial.*
     New York: The Seabury Press.

———. 1976. 'Response to the Panel on Civil Religion', *Sociological Analysis*
     37(2): 153–59.

———. 1989. 'Comment', *Sociological Analysis* 50(2): 147.

———. 2002. 'Epilogue. Meaning and Modernity: America and the World',
     in R. Madsen, W.M. Sullivan, A. Swidler and S.M. Tipton (eds), *Meaning
     and Modernity: Religion, Polity, and Self.* Berkeley: University of California
     Press, pp. 255–76.

Bellah, R.N. and P.E. Hammond. 1980. *Varieties of Civil Religion.* San Fran-
     cisco: Harper & Row.

Bellah, R.N., R. Madsen, W.M. Sullivan, A. Swidler and S.M. Tipton. 1985.
     Habits of the Heart: Individualism and Commitment in American Life. Berk-
     ley: University of California Press.

Billioud, S. and J. Thoraval. 2008. 'Anshen Liming or the Religious Dimension
     of Confucianism', *China Perspectives* 3: 88–106.

———. 2009. 'La Chine des années 2000: nouvelles perspectives sur le poli-
     tique', *Extrême-Orient, Extrême-Occident* 31: 5–31.

Chen, Hsi-yuan. 1999. 'Confucianism Encounters Religion: The Formation
     of Religious Discourse and the Confucian Movement in Modern China',
     Ph.D. dissertation. Cambridge, MA: Harvard University.

Chen Ming 陈明. 2007. '对话或独白: 儒教的公民宗教说随札', 原道 14:
     47–58.

———. 2009. '公民宗教与中华民族意识建构', 文化纵横 6: 92–96.

———. 2012. '儒教: 作为一个宗教', 哲学分析 3(2): 35–55.

Chen Yizhong 陈宜中. 2012. '公民儒教的进路: 陈明先生访谈录', 思想 20: 233–74.

Chen Yong 陈勇. 2007. '公民宗教论综述', 原道 13: 77–89.

Chen Yun 陈赟. 2007. 天下或天地之间: 中国思想的古典视域. Shanghai: Shanghai shudian.

Davie, G. 2001. 'Global Civil Religion: A European Perspective', *Sociology of Religion* 62(4): 455–73.

Ding Yun 丁耘. 2011, '论中华传统的根本特性 — 马克思主义中国化的历史基础', 文化纵横 1: 93–100.

Durkheim, E. 1958 [1950]. *Professional Ethics and Civic Morals*, trans. C. Brookfield. Glencoe: The Free Press.

———. 1960 [1914]. 'The Dualism of Human Nature and Its Social Conditions', in K. H. Wolff (ed.), *Essays on Sociology and Philosophy*. New York: Harper & Row, pp. 325–39.

———. 1964 [1912]. *The Elementary Forms of the Religious Life*, trans. J.W. Swain. London: George Allen & Unwin.

———. 1970 [1952]. *Montesquieu and Rousseau: Forerunners of Sociology*, trans. R. Manheim. Ann Arbor: University of Michigan Press.

———. 1975a [1898]. 'Individualism and the Intellectuals', in *Durkheim on Religion*, ed. W.S.F. Pickering. Routledge & Kegan Paul, pp. 59–73.

———. 1975b [1919]. 'Contribution to Discussion: Religious Sentiment at the Present Time', in *Durkheim on Religion*, ed. W.S.F. Pickering. Routledge & Kegan Paul, pp. 181–89.

———. 2002 [1925]. *Moral Education*, trans. E.K. Wilson and H. Schnurer. Mineola, NY: Dover Publications.

Gan Chunsong 干春松. 2006. 制度儒學. Shanghai: Shanghai renmin chubanshe.

Gan Yang 甘阳. 2007. 通三统. Beijing: Sanlian shudian.

Gehrig, G. 1981. 'The American Civil Religion Debate: A Source for Theory Construction', *Journal for the Scientific Study of Religion* 20(1): 51–63.

Goossaert, V. 2008. 'Republican Church Engineering: The National Religious Associations in 1912 China', in M.M. Yang (ed.), *Chinese Religiosities: Afflictions of Modernity and State Formation*. Berkeley: University of California Press, pp. 209–32.

Gorski, P.S. 2010. 'Civil Religion Today' (ARDA Guiding Paper Series). State College, PA: The Association of Religion Data Archives at The Pennsylvania State University, from http://www.thearda.com/rrh/papers/guidingpapers.asp.

———. Forthcoming. *The Fall and Rise of American Civil Religion: Religion and Politics from Winthrop to Obama*. Princeton, NJ: Princeton University Press.

Gu Yanwu 顾炎武. 1984. 日知录集释, comp. and anno. Huang Rucheng 黄汝成. Shanghai: Shanghai guji chubanshe.

Han Yu 韩愈. 1996. '原道', in 韩愈全集校注, comp. Qu Shouyuan 屈守元 and Chang Sichun 常思春. Chengdu: Sichuan daxue chubanshe, 2662–86.

Ji Zhe. Forthcoming. 'Secularization without Secularism: The Political-Religious Configuration of Post-89 China', in J. Quijada and T. Ngo (eds), *Religion and Communism: Comparative Perspectives.*

Jiang Qing 蒋庆. 2003. 政治儒学: 当代儒学的转向、特质与发展. Beijing: Sanlian shudian.

———. 2004. 生命信仰与王道政治 — 儒家文化的现代价值. Taipei: Yangzhengtang.

Kang Xiaoguang 康晓光. 2004. '仁政: 权威主义国家的合法性理论', 战略与管理 2: 108–17.

Liu Xiaofeng 刘小枫. 2007. 儒教与民族国家. Beijing: Huaxia chubanshe.

Lüchau, P. 2009. 'Toward a Contextualized Concept of Civil Religion', *Social Compass* 56(3): 371–86.

Mathisen, J.A. 1989. 'Twenty Years after Bellah: Whatever Happened to American Civil Religion?' *Sociological Analysis* 50(2): 129–46.

Müller, H.-P. 1988. 'Social Structure and Civil Religion: Legitimation Crisis in a Late Durkheimian Perspective', in J.C. Alexander (ed.), *Durkheimian Sociology: Cultural Studies.* Cambridge, MA: Cambridge University Press, pp. 129–58.

Nakajima Takahiro. 2009. 'Religion et sécularisation en Chine: Pour un confucianisme critique', in Haneda Masashi (ed.), *Sécularizations et Laïcités.* Tokyo: UTCP, pp. 79–92.

Qi Ren 齐仁. 2010. '论中国模式: 中国化马克思主义的历史道路', 文化纵横 10: 16–28.

Richey, R.E. and D.G. Jones. 1974. 'The Civil Religion Debate', in R.E. Richey and D.G. Jones (eds), *American Civil Religion.* New York: Harper & Row, pp. 3–18.

Rousseau, J.-J. 2003 [1762]. *On the Social Contract.* Mineola, NY: Dover Publications.

Wallace, R.A. 1977. 'Emile Durkheim and the Civil Religion Concept', *Review of Religious Research* 18(3): 287–90.

Weber, M. 1922. 'Wissenschaft als Beruf', *Gesammlte Aufsaetze zur Wissenschaftslehre.* Tubingen: J.C.B. Mohr, pp. 524–55.

Willaime, J.-P. 2008. 'Introduction', in E. Durkheim, *Les formes élémentaires de la vie religieuse*, 6th ed. Paris: Presses Universitaires de France, pp. v–xvii.

———. 2009. 'Pour une sociologie transnationale de la laïcité dans l'ultramodernité contemporaine', *Archives de Sciences Sociales des religions* 146: 201–18.

Winston, K. 2005. 'The Internal Morality of Chinese Legalism', *Singapore Journal of Legal Studies* 2005: 313–47.

Yang Shuda 杨树达. 1986. 论语疏证. Shanghai: Shanghai guji chubanshe.

Yu Yingshi 余英时. 2004. '现代儒学的困境 (1988年)', in 现代儒学的回顾与展望. Beijng: Shanlian shudian, pp. 53–58.

Chapter 3

ELEMENTARY FORMS OF WAR

PERFORMATIVE ASPECTS OF YOUTH MILITIA IN SIERRA LEONE

Paul Richards

War and Rite

Durkheim's teaching in *Elementary Forms of Religious Life* (Durkheim 1995 [1912]) scandalized certain sections of French society. Right-wing students demonstrated against their teacher. Professor Durkheim, it was charged, had introduced savages into the Sorbonne, threatening the very basis of French culture and civilization (Richman 2002). Durkheim's work can indeed be seen as a radical alternative to a notion of culture based on the privileged transmission of a literary canon. For Durkheim, culture (or belief) is epiphenomenal. The causal phenomenon is a universal tendency to engage in group ritual action. In the Durkheimian account of religion, prayer causes belief, not the other way round.

This suggestion not only offended the religious but also scandalized those who believed in culture and civilization as the product of an elite tradition. A similar scandal a year later attended Nijinsky, Roerich and Stravinsky's staging of the premiere of the ballet *Rite of Spring* (originally called the *Great Sacrifice*) at the Theatre des Champs Elysees in May 1913. The Parisian audience's riotous reaction resulted not (as often thought) from Stravinsky's modernist score but from Nijinsky's revolutionary choreography, which broke with the light, fantastical traditions of the Russian Imperial Ballet. On stage were raw, stamping peasants hell-bent on human sacrifice. Action, not reason, created human collective values.

Such was Durkheim's line. The performance of a rite generates emotional excitement through which collective representations become fixed: 'We must act, and ... repeat the necessary acts as often as is necessary to renew their effects' (Durkheim 1995 [1912]: 420). Shared ritual activity generates collective emotional energy – *effervescence* – through which the possibility of new understandings of social arrangements becomes apparent. In a much-cited illustration, Durkheim describes how the National Assembly abolished the feudal system in France in 1789 in a moment of passionate sacrificial abandon, resulting in a decision that 'each of its members had refused to make the night before and by which all were surprised the morning after' (Durkheim 1995 [1912]: 212).

But there is hidden danger in what Durkheim calls 'sacred contagion', which he conceives as a societal force unattached in any regular way to material objects or practical concerns. Like an oil slick (Durkheim's metaphor), sacred contagion risks spreading uncontrollably, attaching itself to all that it encounters. If they are not to overwhelm mundane and practical concerns, sacred energies must be controlled. Establishing a regular space for the sacred is thus a core topic in *Elementary Forms*; the text is, in effect, an account of the compositional resources deployed in generating and regulating collective energy. In short, it is a study of ritual dynamics.

Elementary Forms divides these compositional resources into two great groups: the positive and the negative cults. The positive cults involve commitment (sacrifice); the negative cults involve abstention. Between them they grab hold of societal effervescence and mould it into recurrent rhythmic patterns, thus achieving regulatory effects without depleting all-important social energy. Although Durkheim does not address the topic of war explicitly, it is clearly one of the major instances of group cohesive effort to which his analysis can be applied. Considerable investment in the negative cult is required to train fighters (via training drills through which collective order and embodied skills are inculcated, many of which are based on tests of endurance and self-control). Battle then requires an orientation towards the positive cult: acts of leadership, heroism and self-sacrifice are decisive in determining outcomes of an engagement.

Durkheim addresses an additional important group of cult resources in a section termed 'The Piacular Rite and the Ambiguity of the Notions of the Sacred'. Durkheim's translator, Karen Fields, explains that the term covers 'rites conducted on the occasion of death, misfortune or collective crisis' (Durkheim 1995 [1912]: 392). This is true enough, but is perhaps too limited in its scope, depending on how the phrase 'collective crisis' is read. If it is taken to mean 'any severe group difficulty', the point will be obscured. The thrust becomes clearer if we turn the term round to read 'crisis of collectivity'. The crisis in question is the real and present danger that collectivity is about to be utterly lost. The aggressiveness displayed between in-laws at a Mende funeral in southern Sierra Leone, for example, expresses the real fear that two families united by marriage are now about to be sundered by death. It is the end of a social group as its members know it that is at issue in the piacular rite. As will be argued below, a battle group facing annihilation is especially likely to engage in behaviour characteristic of the piacular rite, since the possible extinction of an entire social world is at stake.

Durkheim approaches the topic of the piacular rite by considering rites of mourning. The death of a member is a threat to the group. All feel the loss keenly, and most especially those closest to the dead person. Public mourning engages the mechanism of the piacular rite. Emotions run high, boiling over at times, and the ritual managers of such funerary occasions are hard put to prevent mass disorder. This serves Durkheim's main purpose – to illuminate the connection between reckless, impassioned behaviour and social worlds under threat. Here I extend the analysis of the piacular rite to the theme of civil war, which figured as an important theme in the third part of Durkheim's first book, *Division of Labour in Society* (Durkheim 1964 [1893], henceforth *Division*).

Some scholars argue that *Elementary Forms* represents a break with Durkheim's earlier materialism (Alexander 2005), but my own account posits a red line connecting civil war, as an outcome of a forced division of labour in *Division* (Durkheim 1964 [1893]), with guild rituals as a mode of incorporation within an organized field of skilled work in *Professional Ethics* (Durkheim 1957 [c. 1911]) and cult dynamics as triggers of effervescence in *Elementary Forms* (Durkheim 1995 [1912]).[1] The discussion of the social pathology of a forced division of labour in *Division* makes the connection to civil war explicit. In *Elementary Forms* the connection to civil war is implied rather than stated, but even so the association is clearly implied. Durkheim invokes the vendetta under the category of the piacular rite, and elsewhere in the book cites the Crusades and St Bartholomew massacres of Protestants in France as instances of effervescence run riot.

The outline of a hypothesis about causes of violent atrocity in civil war emerges. If a forced division of labour creates conditions for civil war to take hold (as Durkheim argued in the third part of *Division*),[2] then the triggering mechanism of conflict is a ritualized moment of rage against imminent military defeat and the failure of valued collectivity – namely, the piacular rite. Self-harm, human sacrifice, vendetta or massacre are attempts to stave off or reverse perceived threats to group cohesion.

The Durkheimian approach to ritual dynamics in *Elementary Forms* need not be limited to the problem of terminal crises of collectivity. An approach to understanding the ritual agency associated with many different collective ventures, including training for and prosecution of military campaigns, can evolve from a focus on the kinds of compositional resources to which *Elementary Forms* first drew attention. At heart is the notion that 'collective emotion [energising group cohesion] cannot be expressed without some order that permits harmony and unison of movement' (Durkheim 1995 [1912]: 218). Durkheim was perhaps never fully clear what the mechanism of this ordering might be, but his book lives, I suggest, because recent decades have witnessed the emergence of an experimental framework through which basic hypotheses about group coordination can now be tested. Ethnographers might in turn reconsider how their material on performative competence can best be reformulated to influence the kinds of experimental questions that are tested. Performance in war is a context in which questions are posed most sharply, since the stakes are so high. Here I explore this contextual issue by offering some observations on the performative ritual ordering of the recent civil war in Sierra Leone (1991–2002).

Some Recent Support for
the Basic Durkheimian Hypothesis

In *Elementary Forms*, Durkheim was not explicit about how any mechanism of performative ordering might work, but he hints strongly at a musicological approach: 'Since passions so heated and so free from all control cannot but help spill over, from every side there is nothing but wild movements ... [but then] gestures and cries tend to fall into rhythm and regularity, and from there into songs and dances' (Durkheim 1995 [1912]: 218). In short, Durkheim supposed that effervescence is underpinned by some kind of human capacity to apprehend and respond to a rhythmic gestalt. Recent findings add support to this basic supposition.

First, we can take note of two developments of theory, one within the Durkheimian tradition and the other within the evolutionary tradition. In the 1930s, Durkheim's associate Maurice Halbwachs developed an influential theory of collective memory, much influenced by his work on musicians (Halbwachs 1950). In a group of experienced musicians, according to Halbwachs, the tendency to 'fall into rhythm and regularity' becomes so all-pervading that they play more according to a sense of distributed memory than with reference to score or parts. Halbwachs's pioneering argument continues to be much cited among researchers on memory, improvisation and musicality.

More recently, a number of evolutionary scenarios have been proposed for the selection of basic capacities associated with music and dance, linked to the survival advantages associated with embodied task coordination. Various hunting and gathering techniques may have been favoured by a capacity for rhythmic coordination. A simple contemporary example is the everyday task of cleaning rice in a mortar (van der Niet 2010). It is a job often done by a woman and a child, and woe betide the child who lacks a rhythmic sense of timing.

Cross (2003) has argued that humans, having evolved coordinative capacities, might have developed music and dance as a way of rehearsing or enhancing certain kinds of social interaction. In effect, he builds an evolutionary scenario to support the Durkheimian argument that society was danced into being. Cross envisages this development as maybe having been a separate evolutionary pathway leading to the human capacity for language and symbolic expression. The possibility Cross envisages seems to be enhanced by recent evidence that the human capacity for rhythmic coordination is hardwired in the species rather than being, as some anthropologists have supposed, a culturally acquired characteristic; newborn infants detect a beat (Winkler et al. 2009). It is unclear whether this capacity applies to primates other than humans.

A second important recent set of findings relates to the discovery of a mirror neuron system in humans and some other animals. Seemingly, one agent performing an action is sufficient to prepare neurons in another agent present, or witnessing the action, to take responsive action. Seemingly this preparation takes place through direct replication and not through reflective mediation (Gallese, Keyesers and Rizzolatti 2004). We prepare to copy without knowing why. Other work has suggested that inferring actions from observation of actions rests on a neural capacity for predictive coding; the human brain is wired for Bayesian inference (Wolpert 2007; Kilner et al. 2007).[3]

These kinds of developments have led to the proposal of new unified programmatic frameworks linking music, dance and ritual action to neural foundations (e.g., Dominguez Duque et al. 2009). Gallese (2005) claims that the discovery of mirror neurons provides a common functional mechanism for both body awareness and forms of social understandings, consistent with perspectives offered by phenomenology (Merleau-Ponty, 1962). Turner and Whitehead (2008: 54) specifically envisage a role for a revived Durkheimian perspective in the study of 'feedback relationships between collective representations ... and brain activities which maintain and are maintained by them'. They also note that Mary Douglas's neo-Durkheimian 'grid-group' theory 'may have provided us with a suitable basis for [the] classification of collective representations', which might now in turn become a basis on which to devise experiments in social cognition). Ritual action and 'musical' or dance-based performative activity may provide an especially fruitful empirical field in which to further such studies, and Overy and Turner (2009) have recently edited a collection of work specifically directed towards the investigation of what they term 'the rhythmic brain'. The present essay does not propose to venture into this experimental domain directly, but aims instead to consider how ethnographic data might be used to provide a broader contextualization for such experiments.

The Performative Dimensions of an African War

In examining Australian ethnography at the beginning of the twentieth century, Durkheim was able to make some remarkable inferences about the likely role of group ritual action in forging social bonds. But the work was ahead of its time. Durkheim had some interest in cognitive experimentalism, but the tools of the day were too crude to test the kind of hypotheses his inferences entailed. There was also slippage in regard to the ethnographic underpinnings of his arguments. Complex processes of culture contact made the Australian data harder to interpret as time went by. Nuanced rereadings of this older ethnographic material, though important critical exercises, render the testable hypotheses less readily apparent in increasingly 'noisy' data sets. *Elementary Forms* stands as an inspiring monument to a vision, but a new ethnographic approach is needed to test its embedded hypotheses. The purpose of what follows is to consider whether the ethnography of contemporary warfare might serve as a 'new Australia' in contextualizing questions to be examined by an experimentally grounded neo-Durkheimianism.

The Revolutionary United Front and Its Opposition

The rebellion of the Revolutionary United Front (RUF) was planned by a small group of intellectuals backed by the recently deceased Libyan leader Colonel Gaddafi. The movement's aim was to overthrow the one-party regime of the All Peoples Congress (APC). Gaddafi's motivation appears to have been to add Sierra Leone to a network of client states he sought to expand in the sub-Saharan region. Foundation cadres were trained in Benghazi, took part in the overthrow of Thomas Sankara in Burkina Faso and fought in the civil war in Liberia (on behalf of Charles Taylor). The RUF launched its offensive from Liberia into eastern and southern Sierra Leone in March 1991. Military operations were led by a cashiered army corporal (Foday Sankoh) who had once been jailed for taking part in a coup attempt against the APC. Ideological training was coordinated by Ibrahim Deen-Jalloh, a lecturer from the teacher training college at Bunumbu in Kailahun District.

The movement planned a rapid move through the Sierra Leone interior to strike at the capital. The first targets were the provincial cites of Bo and Kenema, from where the movement hoped to project its appeal to a population alienated by years of corruption and poor governance. In April 1991, Guinean troops were rushed to the defence point Daru under the terms of a mutual defence pact, slowing the RUF advance. Liberian fighters supplied by Charles Taylor committed many atrocities, and the movement lost support in rural districts. The national army, assisted by Liberians opposed to Taylor, pushed the RUF back towards the border, and a stalemate ensued. In 1993 the RUF decided to abandon conventional military tactics in favour of a guerrilla insurgency based on a network of secure camps in isolated areas of forest and swamp grassland. Thereafter, the war was prosecuted with hit-and-run raids and terror tactics.

In its initial advance, the RUF targeted remote villages and mining camps, demanding that the population rally to the movement. Those who refused were either driven off or killed. Many young people joined up, however. The population of the isolated communities from which the movement first recruited fighters had a specific make-up: it targeted larger villages with primary schools, where children were often fostered out from poor families living in the outlying farm areas. There is a long history of exploitation in these areas, which were slave settlements up until emancipation in 1928. Recruits retained an active sense of social stigma and saw the RUF as a potential liberator from generations of disdain. The RUF seized the schools and turned them into training camps for these young recruits as guardians and teachers fled. Other youths were recruited from alluvial mining or logging camps. Frequently these settlements were illegal but sponsored by well-connected members of the elite. The labour force in these camps often knew very well that the country's wealth primarily ended up overseas. Again, they often welcomed the RUF for its message on mining reform.

Post-war studies of ex-combatants confirm the demographic make-up of the RUF. Most combatants were recruited (or abducted) in the first two years of the war in the Liberian border districts. The largest single group (43 per cent) were schoolchildren when they joined the movement. Others were farmers, traders and mine labourers, consistent with the forest edge background just explained. Most recruits became fighters only after ideological and combat training, much of which took place in remote village school sites and later in forest camps. Ideological orientation was in part based on the simple populist youth-oriented rhetoric of the Libyan Green Book, but it also emphasized notions of rural self-reliance adapted from the distinctive Bunumbu curriculum, which trained rural teachers to improvise teaching materials from the natural resources at hand in the expectation that a poor country would never be able to keep classroom teachers in remote villages supplied with lesson materials. Some elements of RUF training were also adapted from training manuals and propaganda materials of the Nicaraguan Sandinistas and from guerrilla tactics used against the Japanese in Korea, as mentioned in Kim Il Sung's biography, a book the North Korean embassy distributed widely in Sierra Leone during the Cold War.

In its later years, the RUF was run by the young recruits brought up in bush training camps and hardened by years of guerrilla combat, who had few exit options, as the army and paramilitary 'civil defence' killed most prisoners of war (Amnesty International 1992). The early intellectual leadership of the movement was thinned out by losses in combat and then by the marginalization of the RUF War Council after an aborted peace negotiation in 1996. The RUF issues that survived the war were mainly those of greatest interest to the conscripts – poor education, farm and mine labour exploitation, and social stigma.

Opposition to the RUF came from three main sources. National business and political elites were major beneficiaries of the alluvial mining system and the labour exploitation associated with it, and would have been excluded from these sources of wealth by a victorious RUF.[4] The international political community was alarmed at the prospect of a new Gaddafi client state. Finally, the international business community was interested in maintaining its access to the country's mineral wealth (including diamonds, but also iron ore, rutile and offshore oil). Business interests invested in both sides of the conflict, but the major bets were placed on the internationally recognized government, brought to power in 1996 by a hastily arranged election facilitated by a British-led coalition of international political and business interests, which excluded the RUF. The APC, earlier deposed in a coup, made no showing, and a coalition led by the formerly banned Sierra Leone People's Party came to power. At first it negotiated with the RUF but, emboldened by international backers, later attempted to reach a military solution.

The Ethnographic Context of the War:
The Case for a Durkheimian Approach

Historically, the Upper West African forest zone has been a frontier of settlement expansion over the past millennium. Compared with the savannah zone to the north, levels of precolonial political centralization remained low. Small chiefdoms formed along trade routes skirting or crossing the forest. More remote parts of the region were settled by decentralized groups. In the north-western sector of the forest, power associations provided some degree of inter-community coordination. The region linking southern and eastern Sierra Leone and north-western Liberia has been termed the Poro Belt after the most prominent of these associations, the male sodality Poro (d'Azevedo 1962). Poro may have been spread by the Mane, a Mande warrior group that expanded westwards towards the Sierra Leone peninsula in the mid/late sixteenth century (Alvares c. 1615), perhaps replacing or absorbing older but comparable power associations.

The power associations of the Upper West African coast can be classed under the institutional category of the sodality. Durkheim used this term, which derives from the Latin *sodales*, to characterize the occupational cults that emerged to meet the organizational needs of productive activities beyond the scope of regulation through the community (to which we can conveniently apply the term 'modality', i.e., parish or family). In the Upper West African forest, induction into power associations is typical for all young men and women approaching adulthood. These associations teach certain basic societal skills and disciplines, including those related to community defence (for men) and childbirth and healing (for women). They also have political functions, with higher grades serving to regulate relations among landowners, warriors, practitioners of key crafts and other 'big people'. Evidence from the late nineteenth century suggests that Poro sometimes also regulated trade (e.g., determining periods of palm oil collection) and coordinated politico-military alliances among neighbouring chieftaincies (Little 1965).

Durkheim's basic point about the sodality is that it serves to organize professional relations through initiation into a cult. The initiate is conscious of having sacrificed something to gain specialized knowledge or professional recognition, and is thereby bound to the group by sacred ties. The sodality thus serves to generate both technical knowledge and religious feelings. The sodality is a vital connection between Durkheim's early and late work – specifically, between *Division* and *Elementary Forms*. The theory is sketched in lecture notes, many times reworked and published posthumously as *Professional Ethics and Civic Morals* (Durkheim 1957). Durkheim worked on this material after the publication of *Elementary Forms*, so his death likely robbed us of a fuller statement about the importance of the sodality (as a melding of work and religion) in the emergence of society 'from below'. It is perhaps regrettable that *Elementary Forms* is so dependent on Australian ethnographic materials, since this focus means that Durkheim's exposition of cult organization is largely determined by the particularities of a hunting and gathering mode of production. It is hardly idle speculation to try to rethink his analysis with materials from the Upper West African forest, where the importance of the sodalities as power associations among 'iron age' farmers and traders is not reduced or obscured by the emergence and superimposition of larger-scale political structures.

Joining a sodality in Upper West Africa generally involves arduous initiation rites that serve to refocus the person through the play of cultic effervescence. All accounts of this cultic effervescence draw especial attention to the role of music and dance. Poro, Sande and similar cults teach skills and disciplines through principles of musical pedagogy. Signals, cries, drum patterns and songs are instantly recognizable triggers of forms of awareness appropriate to conducting sodality business. They immediately halt the mundane world and impose the sacred domain of Poro or Sande time. Non-members instantly flee to their houses, bolting and barring their doors and shutters until the relevant business is achieved and an all-clear is sounded.

Work on the RUF has established that the social shaping of the rebel movement belongs to this more general regional history of sodality dynamics oriented towards the skills of war and mercantile (monopsony) trade (Richards 1996; Peters 2006). The movement created membership by initiation and announced its advance by specific oral signatures. Music and dance (as will be seen) were an inescapable part of its agency on the battlefield. The RUF sought to become a new power association and to transform its captives and recruits for life. The local response was that children abducted by the movement were now irrecoverable for mainstream society. This sense of an irreversible switch of social allegiance and identity reflected a widely shared awareness among forest-edge communities of the huge transformative efficacy of sodality initiation. This pattern in turn underpinned a general suspicion of released RUF inductees, even when these children were family members, locking RUF captives within the movement and vastly complicating the problems of peacemaking. A Durkheimian theoretical perspective seems especially relevant to understanding the dynamics of initiation at the root of the extreme violence and intractability of the Sierra Leone civil war.

The War against the RUF

A military coup deposed the APC government in 1992 and drove the RUF into the forest in 1993. It was widely understood that only mopping-up operations were needed to end the war. The diplomatic community in Freetown believed that by now, violence in the countryside was solely the work of dissident army groups. In 1994, the RUF began to seize foreign hostages, including mine personnel and two British volunteers from a British aid agency, to draw attention to its continuing existence. The hostages raised the profile of the rebel movement.

By 1995, British advisers were engaged in developing a possible rescue plan for the hostages and a more general solution to the rebel insurgency, apparently reflecting British concerns about Libyan influence on the rebellion. An officer of the British overseas secret intelligence service (MI6) was attached to a British-linked mining company as its 'political advisor'. The military regime hired a British–South African security company (Executive Outcomes, EO) to assist with the hostage crisis and provide security for the British mining company. The RUF released the hostages in the hope of furthering a peace process with the government.

Apparently favouring the explanation that the military regime was the main obstacle to peace, the international diplomatic community threw its weight behind democratic transition before a peace deal was clinched with the RUF. For its part, the military regime saw a peace process with the RUF as a way to gain popular acclaim at the polls, but division in the military led to rapidly organized elections that excluded the RUF. This brought to power a civilian coalition largely made up of politicians exiled under the APC. The new regime had little trust in the national army, whose officers were thought to be loyal to either the military regime or the previous APC government. EO canvassed the merits of a military solution against the RUF, contrary to the peace negotiations the new president favoured. EO employed personnel once associated with an apartheid-era special operations unit of the South African Defence Forces familiar with training and supporting groups of local irregulars in 'dirty wars' in Angola and Mozambique. These personnel helped reshape a number of local civil defence forces in Sierra Leone into a counter-insurgency group capable of attacking RUF forest bases.

The plan involved breaking cease-fire agreements with the RUF, which was then engaged in a peace process with the new government in Abidjan. Rebel camps in the forest were encircled and attacked with random shelling and bombing intended to induce demoralization (Hooper 2003). The EO counter-insurgency operatives calculated that the RUF leadership, far away in Abidjan, would be unable to counter the effect of this blitz on a group of abducted schoolchildren. They did not reckon on the solidarity induced by sodality formation. Many rebels were killed. Few prisoners were taken. But the collapse of morale failed to occur. The bonds of initiation into the movement were too tight.

Endgame

The rebel movement's leadership signed a peace agreement in Abidjan on 30 November 1996, perhaps largely because it contained a clause requiring EO to withdraw by the end of the year. Shortly thereafter, in May 1997, government army elements loyal to the APC staged a coup and invited the rebels to share power. British advisers concocted a plan to replace the departed South Africans with British ex-army special forces. Arms were also supplied to civil defence fighters loyal to the deposed elected government. But this support was illegal under international law and a breach of the new Labour government's declared policy of neutrality in the conflict. The option was ended in 1998, when revelations from an investigation were printed by the UK parliament (Legg and Ibbs 1998).

The international community later backed an invasion by Nigerian troops to restore the elected government. Junta forces and RUF units were driven out of the capital into the interior. The RUF leader, unable to return to his fighters in the bush, was detained in Nigeria and returned to Sierra Leone to be placed on trial for treason and condemned to death. A group of leading army officers involved in the junta was tried and executed in October 1998.

International mining capital then helped elements of the disbanded army and its rebel allies rearm and launch a renewed assault on the capital in January 1999. Nigerian peacekeeping forces drove the insurgents back into the interior a second time, and a stalemate ensued. New negotiations resulted in a fragile peace deal, brief deployment of regular British troops (in May 2000), detention without trial of most the RUF political wing and the longer-term deployment of a large UN force, leading to disarmament and the complete cessation of hostilities by 2002.

The rebels in the interior responded to the Nigerian reverses and threats to their leader's life with an outpouring of violence, especially against the rural communities from which the elected government's irregular civil defence forces had been recruited. Effervescent atrocity (notably amputations of limbs of non-combatant villagers, including women and children) spread the infamy of the RUF across the globe. Most of these outrages were committed within the two years 1998 and 1999, when the movement, in retreat, faced clear evidence that its enemies were unlikely to negotiate peace or spare any cadres who surrendered. In Durkheimian terms, this collapse into violent vendetta, by a movement that had initially seen itself as a champion of the rural poor, can be interpreted as the effervescence of the piacular rite, expressive of the rage of a sodality facing imminent extinction.

Dancing a Message?

The rebel Revolutionary United Front produced only one ideological statement of its motivation and objectives, a pamphlet ghostwritten by staff of a conflict resolution agency (International Alert) in 1995 (RUF-SL 1995). Ideological training materials were in short supply. Music and dance, by contrast, were ubiquitous. Combatants prepared for battle with lengthy sessions of song and dance, and enforced dance as a means of 'reforming' groups who rejected their message. The richness of the musical life of the movement must have strengthened the sense that recruits were indeed being absorbed by a powerful new sodality.

The prime encapsulation of the movement's message was its anthem. Sung twice daily in camp, it was a central element in the induction and training of conscripts. Severe punishment was meted out to those who refused or neglected to sing the anthem correctly (Richards 2005, 2007).

> RUF is fighting to save Sierra Leone
> RUF is fighting to save her people
> RUF is fighting to save her country
> RUF is fighting to save Sierra Leone
> Go and tell the president that Sierra Leone is my home
> Go and tell my parents they'll see me no more
> We're fighting in the battlefield, and fighting for ever
> Every Sierra Leonean is fighting for his land
> Where's our diamond, Mr. President
> Where's our gold, APC
> RUF is hungry to know where they are
> RUF is fighting to save Sierra Leone
> [CHORUS]
> Sierra Leone is ready to utilize our own
> All our minerals will be accounted for
> The people will enjoy in their land
> RUF, the saviour we need right now
> [CHORUS]

A middle-aged woman captured by the movement and made a secretary in the RUF War Office, typing battle reports for the leader in the headquarters bush camp, provided this fascinating insight into the motivational power of music in the most adverse conditions:

Q. How often did you have to sing that song?

A. Every day after prayers.

Q. And what happened if you got it wrong, or ... you forgot the words?

A. Well, you will be punished ... beaten. You are forced to learn that, to sing that song.

Q. How would they beat you?

A. You hang, or you touch your toes, or you stretch your arms when they are beating you ... you put your arms down they start again to beat you.

Q. How many times were you beaten like that?

A. [Laughs] For the song? They beat me four times, to know this song.

Q. How can you sing [it] so beautifully, with that memory ... with the memory that this was beaten into you? ... [both laugh].

A. They taught us that song because we have teachers among us. So, after prayers ... for this anthem, you are just forced to sing, whether you are hungry, or you feel discouraged, or someone died ... they don't want to know. All they know that you sing the song on the right time.

When negotiators for the release of hostages arrived at the RUF headquarters camp in Koya Chiefdom in July 1995, the leadership took good care to showcase the movement in performative terms. Negotiators were asked to videotape both a rendition of the anthem and a 'battle display' of the agility of young cadres advancing on a target and setting ambushes. The tape was intended for international media exposure, though very little of it saw the light of day. The negotiators organized a screening in the Department of Anthropology at University College London in October 1995. These elements more effectively projected a sense of the movement and its objectives than did the long, rambling propaganda speech by the RUF leader Foday Sankoh.

A frame of reference is offered by an account of a similar display organized by the Mende warlord Mendegila in the 1890s (at a location only a few miles distant from the RUF video performance a century later, in 1995) for the benefit of the British travelling commissioner T.J. Alldridge:

> Chief Mendigra ... directed his warboys to go through the country ceremony of 'Pulling Kutu'... a display of sword feats. ... A large arena was formed. ... Each warrior ... worked his way, slashing out right and left ... gyrating as he advanced. ... Then having ... worked himself up into a state of frantic excitement, his movements suddenly ceased. ... One of the [warriors], after getting desperately excited, suddenly stopped, tossed his sword up into the air and left the arena, remarking that as there was no one to kill, he could not continue his performance. (Alldridge 1901: 175)

Of particular note in this account is the way the performance – though intended only as a display – was capable of stirring emotions to the point of loss of control. This instance surely illustrates what Durkheim meant when he wrote, 'We must act, and ... repeat the necessary acts as often as is necessary to renew their effects' (cited above).

The RUF seemed to entertain the same idea – that action itself can change orientation and belief, if only applied in strong enough measure – when it repeatedly forced recalcitrant villagers into song and dance, apparently intending to bring dormant or denied feelings of commitment to life. Two such instances, summarized from eyewitness accounts, were included in a conflict mapping report commissioned for the opening of the Special Court on War Crimes in Sierra Leone:

> In early June [1991] [an RUF] commander with his troops came to Benganie [in Pujehun District, south-eastern Sierra Leone] and stating that he was a good dancer, ordered the civilians to dance. Everybody was obliged to attend the dance, except the elderly[;] all doors had to stay open and the dance itself was organized so that the men were to

lead the dance, followed by the drummers, and then by the women at
the end together with the [rebel] forces. One man who defied the order
... was severely beaten and tortured. When the dance started, the men
at the front realised that the women at the back were being raped by the
[rebel fighters]. This dance continued for four nights until the [rebel]
forces left town. (Smith, Gambette and Longley 2004: 493)

In a second account, rebel forces defeated in a battle on the 3rd of
August 1991 retreated across the Moa River to Saama, taking revenge
on civilians for their lack of support:

In one incident, all the inhabitants were were told to undress [and] form
two lines – one for men and one for women – and dance until night-
fall. ... Women were later raped, and those who refused to have sexual
intercourse were killed. (Smith et al. 2004: 495)

Four further extracts from the same source confirm that music and
dance (and the rite-like character of RUF atrocity) were an enduring
feature of the movement. Music and dance were integral elements of
its attempts to bring about a new world by performative means. These
occasions were not simply celebratory moments of exuberance in the
face of success, but (tellingly) equally present under retreat, when
piacular excesses were at their height:

From 16 to 20 June [1995] Guinean forces based in Port Loko Town ...
fired long-range weapons towards Rosent. ... On [the] night of 20 June,
RUF forces danced and fired into the air before leaving on 21 June, ab-
ducting at least six people. (Smith et al. 2004: 192)

[rebels] forced a woman to lay her hand across the log and ... amputated
her hands. ... [They then] forced other abductees to laugh loudly. [The
rebels] punctuated the killing and amputation with song and dance.
(Smith et al. 2004: 199–200)

On 2nd June 1998, [the rebel group] entered Yiffin ... under heavy rain-
fall. Using cutlasses, they tore the corrugated roofing from ... houses,
claiming they were 'repairing' the properties. [They] remained in Yiffin
until [the] next day, singing songs and harassing civilians throughout
the night. (Smith et al. 2004: 176)

Behind their line of advance [on 6 January 1999], RUF forces made
every civilian in the eastern part of Freetown hoist white pieces of cloth
in front of their houses ... to signify their support for peace. Each night,
civilians were forced to burn old tyres in order to light up the city and
to sing peace songs. Some beat drums, while others clapped their hands
or banged empty tin cans together. Some were even forced to dance, especially old people. Those who failed to obey these orders were shot and
killed or had their houses set on fire. (Smith et al. 2004: 543)

Conclusion

Music and dance, it can be concluded, are among the elementary forms of war. Quantitative forms of analysis based on typological categorization and a linear model, relatively powerless to capture the performative aspects of sodality formation and the piacular rite, leave analysts grasping for 'explanation' and 'cause'. Nineteenth-century anarchists talked about the 'propaganda of the deed', and in an age of al-Qaeda atrocity we may need to reconsider this phrase. The modernist composer Karl-Heinz Stockhausen was lambasted for inopportune, seemingly unfeeling remarks about the 9/11 atrocities as a performative event, but perhaps he grasped something important about terror that others missed.[5] He propounded what was in effect a version of Durkheim's provocative hypothesis that actions are capable of generating belief. The world changes as a result of collective action. Durkheim offered ethnographic evidence of effervescence; this chapter has added some evidence of a rather different sort. What now seems most urgently needed is experimental work to probe the cognitive mechanisms through which certain kinds of rhythmic or musical action can entrain emotions and thus shape thought. This is an experimental challenge to be addressed by the new cognitive anthropology. Knowing how piacular rage is drummed into existence is clearly one target for understanding. But a second analytic challenge that may derive from the same source of knowledge is perhaps even more important – namely, knowing how to soothe the savage breast in all of us.

Notes

1. Jeffrey Alexander associates Anthony Giddens with the notion of the unbroken line. Alexander himself believes that Durkheim 'reached his theoretical maturity [only] after a prolonged, if confused, flirtation with materialist forms of structural theory' (Alexander 2005: 136). In fairness, he also points out that Durkheim himself 'never admitted to any radical break in his work at all' (p. 152).
2. Durkheim's argument about civil war in *Division* deserves to be better known than it is. It is understated even in the otherwise excellent recent collection on the Durkheimian theory of violence edited by Mukherjee (2010). Durkheim's basic argument is that a forced division of labour (allocation of jobs according to status and background rather than ability) sends false signals about social worth. This is liable to sustain the

formation of an underclass with little stake in society, and conflict even-
tuates. Durkheim appears to have been reflecting upon the apparent failure of social cohesion in France resulting from educational exclusion
of marginalized groups. The Revolutionary United Front named educational exclusion as its principal cause of war (Richards and Vlassenroot
2002).

3. Bayesian inference is the updating of expectations in the light of experience, named after Thomas Bayes (1701–61).

4. Divisions within the elite, reflecting a factionalized army, were effectively
exploited by the rebel movement in the initial phases of the war.

5. Stockhausen's words are best judged through the full transcript of the
press conference at the Hotel Atlantic, Hamburg, 16 September 2001
(www.stockhausen.org/hamburg.pdf, accessed 21 May 2011).

References

Alexander, J. 2005. 'The Inner Development of Durkheim's Sociological The-
ory: From Early Writings to Maturity', in J. Alexander and P. Smith (eds),
The Cambridge Companion to Durkheim. Cambridge: Cambridge University
Press, pp. 136–59.

Alldridge, T.J. 1901. *The Sherbro and Its Hinterland.* London: Macmillan.

Alvares, M. c. 1615. *Ethiopia Minor and a Geographical Account of the Province
of Sierra Leone,* provisional trans. P. Hair (unpublished, 1990).

Amnesty International. 1992. *The Extra-judicial Execution of Suspected Rebels
and Collaborators.* London: International Secretariat of Amnesty International, Index AFR 51/02/92.

Cross, I. 2003. 'Music and Biocultural Evolution', in M. Clayton, T. Herbert
and R. Middleton (eds), *The Cultural Study of Music: A Critical Introduction.* London: Routledge, pp. 19–30.

D'Azevedo, W.L. 1962. 'Some Historical Problems in the Delineation of a Central West Atlantic Region', *Annals, New York Academy of Sciences* 96(2):
512–38.

Dominguez Duque, J.F., R. Turner, E.D. Lewis and G. Egan. 2009. 'Neuroan-
thropology: A Humanistic Science for the Study of the Culture-Brain
Nexus', *SCAN.* doi:10.109/scan/nsp024

Durkheim, E. 1957. *Professional Ethics and Civic Morals* (based on lecture
notes, c. 1911).

———. 1964 [1893]. *The Division of Labour in Society,* trans. G. Simpson. New
York: Free Press.

———. 1995 [1912]. *The Elementary Forms of Religious Life,* trans. K.E. Fields.
New York: Free Press.

Gallese, V. 2005. 'Embodied Simulation: From Neurons to Phenomenal Experience', *Phenomenology and the Cognitive Sciences* 4: 23–48.

Gallese, V., C. Keyesers and G. Rizzolatti. 2004. 'A Unifying View of the Basis of
Social Cognition', *TRENDS in Cognitive Science* 8(9): 396–403.

Halbwachs, M. 1950. 'La memoire collective chez les musiciens', in *La memoire collective*. Paris: Presses Universitaires de France.

Hooper, J. 2003. 'Appendix: Sierra Leone', in *Bloodsong! An Account of Executive Outcomes in Angola*, 2nd ed. London: HarperCollins.

Kilner, J. et al. 2007. 'Predictive Coding: An Account of the Mirror Neuron System', *Cognitive Processing* 8: 159–66.

Legg, T. and R. Ibbs. 1998. *Sierra Leone Arms Investigation: A Report into the Sandline Affair by Sir Thomas Legg and Sir Robin Ibbs* (ordered printed by The House of Commons, 27 July 1998). London: The Stationery Office.

Little, K. 1965. 'The Political Function of the Poro', parts 1–2, *Africa* 35(4): 349–65 and 36(1): 69–71.

Merleau-Ponty, M. 1962 [1945]. *Phenomenology of Perception*, trans. C. Smith. London: Routledge.

Mukherjee, S. R. (ed.). 2010. *Durkheim and Violence*. Oxford: Wiley-Blackwell.

Overy, K. and R. Turner. 2009. 'The Rhythmic Brain', *Cortex* 45: 1–3.

Peters, K. 2006. 'Footpaths to Reintegration: War, Youth and Rural Crisis in Sierra Leone', Ph.D. thesis. Wageningen University.

Richards, P. 1996. *Fighting for the Rain Forest: War, Youth and Resources in Sierra Leone* (additional material 1998). Oxford: Currey.

———. 2005. 'Green Book Millenarians? The Sierra Leone War from the Perspective of an Anthropology of Religion', in N. Kastfelt (ed.), *Religion and Civil War in Africa*. London: C. Hurst, pp. 119–46.

———. 2007. 'The Emotions at War: A Musicological Approach to Understanding Atrocity in Sierra Leone', in Perri 6, S. Radstone, C. Squire and A. Treacher (eds), *Public Emotions*. Basingstoke: Palgrave, pp. 62–84.

Richards, P. and K. Vlassenroot. 2002. 'Les guerres africaines du type fleuve Mano: pour une analyse sociale', *Politique africaine* 88: 13–26.

Richman, M.H. 2002. *Sacred Revolutions: Durkheim and the College de Sociologie*. Minneapolis: University of Minnesota Press.

RUF-SL. 1995. *Footpaths to Democracy: Toward a New Sierra Leone*. N.p.: Revolutionary United Front of Sierra Leone.

Turner, R. and C. Whitehead. 2008. 'How Collective Representations Can Change the Structure of the Brain', *Journal of Consciousness Studies* 15(10–11): 43–57.

Smith, L.A., C. Gambette and T. Longley. 2004. *Conflict Mapping in Sierra Leone: Violations of International Humanitarian Law from 1991 to 2002: No Peace Without Justice*, preliminary edition for the opening of the Special Court for Sierra Leone (10 March).

Van der Niet, A. 2010. *Bodies in Action: Culture and Body Skills in Post-conflict Sierra Leone*. Leiden: African Studies Centre, African Studies Collection No. 24.

Winkler, I. et al. 2009. 'Newborn Infants Detect the Beat in Music', *PNAS* 106(7).

Wolpert, D. 2007. 'Probabilistic Models in Human Sensorimotor Control', *Human Movement Science*. doi:10.1016/j.humov.2007.05.005

Chapter 4

ELEMENTARY FORMS VERSUS PSYCHOLOGY IN CONTEMPORARY CINEMA

Louise Child

Introduction: The Scholarly Study of Religion and Film

How can Durkheim's *Elementary Forms of Religious Life* contribute to the study of film and television? Recent scholarly debates have questioned whether film should merely be seen as another form of ideological hegemony, or as a place where filmgoers have potentially more creative and subtle engagements with questions of power. These engagements raise questions about tensions between social and individuated personhood that suggest that conceptions of religion and the supernatural, far from being transcended, remain important to the ways in which we negotiate the world.

Lyden goes so far as suggesting that the practice of film viewing can be understood as a religion and that therefore 'the dialogue between religion and film is really just another form of interreligious dialogue' (2007: 416), a view that usefully challenges approaches that see film as merely another form of ideological hegemony, but is perhaps problematic in its stress on filmgoers' viewpoints over the potential insights of theory more broadly (2007: 419). Plate's approach is helpful here, in that he explores both the mythical qualities of film and the ways in which popular culture is employed in ritual activity in the modern world while also distinguishing clearly between these two strands of his work, 'juxtaposing film theory and religious theory in order to highlight the ways both religion and film are engaged in the practice of *worldmaking'* (Plate 2008: 3, original emphasis). Many other analyses of film that employ the concept of myth draw from Campbell's (1956) work on the monomyth, with its emphasis on the psychological implications of the initiation of the hero (Gordon 1995: 78–82).

These previous approaches represent important steps in the development of sociological and psychological analyses of contemporary film and serial drama, and have the advantage of not being obscured by overly rigid and arbitrary distinctions between 'high' and 'low' culture. However, my task here is somewhat different. Rather than exploring the ritual dimensions of audience participation, I utilize key ideas from Durkheim's (1995 [1912]) *Elementary Forms of Religious Life*, in particular his theories about the sacred and *collective consciousness*, to analyse certain characters and themes in two contemporary American television series, *The Sopranos* and *Deep Space Nine*. Both explore, explicitly and in more subtle ways, ideas about collective action and thought, leading me to argue that despite the apparent predominance of psychological models of the individual in modern western culture, a wealth of evidence suggests that collective emotions and symbols are a source of vitality and hope, as well as anxiety and distrust, within those cultural frames.

Gods and Souls in Science Fiction

One of the most significant genres of popular culture that commonly explore ideas about personhood and society is that of science fiction and fantasy. This is partly because fantasy writing and film, by their very nature, give the imagination room to consider possibilities that are not confined to known physical and social realities, enabling their creators to construct philosophical thought experiments and thereby explore moral and social questions in new ways. Moreover, writers such as Ellis have suggested that in addition to creating new mythic worlds, science fiction actually draws from processes whereby scientific discovery and cosmology have already themselves become part of the mythological landscapes of contemporary society. He argues that western contemporary scientific explanations of the origins of the universe, such as the 'Big Bang' theory of star formation, are also cosmogonies, stating that 'we and everything we know are essentially "stardust"' (Ellis 1995: 85). He goes on to suggest that science provides a backdrop for fiction that is comfortable because it is familiar to viewers, allowing them to

resist admitting that we are like all other human communities, in need
of orientating myths and transcendent values. Science fiction enables
us to have our cake and eat it too, to experience a world centred on technology that nonetheless allows for an encounter with cosmic otherness.
Consider this: we are fascinated with space aliens, with familiar-look-
ing men who *fall to earth* because this genre tells us of our beginnings.
By coming into contact with people who are *closer to the stars* than we
are, we are doing nothing other than participating in a mythic experience; through watching space alien films, we are getting in touch with
our roots, exploring the secret, sacred dimension of our scientific world
view. (1995: 85; emphasis in original)

Examining the numinous qualities of aliens (particularly those
that resemble humans), together with their descent from the sky, he
further suggests that these beings evoke the archetypical symbolism
of the sky god (Ellis 1995: 88). I would add that this phenomenon is
particularly significant because the portrayal of gods and goddesses
from any religious tradition is remarkably absent in contemporary
western film (with the notable exceptions of *Jason and the Argonauts*,
1963, and *Clash of the Titans*, 1981). Moreover, science fiction and
fantasy provide examples in which the allusion to gods is not only an
implicit subtext of the portrayal of aliens but is also an explicit issue
that the characters themselves discuss. The *Star Trek* television pro-
grammes and films are a case in point, and the particular series that
I explore here, *Deep Space Nine*, is especially intriguing because the
complex ways in which the programme explores religion intertwine
with ambiguity and tensions related to society, identity and power
that, I suggest, are especially open to illumination through the lens of
Durkheim's work.

Deep Space Nine is named after its setting, a space station adjacent to
a planet called Bajor. The series begins with the arrival of officers and
crew from the United Federation of Planets' military wing, Starfleet. It
is explained that both the planet and the space station were subject to
a brutal occupation by the Cardassians, whose recent defeat and expulsion from Bajor resulted from a prolonged guerrilla war waged by
the Bajoran resistance movement. The territory remains vulnerable,
and Starfleet has been sent to cooperate with Bajoran officials in its
protection. The station quickly becomes a post for intergalactic trade,
diplomacy and petty crime, with its main bar and gambling establish-
ment catering for a wide variety of alien races. Most of these races do
not play the role of 'sky gods' as outlined in Ellis's model, but the station is itself located next to a sacred 'sky' phenomenon, a wormhole
that acts as a portal to another quadrant in space, called the Gamma
quadrant. According to Bajoran religious beliefs, this portal is actu-

ally a celestial temple inhabited by gods known as the Prophets, who guide the Bajoran people by means of artefacts and visions recorded in their sacred texts. This phenomenon, along with the debates about it, allows the series to explore ways in which conceptions of the sacred come into conflict with a world view that is more comfortable with linear problem solving, as exemplified by the members of the Federation. This conflict is not merely played out through debate or military intervention, but it becomes part of the development of a key character's identity.

Starfleet tolerates the Bajoran interpretation but resists it, referring to the Prophets as 'wormhole aliens', but the situation becomes confused when the Starfleet captain in charge of the space station, Benjamin Sisko, enters the wormhole and communicates with the Prophets. He discovers that they are not bound by the usual laws of space and time and reluctantly accepts the Bajoran people's designating him as a religious leader – 'the Emissary' (1001: *Emissary: 46379.1*). Whereas Durkheim's (1995 [1912]: 8–10) exploration of time is largely confined to pointing out its social origins, Hubert (1999 [1905]: 46, 71, 74) takes this argument a step further, exploring the implications of time in myth and ritual and suggesting that the experience of time is related to people's consciousness of the experience. Thus he characterizes sacred time as the result of an exalted collectivity that, being in unison, experiences time without differentiation (Hubert 1999 [1905]: 79; see also Child 2007: 88–89). I would therefore suggest that in this storyline, the relationship between sacred and individuated aspects of human consciousness and being is explored, enabling an internal transformation within Sisko that also has a profound impact on his social and political world.

As the series progresses, it delves into a complex relationship between religion and politics that becomes increasingly ambiguous as the nature of social relations in the Gamma quadrant is revealed. Planets in the Gamma quadrant are subject to an evil tyranny called the Dominion and policed by a ruthless army of genetically engineered soldiers, the Jem'Hadar, whose loyalty is guaranteed by their dependence on a drug dispensed by the diplomatic wing of the Dominion, cloned beings called the Vorta. These two races are controlled by their creators, the Founders, whom they view as gods and therefore obey without question. It is discovered that the Founders are actually shape-shifters, aka Changelings, who, though able to assume myriad shapes including those of animals, humans and plants, are happiest resting together in a liquid form known as 'the Great Link'. Portrayals and descriptions of this 'Great Link', 'a merging of thought and form, idea and sensations' (6004: *Behind the Lines: 51145.3*) are remarkably suggestive of Durkheim's conceptions of collective consciousness, which he describes as a '*sui generis* synthesis of individual consciousnesses ... the product of this synthesis is a whole world of feelings, ideas and images that follow their own laws once they are born' (1995 [1912]: 426). Although the Founders are portrayed as mistrustful intergalactic warlords, twists in the plot indicate that their immersion in collective states of being is not altogether dismissed by the programme makers.

Most notably, not all shape-shifters are located in the Gamma quadrant. One of them – Odo, found and raised in the Alpha quadrant – is the space station's security officer, and has thereby formed close working relationships and friendships with the station's crew. Odo's political affiliations are complex, partly because he was once a security officer under Cardassian rule. Lee, for example, writes that as a representative of social order 'he's made of liquid but he is very rigid', and that because he has no clear allegiance to either of the regimes he negotiates – Federation and Cardassian – his loyalties at times come into question (Lee 2008: 107; 5008: *Things Past: Stardate Unknown;* 2008: *Necessary Evil: 47282.5*). Conflicts between his station identity and his affinity with his species are also explored in some depth. Odo is not only culturally isolated from and curious about other shape-shifters and their transformative abilities, he also experiences an intense longing to experience the 'Great Link' that conflicts with the attractions of other kinds of intimacy possible with his human companions, including sexual love. Odo's decision to remain with humanoids and oppose his own species in the war with the Dominion demonstrates his moral repugnance for The Dominion's political organization, but it also relates to his love for a Bajoran officer, Major Kira.

Odo's resolve is tested when one of the Founders comes to Deep Space Nine and links with him at a time when he is committed to aid a resistance plot to sabotage the Dominion war effort. This linking is depicted as an almost mystical experience that distracts him not only from his duty but from ordinary space and time itself, pointing to the dangers of 'forgetting oneself' in such experiences (6004: *Behind the Lines: 51145.3*). Nevertheless, the programme counterbalances this caution with Sisko's increasing trust in his visionary communications with the wormhole aliens and the positive assistance they provide. Moreover, Odo is not the only character in the series who embodies a collective identity.

The second character through which notions of the person are explored is Lieutenant Jadzia Dax, a member of the Trill species. Trills are distinguished by the fact that some of them have had their humanoid bodies fused with a being called a symbiont that is inserted into their abdomen, a process known as 'joining'. Having a potentially much longer lifespan than humanoids do, the symbionts can sometimes inhabit a series of successive 'hosts'. Each joined Trill therefore has the combined memories, skills and personality traits of their symbiont's previous hosts, a trait with personal, moral and relational consequences. Jadzia Dax keeps promises made by her symbiont's previous hosts, including a blood oath that Curzon Dax took with a group of Klingons to avenge a murder by killing its perpetrator in turn, much to the consternation of her Starfleet captain (2019: *Blood Oath: Stardate Unknown*). She is also bound by taboos prohibiting sexual relationships with the partners of her previous hosts (4005: *Rejoined: 49195.5*). The symbiont can therefore be compared to a soul or totemic principle that is periodically reincarnated within individuals, and for Durkheim this principle is primarily social. He states, for example, that

> the totem is a source of the clan's moral life. All beings that participate in the same totemic principle consider themselves, by that very fact to be morally bound to one another; they have definite obligations of assistance vengeance, and so on, toward each other, and it is these that constitute kinship. Thus the totemic principle is at once a physical force and a moral power, and we will see that it is easily transformed into a divinity proper (1995 [1912]: 192).

Jadzia Dax's joined identity bears some resemblance to Durkheim's (1995 [1912]: 163–66) descriptions of personal totems in that she has had to earn the right to be joined, but it can also be illuminated by his explorations of notions of the soul. Durkheim argues that the notion of soul is bound up with ideas about reincarnation, totems and ancestors (1995 [1912]: 249, 258), suggesting that the idea that the individual is made of distinctly profane and sacred parts, or that individuals contain a spark of divinity within them, is not entirely baseless because

> society, that unique source of all that is sacred, is not satisfied to move us from outside and to affect us transitorily; it organizes itself lastingly within us ... the individual soul is thus only a portion of the group's collective soul. It is the anonymous force on which the cult is based but incarnated in an individual whose personality it cleaves to: It is mana individualized. (1995 [1912]: 266–267)

Further, he argues that the notion that ancestral souls are reincarnated can be explained by the 'perpetuity of the group's life. The individuals die, but the clan survives, so the forces that constitute his life must have the same perpetuity. These forces are the souls that animate individual bodies'. Therefore, each individual person comprises a new body and individual characteristics together with sacred collective forces that are eternal (Durkheim 1995 [1912]: 271).

In the case of Jadzia Dax, this subtle duality of personhood is explored in an extradition hearing held because Curzon Dax, a previous host of her symbiont, is accused of treason and murder. Whereas those who want her to stand trial equate the continuation of memory between Curzon and Jadzia Dax with a continuation of responsibility, Sisko argues that Jadzia Dax cannot be tried for crimes that Curzon Dax may have committed because with each joining, a new, combined person is created. The symbiont does not suppress the host; rather, symbiont and host undergo a total blending and sharing. In an analogy for rebirth that echoes the Upanishads, it is stated that once salt is put into water the two become indistinguishable and inseparable: boiling off the water and placing the salt in a new liquid creates an entirely new entity (1007: *Dax: 46910.1*).

In suggesting that Durkheim's analysis may be instructive for exploring contemporary science fiction, I am not arguing for a precise mapping of totemic religion onto the cosmologies imagined in contemporary media. I am, rather, suggesting that their raising of questions about the potential nature of collective forms of consciousness, society and identity belies the idea that we simply take for granted Freudian conceptions of bounded and impenetrable persons. Although scholars of *Star Trek* like Wagner and Lundeen explore how its storylines present the conundrums of plural selves, they nonetheless suggest, on the grounds of the programme's orientation towards secular humanism, that the purpose of such stories is ultimately to reinforce western cultural assumptions of the 'essential reality of an ultimately stable, bounded self' (Wagner and Lundeen 1998: 79). Moreover, some cultural theorists may dismiss the significance of science-fiction storylines as a simple suspension of disbelief that ends once the programme is over, an argument that is perhaps easier to make concerning a genre that by its very nature makes imaginative leaps. I therefore choose for my next example a programme that remains within the realm of fictional drama but explores settings and characters that are more easily identifiable with observable realities, namely, *The Sopranos*.

Psychology and the Sacred in the Gangster Genre

Ironically, challenges to psychology are often most readily apparent in films and serial dramas that explore psychological ideas and portray the therapeutic relationship. Films and serial dramas such as *Analyze This, Grosse Pointe Blank* and *The Sopranos* draw their comic and dramatic power from the apparently paradoxical notion that violent gangsters may seek redemption through the suburban world of psychoanalysis. Whereas Freud's (1991 [1930]: 303) work arguably explored and sought ways to overcome human beings' predisposition for uncontrolled emotions and criminal deeds in order to advance understanding and civilized behaviour, these films appear to indicate that in the popular imagination, psychotherapy has become associated with the more frivolous 'personal growth' quests of those with sufficient wealth to indulge them.

Television drama, however, has the potential to provide much more than a sometimes-humorous critique of psychoanalysis. Because it sets the analytical process on the stage, together with a range of situations and characters that are spoken about in analysis, drama can offer the therapeutic relationship a sociological setting and context that is particularly open to illumination using a Durkheimian framework. By suggesting that social conflicts in modernity reflect fundamental tensions between the demands of impersonal, indirect and therefore profane social systems on the one hand, and the passions and vitality of the sacred on the other, Durkheim is arguing that the prohibitions and restrictions of social order that produce these tensions both conflict with the sacred and make it possible. The juxtaposition of psychoanalysis with the world of the gangster highlights these complications in ways that suggest the attractions and challenges of the sacred for people (including psychoanalysts) negotiating the modern world even as they reassert the ethical importance of the social order they endeavour to maintain and represent.

The television serial drama *The Sopranos* is a case in point. Created and written by a team led by David Chase, and originally aired without commercial breaks by the U.S. television channel HBO, the series was conceived as both a serial drama, with the gradual and subtle developments of plot and character that this medium at its best entails, and as a succession of one-hour movies, each telling a story in its own right. The plot focuses on a group of New Jersey mobsters and their families, the primary narrative thread being the interaction between Tony Soprano, the head of the mob crew, and his psychologist, Dr Jennifer Melfi. Frequent cuts between these interviews, and scenes showing the action and dialogue of the characters on the broader sociological stage, together with the often amusing and inevitably intriguing ways in which phrases and ideas move and transform between the social contexts of the therapeutic encounter and the characters' home and work lives, provide data for the 'ethnographic eye' in ways the medium of the traditionally written psychological account is challenged to pursue, given its focus on a two-person dialogue recounted from the singular perspective of one of the participants, namely the psychologist.

One of the potential advantages of transposing cultural discussions of the process of psychology from the written medium into drama, therefore, is the ways in which this medium can highlight the fact that psychology takes place within a particular social context, located in this case within the social space of Dr Melfi's office. Meanwhile, there are overflows and disjunctions between that context and the social spaces of Tony's home and the strip club and meat shop he uses as operational bases for his criminal activity. While Dr Melfi's life and work orientate her to goals of social order, Tony's world is one of violence, sexual exploitation and murder, and one of the phenomena that persistently draw the attention of scholars writing about the programme is the puzzling fact that although many features of Tony's life are abhorrent, his character nonetheless engenders a repellent fascination that at times spills over into attraction for viewers and Dr Melfi alike.

It is Dr Melfi who warns Tony about his mother's attempt on his life, a revelation that forces Melfi to go into hiding in one of several incidents in which the series challenges psychotherapy. For example, though she confidently dismisses Tony's sexual advances as a by-product of the process (1006: *Pax Soprana*), the transference phenomena also works in reverse as her own therapist observes with some alarm her use of the phrase 'on the lam' to describe her time in hiding (2003: *Toodle-Fucking-Oo*), her subsequent weight gain and her storming out of sessions uttering a stream of profanities (2005: *Big Girls Don't Cry*) (Gabbard 2002: 47, 79). These things might be seen simply as illustrating her unconscious reactions to the stress of the situation, but at times Tony clearly questions the value of therapy or tries to impose his own power dynamics upon the situation. For example, when his son is caught drunk on communion wine at school and put through a barrage of psychological tests, Tony challenges the Attention Deficit Disorder diagnosis and tells Anthony Junior, 'You're not depressed, you're just sad and angry 'cos you did something stupid' (1007: *Down Neck*).

This contestation of psychology in *The Sopranos* is, I would argue, part of the appeal of the series, but questions remain about audience attractions to tales about violent mobsters. Though one might propose that Tony is an attractive screen character precisely because he is a fictional creation and not a real person, I suggest that this approach evades the question and argue instead that many of the tensions explored can be illuminated by Durkheim's conceptions of the sacred and social solidarity, which help explain the nostalgia that viewers share with Tony for a deeper sense of kinship or blood ties in a fragmented postmodern world.

Blood Symbolism and the Sacred

Exploring the anthropological background of the Sicilian mafia, Blok contends that blood symbolism forges strong bonds and negotiates 'tricky transactions' between various 'kin' groups. This reciprocity extends beyond agnatic and affinal kinship to include ritual kin (such as godparents) and ritual friendships sealed by initiations that include blood symbolism and the violence and death of vendettas (Blok 2001: 87–88). Blood ties are thus forms of solidarity created through powerful bodily and emotional experiences that are often also ceremonial in character.

For Durkheim, the significance of initiation and of ritual action more broadly is located in the ways in which it arouses and directs collective emotions, which, he argues, are fundamental to the functioning of society itself (1995 [1912]: 422). He distinguishes these energies clearly from those that govern the profane world, maintaining that 'the energies at play in one are not merely those encountered in the other, but raised to a higher degree; they are different in kind' (1995 [1912]: 36). Ritual participation in the sacred implies

> a true metamorphosis. Rites of initiation, which are practiced by a great many peoples, demonstrate this especially well. Initiation is a long series of rites to introduce the young man into religious life. For the first time he comes out of the purely profane world, where he has passed his childhood, and enters into the circle of sacred things. This change of status is conceived not a mere development of pre-existing seeds but as a transformation *totius substantiae*. At that moment, the young man is said to die, and the existence of the particular person he was, to cease – instantaneously to be replaced by another. He is born again in a new form. Appropriate ceremonies are held to bring about the death and rebirth, which are taken not merely in a symbolic sense but literally. Is this not proof that there is a rupture between the profane being that he was and the religious being that he becomes? (Durkheim, 1995 [1912]: 37)

Durkheim also points to the significance of blood in initiation, citing examples from the aboriginal Arunta people in Australia to suggest ways in which the shedding of blood is rooted in the conception of this substance as sacred (1995 [1912]: 137). The profound nature of ritual, therefore, derives from its intense immersion of participants in the sacred, and it is the primary means by which people reconnect with the social and emotional energies that make collective consciousness possible.

> The rite serves and can only serve to maintain the vitality of those beliefs and to prevent their memory from being obliterated – in other words, to revitalize the most essential elements of the collective consciousness and conscience. Through this rite, the group periodically revitalizes the sense it has of itself and its unity; the nature of individuals as social beings is strengthened at the same time. (Durkheim 1995 [1912]: 379)

Those energies thus remain with participants, albeit in muted form, long after the ritual is over. Meanwhile, although contemporary western societies are characterized by greater social fragmentation and consequently a less clear demarcation between sacred and profane spheres, the energies of social solidarity – or 'sensual solidarities' (Mellor and Shilling 1997: 173–75) both between and within human beings – continue to be the wellspring that makes social life possible (Mellor and Shilling 1997: 15). Nonetheless, a hunger for more complete immersion in the ritual- and kinship-based collective consciousness at the root of Durkheim's sociological project may to some extent explain our fascination with the Sopranos family.

Despite the military structure of the mafia hierarchy, the bonds between members involve degrees of explicit affection that are unusual in contemporary western depictions of male-dominated spaces. Although homosexuality is treated with extraordinary suspicion in the crew's discourse, male members frequently touch one another, confide in one another and declare love for one another, and this affection is not confined to kinship relations. However, their collective violence may also provide members with opportunities to forge 'blood ties', an idea that could be developed drawing from Girard, whose work on sacrifice suggests equating the sacred with the ebbs and flows of collective violence that in premodern societies play out in blood feuds that are only resolved when deflected onto a sacrificial victim (Girard 1979 [1972]: 7). For Girard, therefore, whatever the actual victim, the symbolism relates to the murder of human beings (1979 [1972]: 10). This mode of analysis obviates the need to question why audiences might identify with Tony as a character (asked by, e.g., Carroll 2004: 122; Harold 2004: 137; Lippman 2004: 149) even though he is a murderer, because as the perpetrator of a series of bloody deeds he becomes the executor of sacrificial violence in a postmodern world.

Moreover, the ritual impurity he accrues through this process places him in danger in several ways, including the anxiety attacks that bring him into Dr Melfi's office, surveillance by the FBI and the attempt on his life ordered by his mother and Uncle Junior.

In Season 2, it is possible to see how the process of deflection onto surrogate victims that Girard describes plays out. Although Tony has become aware of who ordered the hit (when anyone mentions his mother, he replies, 'She's dead to me'), he does not actually exact revenge upon her but instead murders a crew member who has been passing information on to the FBI. I would suggest, however, that Girard's analysis has limited applications in this context. For example, Girard relegates of the notion of the sacred to its violent aspects. His argument that 'violence and the sacred are inseparable' and 'violence is the heart and secret soul of the sacred' (1979 [1972]: 19, 31) presents an incomplete picture when compared with Durkheim's exploration of volatile collective energies that have both positive and negative aspects.

There are similarities between the perspectives of Durkheim and Girard, particularly with regard to notions of volatility, infection and contagion. Girard, for example, likens violence to 'a raging fire that feeds on the very objects intended to smother its flames' (1979 [1972]: 31), suggesting that 'if left unappeased, violence will accumulate until it overflows its confines and floods the surrounding area'. The role of sacrifice is to stem this rising tide of indiscriminate substitutions and redirect violence into "proper channels" (Girard 1979 [1972]: 10). He explores how the 'impurity' violence engenders is thought to have a contagion that goes beyond rational notions of duty or morality, so that

> the notion of ritual impurity can degenerate until it is nothing more than a terror-stricken belief in the malevolent results of physical contact. Violence has been transformed into a sort of seminal fluid that impregnates objects on contact and whose diffusion, like electricity ... is determined by physical laws. (1979 [1972]: 28)

Durkheim too uses the language of electricity and contagion (1995 [1912]: 327–29), pointing to the potential dangers of the sacred forces:

> Does the individual come into contact with them without having taken the proper precautions? He receives a shock that has been compared with the effect of an electrical charge. They sometimes appear to be conceived of more or less as fluids that escape via the extremities. When they enter a body that is not meant to receive them, they cause sickness and death by a wholly mechanical reaction. (1995 [1912]: 192)

He also explores the potential evils of their motility in the context of social revolutions:

> Under the influence of some great collective shock in some historical periods, social interactions become much more frequent and active ... the result is the general effervescence that is characteristic of revolutionary or creative epochs ... stirred by passions so intense that they can be satisfied only by violent and extreme acts: by acts of superhuman heroism or bloody barbarism. (1995 [1912]: 213)

Nonetheless, for Durkheim, 'religious forces are in fact only transfigured collective forces, that is, moral forces' (1995 [1912]: 327). The sacred is not, in and of itself, wedded to violence but is ambiguous, with pure and impure manifestations that can transform into one another with great ease. Social structural prohibitions therefore channel the energies of the sacred, but the moral feeling upon which society relies for its vitality is also located within these forces (Durkheim 1995 [1912]: 415). For Girard, on the other hand, the best defence against a sacrificial crisis is clear social stratification: 'order, peace, and fecundity depend on cultural distinctions; it is not these distinctions but the loss of them that gives birth to fierce rivalries and sets members of the same family or social group at one another's throats' (1979 [1972]: 49).

However, in the case of *The Sopranos* this latter explanation has limited efficacy because Tony's crew are remarkably stratified, with clear roles such as 'Captain' and 'Soldiers'. I would therefore suggest that social solidarity must be brought into the picture, as members are also bound by initiations and oaths remarkably evocative of their Sicilian counterparts. Blok, for example, explores the testimony of Tommaso Buscetta, which suggests that

> initiation into the brotherhood or to be made a man of honour – involved a rite of passage the high point of which was a simple act and formula, as in many other secret societies. Blood from his pricked finger was rubbed on a paper image of a saint, which was set fire in his hand. As it burned, he repeated the following vow: 'May my flesh burn like this holy picture if I am unfaithful to this oath'. Through these rituals of incorporation, blood assumes magical properties of mediation and social cohesion. But blood is also associated with impurity and can impede rather than promote social bonding. The polluting potential of blood is probably at least partly responsible for the often noted exclusion of women from these solidarities – and from secret societies in general. (Blok 2001: 95)

Blok's portrayal of initiation or 'making ceremonies' bears some remarkable resemblances to the episode in which Christopher graduates into the inner circle of the organization. In a preliminary rite that has echoes of a marriage ceremony, Tony asks Christopher to voice any doubts or reservations before the ritual begins, because 'once you enter this family there's no getting out ... it is a thing of honour'. Christopher's finger is pricked with a needle, and Tony presents a card with a picture of Saint Peter on it, explaining that this is his family saint and that as that card burns, so will Christopher's soul burn in Hell if he betrays his friends. Putting the card in Christopher's hands, he asks him to repeat 'May I burn in Hell if I betray my friends' (3003: *Fortunate Son*).

Codes of secrecy, honour and respect are invoked frequently in crew members' conversations, sometimes quite ironically. Underpinning all these practices is a sense of extended kinship based on Italian origination, a nostalgic notion that almost takes on the status of a myth and is sharply drawn out in the episode where the crew visit Italy on a business trip (2004: *Commendatori*). Paulie in particular is overwhelmed by a sense of awe and homecoming, an emotion not reciprocated by his hosts in Naples, who find their American counterparts unsophisticated in manners and food preferences. Tony is also disconcerted to find that the effective leader of the Italian family is a woman, Annalisa, who has no qualms about engaging in confrontational discourse using speech styles he associates with men. He is also intrigued by the fact that she reminds him of a witch, a notion triggered by her engagement with the supernatural, including her burning her nail clippings to prevent her enemies using them to do her harm, and taking Tony to ancient caves that used to house oracles called the Sibyl of Cumae (2004: *Commendatori*). It is here that Tony tells her she reminds him of someone he does not name, but who viewers know is Dr Melfi.

The Sacred in Dreams and Prophetic Psychology

References to oracular or prophetic experiences that sit uneasily with both psychoanalytic discourse and the characters' engagements with organized religion are another way in which the sacred complicates the narrative. In one example from Season 2, Christopher is shot and is technically dead for a moment (2009: *From Where to Eternity*). He awakes to confide in Tony and Paulie that he briefly visited Hell and was told in the vision that this would be his destination upon his final death. Paulie initially consoles him by suggesting that actually Christopher only visited purgatory, where he would have to do a stretch for his sins before finally entering Heaven, but references in Christopher's vision to Paulie's own murders give Paulie nightmares and lead him to consult a psychic. Initially sceptical, Paulie's unease increases when the psychic says that he is surrounded by his victims and makes reference to circumstances of the murders that are unknown to anyone except Paulie himself. Thrown out of the psychic's house, Paulie confronts his local priest, arguing that his payments to the church should have guaranteed him dispensation for his sins and asking for his money back. The priest counters with the argument that Paulie should never have consulted a psychic in the first place, on the grounds that divination is nothing but black witchcraft.

Dreams and visions also play an important part in the primary storylines of Seasons 1 and 2, both of which concern betrayal. Season 1 begins with an exploration of the reasons Tony is referred to a psychotherapist in the first place, particularly his sudden fainting, which cannot be explained physically and is therefore diagnosed as a panic attack (1001: *The Sopranos*). The official head of the family is in jail, and his friend and acting boss Jackie is dying of cancer, leaving a gap in effective leadership. The resulting battle of wills between Tony and his elderly Uncle Junior culminates in an attempt on Tony's life. However, psychology complicates this storyline in several ways. First, Uncle Junior is not acting alone; he frequently confides in Tony's mother, Livia, who uses indirect language to encourage him to order at least two hits, one on an associate of Christopher's (1003: *Denial, Anger, Acceptance*) and the other the attempt on Tony. The closeness of the relationship that threatens Tony's life makes for a dramatic intertwining of psychological revelation and external events in the Season 1 climax. Moreover, the fact that Tony is indulging in psychotherapy is an important factor in Uncle Junior's decision to have Tony killed, as talking therapy is regarded as a puncture in the enclosed discourse that binds organized crime together.

In addition, prior to the attempted hit, Tony experiences a paralysing depression that culminates in a hallucination of a beautiful Italian exchange student whom he takes out to lunch. As she speaks, in his mind's eye he sees her sitting in a rocking chair, nursing a small baby (1012: *Isabella*). When he realizes that she never existed he calls Dr Melfi, who recommends that he stop taking some of his medication and asks him why he might feel the need for the fantasy of a loving caring mother now, given that his own mother frequently makes veiled references to infanticide. Not making the connection, Tony replies, to Dr Melfi's question about his general state of mind, that 'I feel pretty good actually. ... I'll feel even better when I know who took a shot at me' (1012: *Isabella*). In the following episode Tony finally begins to accept Dr Melfi's diagnosis of his mother's borderline personality disorder in an initially violent reaction, followed by an encounter with the FBI where he hears the taped conversations between Livia and Uncle Junior (1013: *I Dream of Jeannie Cusamano*).

Conclusion: The Moral Ambiguities of Kinship, Money and Psychology

This chapter has suggested ways in which contemporary serial dramas explore the attractions and anxieties surrounding modern western understandings of collective life. While on one level both *Deep Space Nine* and *The Sopranos* juxtapose the pleasures of social vitality with assertions of bounded individual identity, their characterizations of the person are also complicated by the fact that social life is not simply seen as effervescent excitement but is also expressed in social order and civic morals. Odo, the character in *Deep Space Nine* who appears able to merge with others of his kind most completely, is also known for his often rigid adherence to rules and regulations at the expense of particular relationships and loyalties. Meanwhile, and more broadly, the military structure of the Federation is an ambivalent feature of the programme. It provides security and a clear chain of command but it also appears as threatening to humans and aliens who prefer a different way of life, because of its insistence on the superiority of Federation 'democracy'.

In *The Sopranos*, tensions between loyalties to kinship and adherence to civil society are more strongly contrasted. For example, although Carmela's anxieties about her marriage to Tony usually focus around his infidelity, at certain rare moments she is confronted with the ambiguity of her choice to stay married to a man whose money comes from violent criminal activity. In her highly sexually charged 'confession' and 'communion' with Father Phil, for example, she says, 'I have forsaken what is right for what is easy, allowing evil into this house', referring to the potential corruption of her children, which she has ignored for the sake of their material well-being. Interestingly, in the same episode the language of vows is used thrice more. On the morning after the foregoing incident (the sexual tension of which was broken by Father Phil's fit of violent vomiting), she reassures Phil that nothing untoward has happened with the rhetorical question 'Is there a commandment against eating Ziti?' and sarcastically tells him, 'Don't forget your sacrament kit or whatever.' The third instance comes in a parallel story, in which Tony finds and murders an informant he happens across while taking his daughter to tour prospective colleges, telling the man, 'You took an oath and you broke it' (1004: *Meadowlands*).

While the language of loyalty and oaths sustains Carmela's complicity in her relationship with Tony, the language of psychology comes into question when she goes to see a psychiatrist recommended by Dr Melfi. Complaining about Tony's infidelity, she nonetheless assures herself that he is a good man, to which the psychiatrist replies, 'You tell me he's a depressed criminal, prone to anger, serially unfaithful. Is that your definition of a good man?' When she protests that she thought psychiatrists were not supposed to be judgemental, he counters, 'Many patients want to be excused from their current predicament because of events that occurred in their childhood, that's what psychiatry has become in America' and, on discovering that her husband's crimes are organized crimes, advises her to renounce her role as an accomplice and enabler – 'take the children, what's left of them, and go' – explaining that 'I'm not charging you because I won't take blood money and you can't either' (3007: *Second Opinion*).

This statement not only starkly questions Carmela's choices, it also invites the viewer to reconsider Dr Melfi's role and any amusement engendered by Tony's way of often interpreting her advice not as a vehicle for reform but as ideas to help him to be a more effective gangster. The fact that Tony undergoes therapy for five seasons without ever seriously contemplating renunciation of his violence suggests the limitations of confrontations with the past if they are unaccompanied by the assumption of moral responsibility in the present. Dr Melfi therefore walks a thin line in her attempts to represent the necessary restraints of civil society, not least because the violence she seeks to restrain and transform through rational and emotional insight is supported by the emotional and social attractions of kinship and solidarity, as well as those offered by rationalized discourses and vast sums of money.

A character that epitomizes these tensions is Ralph Cifaretto, a high earner in Tony's crew who nonetheless is desperate, both to earn promotion to Captain, and to gain respect through alliances of kinship and blood with Tony. He dates Tony's sister, Janice, and had earlier tried similarly to use his relationship as 'stepfather' to Jackie Aprile (Jackie Junior), the son of a close friend and associate of Tony's who died of cancer earlier in the series. Ralphie encourages Jackie to take an interest in Tony's daughter, Meadow, and incites him to try to make a name for himself committing petty crimes, a course of action that Tony wants to discourage because he had promised the boy's father that he would keep Jackie away from organized crime. However, Christopher, Tony's 'nephew' and primary assistant, is confused by the situation and reminds Tony that Jackie is 'the heir apparent' (3003: *Fortunate Son*). Ralphie's plans to join Tony's kin ultimately fail, but he is promoted to Captain because of his high earning power and escapes the full force of Tony's wrath for the whole of the third season, despite Tony's deep discomfort with the extent of Ralphie's unbridled ambition, his encroaching on other crew members' territory and his casual beating to death of a young girl outside the strip club Tony owns, where she worked (3006: *University*). Only in Season 4 is Tony incited to a murderous rage when a horse owned by Ralphie, which Tony has developed an affection for, is killed in a fire that Ralphie arranged in order to claim the insurance money. When Tony accuses Ralphie of cooking the horse alive, Ralphie argues that it was just an animal and a potential financial liability, adding that Tony neither complains about the fat envelopes of money Ralphie hands to him nor asks where that money has come from. 'What are you,' Ralphie asks, 'a vegetarian? You eat beef and sausage by the ... cartload!' (4009: *Whoever Did This*).

These words are a trigger for Tony, partly because they remind him of a scene recounted earlier to Dr Melfi in which, as an eleven-year-old child, he witnessed the owner of a meat shop being threatened for failing to repay a loan to Tony's father, who proceeds to hack off the shop owner's finger. Shortly after this incident young Tony has his first panic attack later that evening, when his mother displays great pleasure with the free meat Tony's father brings home. Dr Melfi links this incident with puberty, 'witnessing not only your mother and father's sexuality, but also the violence and blood so closely connected to the food you were about to eat and also the thought that someday you might also be called upon to bring home the bacon, like your father' (3003: *Fortunate Son*). In this sense, it could be argued that a cluster of issues around sacrifice and eroticism that both intersect and conflict with money and murder is brought to a climax by Ralphie's murder. Just when Tony wants to assert his own sense of solidarity and respect for innocent life, he is reminded of his own mercenary nature, even as viewers are reminded that the effectiveness of psychological discourse is limited and constrained by the extent to which it can be wedded to moral discourse. In the words of Dr Melfi's ex-husband, Richard: 'you call him a patient – the man's a criminal, Jennifer, and after a while you're going to get beyond psychotherapy with its cheesy moral relativism. Finally you're going to get to good and evil. And he's evil' (1008: *The Legend of Tennessee Moltisanti*).

References

Blok, A. 2001. *Honour and Violence*. Cambridge: Polity Press.

Campbell, J. 1956. *Hero with a Thousand Faces*. New York: World.

Carroll, N. 2004. 'Sympathy for the Devil', in R. Greene and P. Vernezze (eds), *The Sopranos and Philosophy: I Kill Therefore I Am*. Chicago and La Salle, IL: Open Court. pp. 121–36.

Child, L. 2007. *Tantric Buddhism and Altered States of Consciousness: Durkheim, Emotional Energy and Visions of the Consort*. Aldershot: Ashgate.

Durkheim, E. 1995 [1912]. *The Elementary Forms of Religious Life*, trans. and intro. Karen E. Fields. London and New York: The Free Press.

Ellis, C.S. 1995. 'With Eyes Uplifted: Space Aliens as Sky Gods', in J.W. Martin and C.E. Oswalt Jr (eds), *Religion, Myth, and Ideology in Popular American Film*. Boulder, CO: Westview Press, pp. 83–93.

Freud, S. 1991 [1930]. 'Civilization and Its Discontents', in *Penguin Freud Library Volume 12, Civilization, Society and Religion*, trans. J. Strachey, ed. A. Dickson. London and New York: Penguin,

Gabbard, G.O. 2002. *The Psychology of the Sopranos: Love, Death, Desire and Betrayal in America's Favourite Gangster Family*. New York: Basic Books.

Girard, R. 1979 [1972]. *Violence and the Sacred*, trans. Patrick Gregory. Baltimore and London: John Hopkins University Press.

Gordon, A. 1995. '*Star Wars*: A Myth for Our Time', in J.W. Martin and C.E. Oswalt (eds), *Screening the Sacred: Religion, Myth, and Ideology in Popular American Film*. Boulder, CO: Westview Press, pp. 73–82.

Harold, J. 2004. 'A Moral Never-Never Land: Identifying with Tony Soprano', in R. Greene and P. Vernezze (eds), *The Sopranos and Philosophy: I Kill Therefore I Am*. Chicago and La Salle, IL: Open Court, pp. 137–40.

Hubert, H. 1999 [1905]. *Essay on Time: A Brief Study of the Representation of Time in Religion and Magic*, ed. R. Parkin and J. Redding. Oxford: Durkheim Press.

Lee, S. 2008. 'Is Odo a Collaborator?', in J. Eberl and K.S. Decker (eds), *Star Trek and Philosophy: The Wrath of Kant*. Chicago & La Salle, IL: Open Court, pp. 105–15.

Lippman, M. 2004. 'Know Thyself, Asshole: Tony Soprano as an Aristotelian Tragic Hero', in R. Greene and P. Vernezze (eds), *The Sopranos and Philosophy: I Kill Therefore I Am*. Chicago and La Salle, IL: Open Court, pp. 147–56.

Lyden, J.C. 2007. 'Interreligious Dialogue and Film', in J. Mitchell and S.B. Plate (eds), *The Religion and Film Reader*. New York and London: Routledge, pp. 416–20.

Mellor, P.A. and C. Shilling. 1997. *Re-forming the Body: Religion, Community and Modernity*. London: Sage.

Plate, S.B. 2008. *Religion and Film: Cinema and the Re-Creation of the World*. London and New York: Wallflower Press.

Wagner, J. & J. Lundeen. 1998. *Deep Space and Sacred Time: Star Trek in the American Mythos*. Westport, CT, and London: Praeger.

Filmography

Armitage, G. 1997. *Grosse Pointe Blank.*
Berman, R. and M. Piller. 1993–1999. *Star Trek: Deep Space Nine.*
Chaffey, D. 1963. *Jason and the Argonauts.*
Davis, D. 1981. *Clash of the Titans.*
Ramis, H. 1999. *Analyze This.*
Chase, D. 1999–2006. *The Sopranos.*

PART III

Collective Minds

Chapter 5

DURKHEIM'S SACRED/PROFANE OPPOSITION

WHAT SHOULD WE MAKE OF IT?

N.J. Allen

Durkheim the theorist has always been difficult to pigeonhole. In the subtitle to *The Elementary Forms of Religious* Life,[1] the reference to Australian Aborigines connotes evolutionism (I prefer the label 'world-historical' – but no matter); yet the famous four-line italicized definition of religion (1968 [1912]: 65) points in two other theoretical directions. It ends with religious beliefs and practices uniting adherents into a single moral community – this is functionalism. But it starts with the beliefs and practices forming a system relating to sacred things, that is, to things that are set apart (i.e., from profane things) and forbidden or tabooed. The sacred/profane binary opposition foreshadows the structuralism of the 1950s and 1960s.

Several approaches come to terms with this opposition. First, one can ask how Durkheim is using it. Many have attempted summaries of this sociological masterpiece, so I content myself with two quotations. In the first, 'The distinctive feature of religious thought is the division of the world into two domains, one containing all that is sacred, the other all that is profane' (1968 [1912]: 50f.), he is proposing a dichotomy of the thinkable. In the second, 'There does not exist in the history of human thought another example of two things so profoundly differentiated, so radically opposed one to another' (53), they are more profoundly opposed than good and evil. These formulations seem to me unnecessarily rigid. Since he admits degrees of sacredness

(52), Durkheim could surely have left more room for contexts where the sacred and profane par excellence form the poles of a continuum – although light and dark form an opposition, sometimes one has to recognize twilight. From this point of view the profound opposition would be between the two poles.[2]

A second approach would trace the development of the opposition in Durkheim's earlier writings, also taking into account his immense debt to his nephew, Marcel Mauss, and other collaborators at the *Année sociologique*. Two texts merit special note. The 1899 essay by Hubert and Mauss (1968 [1899]) argues that sacrifices of all sorts consist in establishing communication between the sacred and profane worlds via a victim that is destroyed during the ceremony (302). Second, in 1906 Mauss (with H. Beuchat) contrasted two lifestyles practised by Eskimos and certain other societies: in the winter the population congregated and lived an intense religious life; in the summer it dispersed and minimized religious activity – a contrast that can easily be rephrased in terms of sacred and profane (Mauss 1973 [1906]). Though private letters to Mauss at the time show that the debt was recognized by his *Année* collaborators, later commentators have sometimes ignored it, no doubt because of their intense focus on the uncle (e.g., Jones 2005; cf. Fournier 2007: 766f., 795).

Third, one can ask what later writers have made of the opposition. For instance, within anthropology, drawing on his own experience, Evans-Pritchard said (1965: 65) that he had never found the sacred/ profane dichotomy of much use in either formulating fieldwork-testable questions or classifying observed facts.[3] An American collection of articles by sociologists and religionists called *Defining Religion* (Greil and Bromley 2003) makes a few references to *Elementary Forms*, but none of its contributors engages seriously with the definition offered by the book. The definition fares slightly better in a more recent collection where, in addition to occasional allusions, one of the twenty-four contributors cites it and gives it a paragraph of commentary (Davie 2009: 175). Other scholars are more enthusiastic. For instance, Massimo Rosati (2007) usefully summarizes the work of Roy Rappoport and Jeffrey Alexander, two U.S. theorists who have built on the Durkheimian sacred.

A fourth approach could focus on analytical vocabulary. How many languages have words for *sacred* and *profane*? And if not many, does it matter? Anyway, are they the best terms? Profane seems awkward nowadays (if only because of the irrelevant term profanity), and one can toy with alternatives: mundane, worldly, secular, this-worldly, everyday, ordinary... The profane is left implicit in Durkheim's definition, and he uses the term in various ways (Pickering 1984: 133ff.). As for sacred, a list of semantic neighbours could include holy (in French, *saint*, sometimes used by Durkheim himself),[4] religious (though it would be tautologous to define religion as concerned with religious beliefs), and other-worldly (which lacks the element of taboo). This fourth approach could help to link *Elementary Forms* to other bodies of literature – on secularization, for instance.

But my approach here is to relate Durkheim's opposition to four themes that have interested me. My conclusion is that it is at least a useful mental tool, capable of suggesting worthwhile questions. I start with a question about the very notion of opposition.

Markedness

In 1985 I found myself discussing Louis Dumont's notion of hierarchical opposition as distinct from non-hierarchical or equistatutory opposition; I thought it resembled the linguists' notion of markedness, especially as used in semantics (Allen 1985). Both ideas concern an asymmetry that is very common in pairs, whereby one member is somehow more fundamental, widespread, valued or inclusive than the other, so that it seems natural to treat the first as a conceptual starting point and to derive the second from the first rather than vice versa. If the first is multipurpose, the second is specialized. Thus, whether a line is long or short, we ordinarily ask how *long* it is: *long* refers to the dimension of length as well as to an assessment within the dimension, whereas *short* seldom refers to a dimension. Though not in this case, in many others the asymmetry is reflected in the morphology, the fundamental member being a single lexeme, the derivative one consisting of the same lexeme preceded by a negative prefix, as in pure versus impure (the basic concepts in Dumont's analysis of Hinduism). Hence the analytical terminology: the fundamental term is unmarked, the narrower one marked by the prefix. At least in English, when the terms are paired, it usually sounds natural to put the unmarked first. One says 'pure and impure', 'long and short', rather than the reverse. Still, the analysis is not applicable to all pairs. Moreover, different criteria of markedness do not always coincide, and a change of context may reverse the allocation. But the interesting point is how often the asymmetry *is* present.

In 1985 my focus was on Dumont, and I did not discuss the sacred/profane opposition as such. But I could well have recalled Hertz's 1909 essay, which presents the sacred as belonging in a single category with the right hand, the male sex and the sky above, as opposed to the profane, left hand and earth beneath (Hertz 1928 [1909]: 96–98). Mauss later thought that the binarism of the early *Année* work – including Hertz's, though it had served as a useful starting point – was excessively simple; it abstracted the contrasted elements from contexts that were more complex (Mauss 1968–1969 II: 143–48; Allen 2000: 120, 142). Nevertheless, Hertz's idea is worth pursuing. It presents the sacred as unmarked – prior and valued – as distinct from the profane, which is secondary, derivative, devalued. Perhaps worlds such as he was discussing *have* often been, to their members, fundamentally sacred and only derivatively profane. Of course profane or this-worldly activity takes place, but it would be against the background of the sacred or within the setting it provides.

Such an attitude might be recognizable synchronically – religion would (at least in principle) embrace or pervade the rest of social life; or it might be recognizable diachronically, in so far as the mythology moved from the primordial sacred (from dream time or divine creation) towards the here-and-now, with its observable settlements and institutions. The commanding position of religion is of course a very Durkheimian doctrine: 'If religion has given birth to everything that is essential in society, it is because the idea of society is the soul of religion' (599; cf. Pickering 1984: 267).

But in today's apparently more secularized or disenchanted world, is the sacred still unmarked relative to the profane? There are many, and not only among practising scientists, who hold that a this-worldly or physical science approach is or should be the default position, the starting point or basis for a contemporary world view, onto which an element of the religious or 'spiritual' may be added as a sort of optional extra for those who fancy it. Here the sacred or other-worldly becomes the secondary element, the marked term in the opposition. Accordingly (they might say), world-historical narratives now reverse the course taken by myth: they start, not with supernatural creators, but with the evolution of the cosmos and biosphere, and ask how, why and when the sacred and the gods made their – doubtless fleeting – appearance in human imaginations. 'Natural versus supernatural' should replace sacred versus profane, effectively reversing it at the same time.

On the other hand, in Durkheim's view, the sacred is always with us, and if the gods have died (they have nonetheless proved more resistant than used to be expected), the sacred has taken refuge in the cult of the individual. Perhaps a broader formulation would be better, allowing the sacred to take refuge in any values regarded as ultimate

– in human rights, nature, the nation, revolution, the constitution, science, truth, or whatever. In any case, humans are social beings and will always need some sort of ultimate values, however multiple, fluctuating and contested. Personally, despite the difficulty in pinning down what is sacred in the modern world, I side with Durkheim, and doubt whether thoroughgoing reversal of his opposition is a tenable position. But my more general point is that markedness offers an interesting angle of approach to the paired concepts and to their long-term history.

Indo-European Cultural Comparativism

The discussion has to start with the forerunner of the philosophical ambitions of *Elementary Forms:* Durkheim and Mauss's essay *Primitive Classification* (1903), which was subjected to regrettable and uncomprehending criticism in the Introduction to the English translation (Allen 2000: 39ff.). What makes a classification a 'primitive' one is that it homologizes or superimposes classifications of different domains. *We* see clans, cardinal points, elements, colours, ritualists as belonging to separate domains, but many societies recognize correlations or correspondences between them.

In the Indo-European (IE) field one can start with Dumézil (died 1986), who, though he never cited *Primitive Classification,* was surely influenced by it indirectly. Dumézil characterized the proto-culture ancestral to the various cultures of the older IE-speaking world as possessing what he called a trifunctional ideology – and what a Durkheimian could call a triadic form of primitive classification. Take for instance the categories of the twice-born (i.e. initiates) in Hindu normative literature: they are classified into priests, warriors and producers, typically listed in that order as a descending hierarchy. Numerous such ranked triads can be assembled from India and elsewhere in the older IE world, and if their elements are ranged in order across a page, one triad below another, the analyst can abstract from each column the common factor or factors that give it a degree of unity. In Table 5.1 I give two of Dumézil's many formulations of these unifying factors, followed by his labels for them (in bold) and my abbreviations for those labels. The question now arises whether, if F1 covers priesthood and sacred power, F2+F3 cover the profane.

The problem is that, in case after case, Dumézil's schema turns out to be too compressed (Allen 2011). In focusing on the core of the hierarchy, his analyses often ignore its extremes; in so far as the summit of

Table 5.1. Dumézilian or trifunctional analysis of the three twice-born Hindu estates

Priest	warrior	producer
magical & juridical sovereignty	warrior force	fecundity
sacred power	force, offensive or defensive	means of economic & genetic continuity
first function (F1)	**second function** (F2)	**third function** (F3)

the hierarchy is taken into account, its analysis is unsatisfactory. To revert to the Hindu case, we need at the bottom end a devalued category for serfs or non-initiates, and at the top a valued category for the king, who cannot be convincingly assimilated to either priest or warrior. Despite their remoteness in a linear hierarchy, both these additions to the schema are heterogeneous relative to the core categories. To the twice-born, neither is an ordinary human being: the king is ideologically transcendent;[5] the serf is ritually excluded. The heterogeneity that they share justifies allotting them to a single function, but this function needs to be subdivided into two aspects to take account of the different value attached to king and serf. Thus F4+ covers other valued outsiders, such as founders, creators and deities, as well as kings, and F4- covers enemies, whether human or supernatural, as well as ritual outsiders. The pentadic schema rests on detailed arguments and evidence from the IE world, but it turns out to fit Durkheim's opposition much better than Dumézil's does, and in two ways.

Taken as a whole, F4, set apart from the other three, corresponds to the sacred, set apart from the profane. This statement deliberately ignores Dumézil's link between F1 and the sacred, which I see as oversimplified. His fuller definitions of F1 emphasize rather intelligence and knowledge, including knowledge of how to *deal with* the sacred. In so far as sacredness inheres in a priest, I think it is largely because of what Durkheim calls its contagiousness (458f.). Despite what is said in Sanskrit texts that assimilate priests to gods, divine kings, who are expressions of society as a whole, make more sense comparatively than divine priests. Priests and priestesses typically 'mediate upwards from the people to God', offering sacrifice on behalf of the people (Cunningham 2009: 288).

As for the two contrasting aspects of the fourth function, valued and devalued, they parallel Durkheim's contrast, derived from Robertson Smith, between two types of sacred thing that are nonetheless closely allied (431, 454, 584): that which is pure, auspicious or positive, and that which is impure, inauspicious or negative.[6] As both theorists were aware, the dualism was already present in the semantics of Latin *sacer*. Sacredness goes beyond purity, but this only qualifies the parallel between the two bodies of theory; it does not destroy it. One might wonder whether the parallel arose because *Elementary Forms* influenced my interpretation of the structures present in the IE material, but I doubt it; if it did, I believe the influence was subconscious.

In any case, the parallel prompts certain observations. Thus in the Rigvedic myth of origin of Hindu social structure, Purusha, the Primal Being/Person, is divided into four parts, three of which (head, arms, thighs) give rise to the twice-born while the fourth (feet) gives rise to the devalued Shudra or serfs. I suggested above that twice-born and serfs paralleled respectively two of Durkheim's categories, namely profane and impure sacred. But these two categories are not always sharply contrasted: Hertz, for example, could write of their 'natural affinity and near equivalence'. The two notions, he says, come together 'and form, in opposition to the sacred, the negative pole of the spiritual world' (1928 [1909]: 90). Similarly, although the gap between twice-born and excluded is as fundamental in practice as it is conceptually (Allen 2007), the four social categories are aligned both in the myth and under what became the standard term *varna*, 'estate'. In these contexts what can be seen as a triad appears instead as a duality – precisely the situation Hertz was envisaging. Perhaps Durkheim's failure as analyst to give a precise definition of the profane reflects a grey area in the real world.

The top end of the Indo-European hierarchy presents a comparable theoretical issue. If the term sacred is covered primarily by F4+ and only secondarily by F1, the application of the term *religion* becomes problematic. It seems that the analyst needs to distinguish two aspects of the concept: religion as embodied in sacred beings, including kings and gods; and religion as expounded doctrinally and expressed in cultic activity by ordinary human priests (however pure they may be). The gap separating the two aspects can be approached in various ways. In Dumézil's language it is the gap between the encompassing ideology and one of the functions that compose the ideology. In Mauss's language it is the gap between two sorts of social fact (or social phenomena), which he classifies as 'total' ('general' being a less satisfactory label) and 'religious' (Allen 2000: 143–145). In writing on this, I did not at that time appreciate that the gap is implicit in Durkheim's definition of religion. The definition recognizes sacred things on the one hand, and the community on the other, with the beliefs and practices that (in various ways) relate to those things. 'Religion' straddles the gap.

Kinship

My third theme relates our opposition to a theory of kinship that I have labelled tetradic (Allen 2008). Logically, the simplest way to structure a *whole* society on the basis of kinship is to divide it into four sections linked by rules of marriage and recruitment; the four sections are congruent with four kinship terms, each of which refers to one of the four types of relative recognized by ego. The simplicity of the structure suggests that it (or something similar) was the earliest distinctively human kinship system. I see two sorts of link between the theory and the sacred/profane opposition. On the first I shall be particularly brief, since I covered it in 2008 and previously.

Drawing on Mauss and his study of the Eskimos (noted above), Durkheim associated religion with periods of tribal demographic concentration. The famous effervescent assemblies, with their ritual and artistic creativity, contrasted with the humdrum subsistence-oriented lifestyle of the dispersed hunter-gatherer bands. But, one can ask, in which of these phases would early humans invent and institutionalize a tetradic kinship system? The answer has to be in the concentrated phase, if only because the system organizes the society as a whole. Tetradic theory proposes that the structure devised at or for the concentrated phase came to replace whatever practices prevailed in the dispersed phase.

A different and new question is whether our opposition can plausibly be incorporated in the tetradic model – of which we need a slightly fuller account. Imagine a demographically isolated society, where everyone is related to everyone else. Split it first into endogamous generation moieties that exchange children; then crosscut this set-up with exogamous descent moieties. It does not matter whether we start by opting for descent moieties that recruit in the female line (the option I follow below) or in the male line, since in either case the outcome is a social structure consisting of four exogamous sections organized into three types of moiety (or pairs of sections) – generation, matri and patri. The model-builder is at liberty to associate the sacred/profane opposition with one or another of the types, but to do so seems unprofitable.

The interesting question arises when one shifts from the socio-structural to the egocentric perspective, situating ego in one quadrant and thus turning the quadrants into categories of relatives. Thinking as they did, in terms of descent moieties, the early *Année* (Durkheim 1898) saw ego's moiety as sacred, the other as profane; and Hertz (1928 [1909]: 90) did likewise, proposing that later in world history this 'reversible dualism' was replaced by stratified hierarchical social structures in which sacred strata outranked profane ones.

Tetradic theory can offer two distinct approaches. Let us first consider male ego's primary relatives (those in the nuclear family), in the light of Figure 5.1.

If ego and his sister are in the lower left quadrant, his mother is in top left and his father and daughter in top right. Forbidden to marry within these three categories (which would count as incestuous), he takes his wife from the only remaining one (bottom right), which incidentally contains his cross cousins, among other relatives. In other words, three quadrants contain the closest relatives of an unmarried ego, and in that sense are familiar, this-worldly, profane. The fourth quadrant contains his bride and the unfamiliar world she opens up – that of ego's direct affines. So can one interpret these affines as sacred? The three familiar groups could not exist without the 'outsider' fourth, which contains two of the four grandparents. Moreover, as outsiders to ego's natal family and therefore essentially strangers, affines are often viewed with an ambivalence that recalls the opposition between pure and impure sacred: a spouse and his or her people can be a blessing or a curse. Across the world, ambivalence towards a spouse's group is quite often reflected in 'joking relationships' that, as some theorists recognize, are one in a set of four distinct attitudes towards different categories of relatives (Allen 1989: 52).[7]

I have often wondered whether tetradic theory, with its time scale on the order of fifty millennia, can be related to the IE pentadic theory, with its time scale on the order of five millennia. If our first approach is on the right track, the sacred/profane opposition would provide one such link; strikingly, in both theories the profane is represented by three separate groups.[8] However, there is a second approach to envisaging the link. Rather than locating the sacred in one component of a tetradic society, one could locate it in the whole society – in what

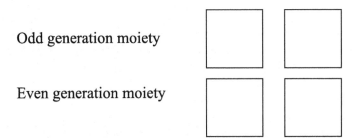

Odd generation moiety

Even generation moiety

Figure 5.1. Endogamous even/odd generation moieties, cross-cut by exogamous descent moieties

transcends all the four components. This approach (which I prefer) accords better with both the IE case and Durkheim's suspicion that totality was the category par excellence (629). It also leads on to my final theme.

God as Society Hypostasized

This final topic has interested me less as a teacher or researcher than as an anthropological man-in-the-street – more or less a Durkheimian, but one who is only too aware of his lamentable unfamiliarity with theology or philosophy. The topic certainly concerns the sacred/profane opposition, since Durkheim linked this opposition very closely to two others: that between God and man, and that between society and individual. In his view, God is only the figurative expression of society (1968 [1912]: 323). After assembling a good number of quotations, many from outside *Elementary Forms*, Pickering summarizes Durkheim's position: 'The reality is society and God [is] the symbolic (figurative, transfigured, hypostasised) expression of it' (1984: 232). It seems to me that this view is too seldom taken into account, particularly by those who engage in public debate about the existence of God. The debate tends to be conducted in extra-Durkheimian or pre-Durkheimian terms, as if the only possible answers were 'yes, God exists', or 'no, he doesn't' – as if the only choice lay between theism and atheism.[9]

The similarities between God and society are many, but they are difficult to classify. For a start, both entities find themselves subjected to destructive criticism, often dismissed as myths, empty fictions or illegitimate or unhelpful reifications. But even for those who accept them, a comprehensive definition is elusive, perhaps impossible. Within a religious community, believers do not necessarily view God in identical ways, nor do members of society necessarily have a common view of what it is they belong to. In both cases the view of insiders and outsiders may well be discrepant. One can come at either entity locally or globally – as 'our God', or as ruler of the world; as 'our society', or as the human family. If society and the phenomena that constitute it are both entities sui generis (Durkheim 1988 [1895]: 82, 101), then so is God.[10] Not being three-dimensional, both resist satisfactory visual representation (God the father with his white beard, Holy Spirit as dove, frontispiece to Hobbes's *Leviathan*). But most people, most of the time, are happy to use the concepts without worrying over definitions. Paradoxes are readily accepted: God is transcendent and immanent;

society is external to us but interiorized. An element of indefinability or vagueness may even be acknowledged, whether gladly or wryly (God moves in mysterious ways; the pressures of society operate on all of us, even sociologists, one way or another).

Both God and society are conceived as agents. Both exercise authority. Both propose systems of values, though these too may be hard to define, and how they should be acted out in particular contexts is usually arguable. Both can or should be 'served' and can be regarded with gratitude. Both offer punishments and rewards, though which of these receives more emphasis can vary. God shares his domain with the Devil; society contains criminals as well as positive role models. If theodicy presents theoretical problems, so do the imperfections of society. But on the whole, it is the positive aspects that are emphasized in both cases. Ideally, God provides order, justice and support for individuals, and so does society. Going only a little beyond Durkheim's words, one can say that God is love, and society is solidarity (the bonds that unite men one with another).

To a believer, any such list of similarities, however long and richly elaborated, omits the one thing that really matters, namely, that God existed before human society and continues to exist outside it. Thus, according to Pickering, a careful and usually a sympathetic expositor of Durkheim, Durkheim's position 'lacks empirical support from the experiences of those who are religious'. 'The great illusion which arises out of Durkheim's position is that the believer or practitioner does not know what is happening. ... Only the scientist or sociologist knows' (1984: 241, 222).[11]

Counterarguments can of course be advanced, but I comment only obliquely. In leaving no theoretical space for the existence of what the believer experiences and interprets as something outside society, are scientists/sociologists being arrogant? Perhaps they are, but no more so, I think, than a scientist/anthropologist who analyses a society that believes in reincarnated ancestral spirits or witchcraft but who leaves no theoretical space for the existence of such entities. One advantage of the Durkheimian position is that, by acknowledging the background of truth in all religions, it helps one minimize at least that form of arrogance.

Theoretical arguments about the God-society relationship will not be settled easily or soon. It has even been argued (Bauman 2005: 378) that in the century since *Elementary Forms* appeared, 'society' has changed so radically as to undermine whatever plausibility and cognitive usefulness Durkheim's grand vision once possessed. Personally I doubt this claim and regard the relationship as still worth exploring.[12]

One possible approach is to concentrate on exactly what it means for something to exist 'outside society'. To a Durkheimian, social facts include ways of feeling, and one might ask how believers, without the help of society, are to know what their experiences are experiences *of*. Another approach could look at contexts in which the theological and sociological sorts of discourse come close to each other. For instance, at a funeral, presentations of the life of the deceased can be expressed in terms of service to either God or the social group, and translation between the two modes of expression is often so easy that one scarcely notices which has been used. Similarly, in cases of civil disorder, whether the rioters are condemned as lacking respect for the authority of religion or of society, the accusations may be couched in almost identical terms. From this point of view, the gap between Durkheimian and religious formulations is much smaller than is usually assumed. A good deal has been written about the influence of Judaism and/or Christianity on Durkheim, but much less on the sense in which he actually *is* religious. His view of society can be fragmented analytically, as by Lukes (1973: 20–22), but to believe in society is to believe in *something*.

So let me end by risking a cursory formula. Of the three main founding figures in sociology, Marx was not deeply interested in religion. Weber was, and he had much of interest to say, but his disenchanted and religiously unmusical rationalism is too close to the common sense of contemporary individualism to raise the deepest issues. Durkheim continues to challenge us, and the sacred/profane opposition lies at the heart of this challenge.

Notes

Special thanks to Sondra Hausner for helpful comments.
1. Though I use the English title, in this chapter bracketed numerals that are not dates are page numbers in the French edition.
2. Cf. James (2003: 200): 'The Durkheimian dichotomy obscures the shadings of ceremoniality that pervade all arenas of social action.'
3. But in his book on Nuer religion, Evans-Pritchard (1956) focuses the first two chapters on the sacred (the world of gods and spirits), and only then moves to the human world and its communication with the sacred via sacrifice. Is he not subconsciously using the dichotomy?
4. Cf. Fields (2005: 173), who suggests that *saint* is left over from an earlier phase of Durkheim's theorizing.
5. Embodying the gods of the eight cardinal points, he is effectively immune to impurity (*Manu* 5.93–7).

6. The contrast is sometimes referred to, with conscious reference to Hertz, as right sacred versus left sacred (Riley 2005).
7. The idea for the proposed link between sacredness and kinship was suggested to me by a discussion of Lowland South American societies (Rivière 2004) that links affinity with otherness and creativity, but also with symbolic exchanges that may involve love or violence. In the context of concentric dualism, says Rivière, 'the inside is associated with familiarity, kin and safety, the outside with the other, affines and danger'.
8. A hypothesis to align the two triads might start from ego as child and associate the odd-level sections with F1 and F2 (respectively authoritative/disciplinary and defensive/supportive), and ego's own section with F3 (junior, but holding promise of producing the next generation).
9. Durkheim is sometimes described as agnostic, for instance in the first paragraph of Swain's introduction to his translation, or by Fournier (2007: 513). But Durkheim knew better than most what his personal beliefs were about the existence of God, and explicitly preferred the label 'rationalist' (Fournier 2007: 717).
10. The Latin phrase 'of its own (unique) type' was also used by Comte (cited in Lukes 1973: 81).
11. With the second quotation compare the following, from a non-Durkheimian psychologist: 'Only privileged minorities enjoy atheism ... atheism is a luxury of the elite' (Barrett 2004: 118).
12. It may be true that French society in the early twentieth century was (or felt) more stable than today's society, but Durkheim was not unaware of the flux or fluidity of social life. At the end of chapter 2 of the *Rules* (1988 [1895]: 137–39), he talks of research on the social domain needing to start with terra firma and then move forward gradually to 'encompass that fugitive reality which the human mind will perhaps never be able to apprehend completely'. Here he is contrasting social life in its crystallized or consolidated forms with social life embodied in events.

References

Allen, N.J. 1985. 'Hierarchical Opposition and Some Other Types of Relation', in R.H. Barnes, D. de Coppet and R.J. Parkin (eds), *Contexts and Levels: Anthropological Essays on Hierarchy* (*JASO* Occasional Papers 4). Oxford: JASO, pp. 21–32.

———. 1989. 'Assimilation of Alternate Generations', *JASO* 20(1): 45–55.

———. 2000. *Categories and Classifications: Maussian Reflections on the Social.* Oxford: Berghahn Books.

———. 2007. 'The Close and the Distant: A Long-term Perspective', in G. Pfeffer (ed.), *Periphery and Centre: Studies in Orissan History, Religion and Anthropology.* Delhi, Manohar, pp. 273–90.

———. 2008. 'Tetradic Theory and the Origin of Human Kinship Systems', in N.J. Allen, H. Callan, R. Dunbar and W. James (eds), *Early Human Kinship: From Sex to Social Reproduction*. Oxford: Blackwell, pp. 96–112.

———. 2011. 'The Indo-European Background to Greek Mythology', in K. Dowden and N. Livingstone (eds), *A Companion to Greek Mythology*. Oxford: Blackwell, pp. 341–56.

Barrett, J.L. 2004. *Why Would Anyone Believe in God?* Lanham, MD: AltaMira Press.

Bauman, Z. 2005. 'Durkheim's Society Revisited', in J.C. Alexander and P. Smith (eds), *The Cambridge Companion to Durkheim*. Cambridge: Cambridge University Press, pp. 360–82.

Cunningham, L.S. 2009. 'Holy Men/Holy Women', in R.A. Segal (ed.), *The Blackwell Companion to the Study of Religion*. Oxford: Wiley-Blackwell, pp. 285–93.

Davie, G. 2009. 'Sociology of Religion', in R.A. Segal (ed.), *The Blackwell Companion to the Study of Religion*. Oxford: Wiley-Blackwell, pp. 171–91.

Durkheim, E. 1898. 'La prohibition de l'inceste et ses origines', *Année sociologique* 1: 1–70.

———. 1968 [1912]. *Les Formes élémentaires de la vie religieuse: Le système totémique en Australie*, 5th ed. Paris: Presses Universitaires de France.

———. 1988 [1895]. *Les règles de la method sociologique*. Paris: Flammarion.

Durkheim, E. and M. Mauss. 1903. 'De quelques formes primitives de classification', *Année sociologique* 6: 1–72.

Evans-Pritchard, E.E. 1956. *Nuer Religion*. New York and Oxford: Oxford University Press.

———. 1965. *Theories of Primitive Religion*. Oxford: Clarendon Press.

Fields, K.E. 2005. 'What Difference Does Translation Make? *Les formes élémentaires de la vie religieuse* in French and English', in J.C. Alexander and P. Smith (eds), *The Cambridge Companion to Durkheim*. Cambridge: Cambridge University Press, pp. 160–80.

Fournier, M. 2007. *Émile Durkheim*. Paris: Fayard.

Greil, A.L. and D.G. Bromley (eds). 2003. *Defining Religion: Investigating the Boundaries between the Sacred and Secular*. Amsterdam and London: JAI.

Hertz, R. 1928 [1909]. 'La prééminence de la main droite: Étude sur la polarité religieuse', in *Mélanges de sociologie religieuse et folklore*. Paris: Presses Universitaires de France, pp. 99–129.

Hubert, H. and M. Mauss. 1968 [1899]. 'Essai sur la nature et la fonction du sacrifice', in M. Mauss, *Œuvres, I–III*, ed. V. Karady, vol. 1. Paris: Minuit, pp. 193–307.

James, W. 2003. *The Ceremonial Animal: A New Portrait of Anthropology*. Oxford: Oxford University Press.

Jones, R.A. 2005. 'Practices and Presuppositions: Some Questions about Durkheim and *Les formes élémentaires de la vie religieuse*', in J.C. Alexander and P. Smith (eds), *The Cambridge Companion to Durkheim*. Cambridge: Cambridge University Press, pp. 80–100.

Lukes, S. 1973. *Émile Durkheim: His Life and Work, a Historical and Critical Study*. London: Allen Lane.

Mauss, M. 1968–1969. *Œuvres, I–III*, ed. V. Karady. Paris: Minuit.

———. 1973 [1906]. 'Essai sur les variations saisonnières des sociétés eskimos: Étude de morphologie sociale', in *Sociologie et anthropologie*. Paris:
Presses Universitares de France, pp. 389–477.

Pickering, W.S.F. 1984. *Durkheim's Sociology of Religion: Themes and Theories*.
London: Routledge and Kegan Paul.

Riley, A.T. 2005. '"Renegade Durkheimianism" and the Transgressive Left
Sacred', in J.C. Alexander and P. Smith (eds), *The Cambridge Companion to
Durkheim*. Cambridge: Cambridge University Press, pp. 274–301.

Rivière, P. 2004. 'The Amerindianization of Descent and Affinity', in R. Parkin and L. Stone (eds), *Kinship and Family: An Anthropological Reader*. Mal-
den, MA, and Oxford: Blackwell, pp. 104–9.

Rosati, M. 2007. 'Recovering Durkheim's "Second Program of Research": Roy
Rappaport and Jeffrey C. Alexander', *Durkheimian Studies* 13: 105–21.

Chapter 6

DURKHEIM AND
THE PRIMITIVE MIND

AN ARCHAEOLOGICAL RETROSPECTIVE

Clive Gamble

Like every human institution, religion did not commence anywhere.
– Emile Durkheim, *The Elementary Forms of the Religious Life*

Durkheim's impact on archaeology, and in particular its earliest branch – the Palaeolithic – is only now starting to be felt, 100 years after the publication of *The Elementary Forms of the Religious Life*. Given his sustained impact on the fields of sociology and anthropology, the decision of his archaeological contemporaries and their successors to proceed with very few nods in his direction is worth investigation. In this chapter I explore the proposition that archaeologists have managed to live without him for so long because they were wedded to the un-Durkheimian view that religion is a separate and different type of social activity. They were set on this course by the trappings of religion – burials, grave goods, statues – and the interpretive opportunities these presented to a material science such as Palaeolithic archaeology. I suggest instead that considering some of the basic propositions of *Elementary Forms* in the deep-time perspective that archaeology provides would rather considerably enrich the study of the deep hominin past. In particular, through Durkheim we begin to understand the variety of moral codes that underpin society as well as the collective spirit that drives us to be social.

Ten Years before *Elementary Forms*

The development of Palaeolithic archaeology over the last century might have taken a different turn if archaeologists had absorbed Durkheim's insights into the social basis of actions. The decade before the publication of *The Elementary Forms of the Religious Life* was an especially lively one for Palaeolithic archaeology. It started with Spencer and Gillen's *Native Tribes of Central Australia* (1899), which would profoundly impact not only Durkheim but also W.J. Sollas's 'living prehistory' and his influential book *Ancient Hunters and Their Modern Representatives* (1911). In this work Sollas compared the Lower Palaeolithic of Europe to the technology and society of the Tasmanians, the Middle Palaeolithic to the Australians and the Upper Palaeolithic to the apparently more advanced Inuit and San peoples of the Kalahari.

Sollas was following a path well trodden in Oxford tradition. Much earlier, Edward Tylor had been impressed by a Tasmanian stone tool that Thomas Dawson brought to the Taunton Museum in 1860 (Murray 1992). The pattern of stone flaking linked it directly, in his view, to Pleistocene-age material from Clermont in France (Tylor 1865: 193). Moreover, 'Native Tasmanian life presents a picture of man at perhaps the lowest intellectual and industrial level found among tribes leading an independent existence, on their own land and after their own manner' (Tylor 1894: 148). The idea that the Palaeolithic of Europe could still be encountered had carried the day.

Other archaeological discoveries in the decade before *Elementary Forms* added a new dimension to Tylor's Palaeolithic basement for society. In 1901, thanks to the energy of the young priest Henri Breuil, the polychrome cave art of Font de Gaume and the engravings of Les Combarelles near the village of Les Eyzies, Dordogne, were not only discovered but authenticated as Pleistocene art. The next year saw the older find of Altamira in Cantabrian Spain added to that list. Engraved and carved bone, as well as beads and other ornaments, had been commonplace in excavations in southwest France since the 1860s, but the addition of painting to their accomplishments raised the stakes in terms of mental ability and the symbolic reach of Upper Palaeolithic people.

Then in 1908 came two very different key discoveries. A skeleton in a pit was excavated by three clerics (the Abbés Amédée and Paul Bouyssonie and Abbé Bardon) in the appropriately named cave of La Chapelle-aux-Saints near Brive. Associated with Middle Palaeolithic stone tools, the skeleton became the classic Neanderthal following an exhaustive, albeit biased (Hammond 1982) study by Marcellin Boule (1911, 1912, 1913). That same year a small limestone female figurine was excavated from the Upper Palaeolithic site of Willendorf, near Linz in Austria. The proportions of this 'Venus of Willendorf' excited much comment, and the object achieved instantaneous iconic status for Palaeolithic symbolism.

Much later, in his short book *Les religions de la préhistoire*, André Leroi-Gourhan (1964) listed four lines of archaeological evidence for recognizing Palaeolithic religion. The list included burials, bone cults, religious art, and ceremonies inferred from objects. The Willendorf figurine was an example of this last category, along with beads and other ornaments, some of them obtained many hundreds of kilometres from where they were found, indicating the possibility of a form of Stone Age pilgrimage. Along with the predominantly animal art from the painted caves of France and Spain, these objects came to represent instances of totemism and magic that, in the intellectual parlance of the time, acted as proxies for religious life.

Palaeolithic Religion

The archaeological discoveries of this decade comprise two strands. First was the close involvement of French priests in human origins. Breuil (1877–1961) would become the most important of them for his contribution to Stone Age systematics and documentation of cave and rock art from Europe and South Africa. Supported by the Catholic Church in his research, Breuil achieved independence such that he never served in a parish, nor was his work ever censored. His occasional collaborator, the Jesuit priest Pierre Teilhard de Chardin (1881–1955), sought to reconcile evolutionary evidence with religious belief, but the Church could not abide by this approach. De Chardin's *Le phénomène spirituel* (1937) was banned outright. Over a long career, Breuil never received such censure and became the world's most famous prehistorian, a safe handler of the evidence of human evolution and a champion of the French Palaeolithic as a source of national pride.

The second strand was the nature of the discoveries. The reason La Chapelle-aux-Saints struck such a chord was its resemblance to Christian burial practice. Although the body was not laid out but buried with legs drawn up, its placement – in a rectangular, straight-walled, flat-bottomed 'gravepit' – was recognized as so important that the three abbés had a notary public witness their description as truthful and accurate. This evidence of a deliberate burial has, despite critiques (Gargett 1989), stood the test (Pettitt 2011). Its lasting significance, confirmed later by similar discoveries, is that it was *not* a burial of *Homo sapiens*. On this evidence, it appears, some form of religious life preceded the appearance of our own species – just as, Durkheim was to argue from ethnography, older forms of religious activity existed prior to Western religions. But there the parallel stops. Durkheim did not accept the argument of primitivism, declaring instead that man is man and distinct from animals and lesser beings. In other words, he provided no comfort for those who looked to the present to provide a historical veneer over the ancient past.

In summary, on the one hand Palaeolithic religion was defined by a reading of ethnography that stressed difference, while on the other the close involvement of a western Christian tradition saw to it that the evidence was sifted for the familiar paraphernalia of religious life. As a result, the missionaries in originsland who had set up their tent before 1912 were unreceptive to the Durkheimian call. The suggestion that religion would be familiar not because it was Christian but because it was social countered the very premise of the grail they sought.

Totems and Archaeological Cultures

Durkheim, as many have commented (James 2003; Kuper 1988), was concerned with issues of identity and morality applied to social phenomena. He questioned the contemporary view that society derives its moral force from the family and religion. In his search for alternative sources of moral authority, he emphasized the importance of ancestral totems as collective emblems for the group and argued that 'totemism and the clan naturally imply each other' (Ucko and Rosenfeld 1967: 123). He drew on Australian ethnographies to demonstrate the importance of abstract thought 'that enabled the Australian to imagine who he was by imagining his relations with other Australians and the natural world' (James 2003: 13). As discussed by Kuper (1988: 118–19), groups assembled to access seasonal resources, and when they did so it was under the auspices of a common emblem, the totem. The sentiments aroused as the product of group activities – what Durkheim called *effervescence* (Allen 1998) – were then transferred to the emblem itself. This was a religion without gods (unless the totem was one) and independent from family, since it was the group that counted. Morality, then, could be defined as the subordination of the individual to the interests of the group (Kuper 1988: 119). Moreover, the distinctive traits of humanity encoded within Durkheim's banner of religion were reason, identity and community (James 2003: 13). If archaeologists read *Elementary Forms* when it was published, and there is no evidence from their citations that they did, then all they took away was the juxtaposition of a primitive culture, Australian, with their own civilized society. However, Tylor and Sollas had made the same concurrence without the benefit of Durkheim's text. Furthermore, the notion of symbolic thought as the hallmark of humanity was hardly new. Symbolic thinking as understood by archaeologists at the time did not, however, involve imagining the relations between people and nature but rather was an instance of the triumph of rudimentary rationalism: the ability to make sense of a substitution, for example, such as the totem for the clan or the emblem for the group.

Yet it is difficult to be precise about their arguments, for two reasons. First, archaeologists rarely discussed Palaeolithic society, and recourse to ethnographic examples was the norm (Gamble 1999: chaps. 1 and 2). Hence we find descriptions of Palaeolithic *hordes* without any further elaboration. A name is sufficient. And second, many scholars of social evolution followed the line of Gordon Childe (1951: 85), who when discussing society was inclined (perhaps because he was born Australian) to dismiss everything before the Neolithic. Unfortunately, his judgement that one cannot infer society from the 'scraps' of Palaeolithic evidence has a long and continuing legacy (e.g., Renfrew 2007). Totemism (not of the Durkheimian variety) had a tenacious, if unrecognized, hold on the archaeological imagination because, as Kuper (1988: 121) claims, it was anthropology's one agreed-upon myth for the origin of society; it served as a foundation narrative for rationalism. In this regard Childe's classic definition of an archaeological culture as the recurrence of associated traits in time and space that formed the material expression of a 'people' (1929: v–vi) has a hint of Durkheim about it. It implies that when group activity becomes linked to emblems, then cultural persistence, in the guise of tradition, invariably follows.

Palaeolithic examples of Childe's concept are common. The wide distribution of Willendorf-type figurines is one instance of an icon-led Gravettian culture (Gamble 1982). More complex, polythetic cultures produce ethnic labels such as the Aurignacians and Magdalenians (Djindjian, Kozlowski and Otte 1999), as do the five Neanderthal tribes of Southwest France, defined by the proportions of tool-types and knapping techniques in excavated collections (Bordes 1972). However, all these examples feature a rational rather than a relational understanding of social forms. The archaeologists' persistence is due to their expectation of the iron hand of tradition and a respect for making things in time-honoured ways, whether enshrined in a stone tool or an engraved bone. The tradition continues. For example, Foley and Lahr (2011) have viewed the proliferation of human cultures as the result of boundary-making between human communities that arise from three processes:

1. Fission, by which kin-based communities reproduce themselves over generations;
2. The differential impact of ecology on the rate of fissioning; and
3. unique human cognitive capacity to generate socially transmissible behaviours that structure the outcome of that fissioning.

When viewed geographically, cultural diversity as a consequence of fissioning is greater in the tropics than elsewhere (Binford 2001; Collard and Foley 2002). This observation leads to Foley and Lahr's general proposition that 'human cultures, as communities of individuals, form when boundaries begin to occur within such communities, and when, through both adaptive and neural mechanisms, the traits of each community – from language to decoration to technology – begin to diverge' (2011: 1085).

These accounts do not, however, relate the sense of collective action and imaginative capacity that brings people, things and landscapes into relation with each other. These archaeological cultures are not societies in Durkheim's sense. Glimpses in the literature are rare and apologetic because the authors know they are straying from the rational description of evidence.

A good example (Figure 6.1) of their cautious approach to anything approaching a social interpretation comes from Breuil and is addressed to the 'ordinary reader'. In *Beyond the Bounds of History* (1949) he provides his own illustrations to imagine the contexts of ritual activity inspired by those four lines of evidence listed by Leroi-Gourhan (1964). One of these is a cave art 'sanctuary', which he interprets as a tribal reunion that took place in the winter (Breuil 1949: 79–83). The purpose of the gathering is to

> initiate the young people in their new obligations as adults and instruct them in the traditions of the tribe. On such occasions magico-religious ceremonies are also performed, including masked dances and invocations to celestial beings or spirits designed to ensure the multiplication of game, the destruction of wild beasts and good fortune in forthcoming hunting expeditions during the summer. (1949: 79)

The licence Breuil allows himself in a popular book was not matched in his academic writings where, as Ucko and Rosenfeld (1967: 129)

Figure 6.1. Breuil's illustration of a religious ceremony in the Upper Palaeolithic.

point out, his interpretations of cave art were neither original nor well thought out.

The Stratified Mind

What of those cognitive abilities that Foley and Lahr (2011) address? The model of a stratified mind (Gamble and Moutsiou 2011) dominated the second half of the nineteenth century and juxtaposed, yet again, the primitive and civilized. It was clearly set out by the archaeologist and ardent evolutionist Augustus Lane-Fox (from 1880 Pitt-Rivers) in his paper on how to organize a museum collection (Lane-Fox 1875).

As a topic of archaeological discussion, the primeval mind was as rare as Palaeolithic religion, but not so for Lane-Fox, who applied the principles of stratigraphic excavation to its prehistory. He divided the mind into two historical components: the *automaton* mind of habit and the *intellectual* mind of rational thought. Tasmanians and Australians had once possessed an intellectual mind, as shown by their technological solutions to the challenges of their environments. However, these had long since become automatic actions and now were simply performed as mental drills, a process described by Bagehot (2007 [1872]). For Lane-Fox there were three strata to the mind: (1) primitives, (2) children, women and workers, and (3) socially dominant men like himself. From this standpoint he provided the cognitive underpinning for the subsequent notion of an archaeological culture that, as we have seen, shelters under the concept of the emblemic totem, bound by unrelenting tradition:

> In the earliest phases of humanity ... things themselves are handed down unchanged from father to son and from tribe to tribe, and many of them have continued to our own time, faithful records of the condition of the people by whom they were fabricated. (Lane-Fox 1875: 303–4)

At first sight *Elementary Forms* offers some support for this model and Lane-Fox's 'philosophy of progress' from simple to complex. Drawing on ethnological studies, Durkheim characterized 'lower societies' where 'everything is common to all. ... And while all is uniform, all is simple as well' (Durkheim 1915 [1912]: 18). But he departed significantly, leaving the archaeologists to their own devices, in his presentation of all intellectual life as a duality of individual and social beings. Such duality applies to simple and complex societies, 'lower' and 'civilized' alike, and recognizes no division by occupation, age or gender. There is no innate difference in reason but only historical circumstances, which need addressing if an understanding of what generates religious behaviour in all its forms is to be achieved. For example, he dismisses both rational and empirical views that account for mythologies and concludes that 'far from being engraven through all eternity upon the mental constitution of men, they depend, at least in part, upon factors that are historical and consequently social' (Durkheim 1915 [1912]: 25).

Social Brains and a Distributed Mind

How different research into human origins might have been, if Durkheim's thesis that 'religion is something eminently social' (1915 [1912]: 22) had found a place in early Palaeolithic research. Instead, pioneering archaeologists such as Breuil and Lane-Fox saw the symbol as innate to the human mind; determining religious behaviour thus depended upon material proxies whose pedigree could be traced to contemporary institutions. Consequently, there was little discussion about either Palaeolithic society or religious behaviour. Durkheim could have been aiming at Breuil when he criticized rationalists who believed that the mind's power to transcend is an inherent feature of human intelligence and that a divine reason sits above the reason of individuals (Durkheim 1915 [1912]: 27). In particular his core concept of collective representations, the result of an 'immense co-operation, which stretches out not only into space but into time as well' (Durkheim 1915 [1912]: 29) would have provided a very different framework for the study of issues such as the evolution of language, reciprocal exchange, symbolism, cooperation and society.

But perhaps the steady accumulation of evidence, its scientific dating and the opportunity to consider a digested *Elementary Forms* has its own advantages. A solid body of evidence was needed to counter claims of unwarranted speculation, and archaeology needed to be cured of the inappropriate use of ethnography. Older and wiser, it is certainly not too late to return to Durkheim's insistence that the whole of social activity underpins the variety of activities observed by archaeologists and anthropologists. To do so requires that we stop thinking about religion as a separate and different form of behaviour. In the same way we must also elide the distinctions between other areas of activity such as hunting or technology and recognize that they all draw their inspiration from the same social source (Gamble 1999).

This standpoint also opens up a wider view of society than the one Durkheim proposes for humans, since it now broadens his vision to include the collective action of animals. Here the ability to be social is not innate, or hardwired into brains, but rather the outcome of performance and negotiation by individuals and groups. What distinguishes chimpanzee or elephant social life from that of humans is, as Durkheim argued for humans alone, contingent on their history rather than part of the essence of these animals. Once this is acknowledged, the neglect visited upon the social lives of our large-brained hominin ancestors seems perverse indeed.

The advantages of rediscovering Durkheim lie in the concept of the social brain (Dunbar, Gamble and Gowlett 2010; Runciman 2009), deliberately so named because it identifies social life as the operative dynamic in hominin evolution, a dynamic that not only has transformed the hardware of cognition but also explains the variety of collective representations arising from these modifications in deep hominin history. The social brain also serves as a framework for the interdisciplinary investigation of human evolution, which is as concerned with traditional issues, such as what they ate, as with how they interacted.

To play its part in this endeavour, archaeology can now draw not only on Durkheim's agenda of the moral underpinnings of society but also the relational, rather than rational, construction of cognition (Gamble 2010). The latter is summed up in the distributed mind model, where humans are constituted by their environment and, crucially, the materials and objects they interact with, as much as by their minds. Consequently, the Palaeolithic hand axe is as much a part of mind as the brain's neurons or the hominin's big toe (Gosden 2010). Cognition is distributed throughout the world rather than being the sole property of brains that act upon the world and by doing so become classified as minds.

To further illustrate this change in emphasis, Figure 6.2 presents a map of the social brain. At the core of the social brain are the resources of the senses and material world that are common to hominins and all other animals besides. It is the aesthetics of materials – their touch taste, smell, appearance and sound – that can be transformed through performance and negotiation into social bonds of variable intensity and commitment. This is the core around which social life is

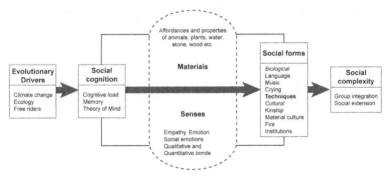

Figure 6.2. A map of the social brain emphasizing the core of materials and emotions that arise from a model of extended cognition and distributed mind (Gamble, Gowlett and Dunbar 2011: Figure 1).

scaffolded. The outcomes of these social lives vary greatly, and some examples are given in Figure 6.2; they range from language and crying to kinship and fire.

The task of archaeologists has also changed. No longer are they looking just for a well-dated material proxy of these social forms as they once did in the search for Palaeolithic religion (as in the excavation at La Chapelle-aux-Saints, for example). Instead, as Durkheim reminds us, 'like every human institution, religion did not commence anywhere' (1915 [1912]: 20). What has been subject to historical processes has been the differential selection of the available resources. For example, Aiello and Dunbar (1993) have argued that language is at least 500,000 years old, and that it evolved to meet the requirements of larger social groups as inferred from the relationship between brain and group size in primates. Dunbar (2003) has extended this analysis to consider advanced levels of intentionality for hominins of a similar age. Although the implication of collective representations supported by language and a theory of mind is obvious, the trail goes cold when it comes to finding appropriate artefact proxies for such a shift in large brained hominins 500,000 years ago. Instead I have argued (Gamble 2010; Gamble, Gowlett and Dunbar 2011) that these early hominins amplified their emotions, rather than merely transforming materials, into the myriad forms of human culture that we simply take for granted and through which we chart our historical journeys. Some examples of the amplifying mechanisms are provided in Table 6.1.

The development of containers is an example of this process. Such forms – houses, cars, clothes, cups, kinship categories – are so common today that they automatically structure the way we think about the world (Lakoff and Johnson 1980, 1999). Through our bodies we appreciate the sensations of containment, and we apply such experiences to the business, and performance, of making relations with the world. Things bring comfort (Miller 2008), and they are able to do so primarily because they contain memories and thereby enshrine our relations to each other. Archaeologists would be unable to identify recurrent patterns in their data, if not for the Palaeolithic practice of creating sets and nets by the exchange of materials like shells and amber, and then further amplifying these relations across time and space through their transformations into items of material culture such as beads and necklaces that encircle, and so contain, the body.

The three movements are chronologically broad and subsume many hominin species. If there is a characteristic that distinguishes *Homo sapiens* from other hominins it is neither the size of their brains nor the quality of their spear points, but rather that they were a well-

Table 6.1. An outline of social evolution with a Durkheimian perspective from the beginnings of technology 2.6 million years ago

Technological movements	Age, years ago	Material metaphors	Amplifying mechanisms	Examples	Markers
Short Answer	20,000–6,000	Containers/instruments	Population numbers	Institutions	Sedentism and agriculture after 10,000 years ago
Common Ground	100,000–21,000	Instruments and Containers	Social and geographical extension	Myth, kinship and kinshipping	Global expansion after 60,000 years ago
Long Introduction	2,600,000–101,000	Instruments/containers	Social emotions | Primary emotions	Language, dance, music, crying, laughter, focused gaze	Big-brained hominins after 600,000 years ago

For further details see Gamble (2007: chap. 7), Gamble (2010) and Gamble, Gowlett and Dunbar (2011).

wrapped species, contained – like a medicine bundle from North America or a burial from ancient Egypt – by layers of stuff and significance. By comparison, the body in the pit at La Chapelle-aux-Saints, and Neanderthal culture generally, is defined more by instruments than containers; as a result, we can trace only limited levels of wrapping (Gamble 2007). In other words, the relations scaffolded around that core of emotions and materials (Figure 6.2) had a different expression. There is no need to imply a difference in intelligence or in a concept from cognitive science such as working memory (Wynn and Coolidge 2004).

Instead, what we see between hominins such as Neanderthals and *Homo sapiens* is a diversity of relations, imagined and real. Paraphrasing James (2003: 13), sociability has always been the distinctive hominin means of knowing. Part of that sociability is our ability to imagine relations with others and the natural world. Following the model of the distributed mind, hominin imagination has always been implicated in technology. However, the mainspring for that technology has always been the experiences of the body rather than just the reason of the mind as is often argued. Therefore, as Table 6.1 shows, the shift to containers as the dominant material form during the Common Ground (Gamble 2007: 169–175) era of deep hominin history (100,000–21,000 years ago) amplified the content and contexts of social relationships between hominins.

This is where Durkheim's collective representations come into play. We are, as James (2003) has argued, ceremonial animals. Our love of performance and coordinated activity rewards us chemically through opiate surges and materially through our association with others. Just as containers assume ascendancy in human culture during the Common Ground (Table 6.1) and explode in the subsequent Short Answer (21,000–6000 years ago), so too did the intricacy and complexity of performances. The difference between the La Chapelle-aux-Saints burial of an infirm Neanderthal dated to between 40,000 and 60,000 years ago, and the human double burial of an adolescent and child at Sunghir from Vladimir in Russia, dated between 23,000 and 27,000 years ago (Pettitt 2011: Tables 6.2 and 5.1), is entirely about the performance associated with each and not about the inherent abilities of the two species. Neither is an example of Palaeolithic religion, unless understood through a Durkheimian lens. Both are instances of sociability based on cooperation that created collective representations of the relations between all the elements of their worlds: people, things, materials and places.

The Moral Neanderthal

Earlier I discussed the role of *Elementary Forms* in establishing an alternative moral interpretation of Palaeolithic society, one based on cooperative action rather than the institutions of family. This adjustment would also involve a redefinition of religion. Cooperation is usually demonstrated through economic and technological evidence, supplemented by collective rituals such as burial. However, this analysis can be extended by adopting a social brain perspective and applying it to a theory of mind for primates and hominins. Theory of mind depends on the imaginative ability to believe in something that is not referable to immediate experience, and to conduct social activities accordingly. In terms of levels of intentionality, many animals achieve level 1, self-awareness. Among primates, only chimpanzees have been claimed to reach level 2, where recognizing another mind and adjusting activities provides the test. Even here the majority view is that chimpanzees do not have a fully developed theory of mind and certainly cannot reach level 3, as humans easily do, where chains of beliefs are ascribed to others. As anyone knows who has had a car that failed to start on a damp day, and a nine o'clock lecture to give, it is all too easy to ascribe intentions to objects as well as people. Level 4 upgrades the belief system to the worlds of myth, ancestors and religious intervention. Some examples are given in Table 6.2.

Table 6.2. Levels of intention after Cole (2008)

Level 1	Level 2	Level 3	Level 4
Ego is self aware	Ego recognizes another person's belief-states as similar/different to theirs	Ego wants another person to recognize Ego's own belief state	Ego believes that the group understands that another person recognizes Ego's own belief states
Dave (the re-enactor) *believes* he is a Crusader	Dave *believes* that Ben (a fellow re-enactor) *thinks* he is a Crusader	Dave *desires* that Ben *believes* that Dave *thinks* he is a Crusader	Dave *knows* that the re-enactment group are *aware* that Ben *believes* that Dave *thinks* he is a Crusader

Source: Gamble 2010: Table 2.

The question from a Palaeolithic perspective concerns the levels of intentionality achieved by the large-brained hominins such as Neanderthal and *Homo heidelbergensis* dating to a rise in brain size after 600,000 years ago (Rightmire 2004). Dunbar (2003), for example, has used comparative data on group and brain size to predict at least level 3 for all these hominin species. McNabb (2007), using Palaeolithic data on technological competence, agrees. This suggestion of course does not mean that these early hominins 'got religion' but rather that they possessed the more fundamental Durkheimian property of social imagination – without, as we have seen, the commitment to render their actions as material representations of such a collective activity.

Another way to look at this issue is to consider the social emotions. Primary emotions are common across species and include those with survival value, such as fear, anger and contentment. The secondary, or social, emotions require a level 2 theory of mind (Table 6.1) and the recognition of someone else's belief states as similar and/or different. The social emotions of guilt, pride and shame and the social tactics of cheating, boasting and lying would not exist without a theory of mind (Gamble 2010). This moral richness of human social life is accomplished when the interests of the individual become subordinated to those of the group (Kuper 1988). It does not require religion as such, but it does depend on the social basis of human cooperation as argued in *Elementary Forms*, which in Durkheim's rendering can be understood as religion writ large.

Of course, the tactical deception literature on chimpanzees and other great apes (de Waal 2006) might suggest that they do have theory of mind. However, another component of *Elementary Forms* rules out this possibility: Humans, and by inference hominins, engage with others through these social emotions and tactics in absentia. Further-

more, we engage though our amplified material and emotional core
(Figure 6.2), which, as already noted, exemplifies Durkheim's 'immense co-operation' that can cross time and space. Religious symbols,
those items that some like Breuil see as resembling the tokens of Palaeolithic pilgrimage, are obvious examples. But once it is acknowledged that it is social rather than religious – in the specific sense of,
say, Christian – behaviour that underpins morality and identity, then
some very substantial barriers to understanding the commonality of
our ancestors begin to fall.

Conclusion

In January 1960 Claude Lévi-Strauss gave his inaugural lecture to
the Collège de France. Durkheim occupied a prominent part in his
talk; Lévi-Strauss (1967: 8) delighted in pointing out that France, unlike other countries, had failed to commemorate the centenary of his
birth two years earlier. A footnote records that this was rectified at the
Sorbonne later that month.

I doubt that in 1960 any archaeological publication would have
referred to Durkheim or to *The Elementary Forms of the Religious Life.*
A quick trawl through some recent publications reveals similarly slim
pickings (Dunbar, Gamble and Gowlett 2010; Guthrie 2005; Pettitt
2011). In their analysis of religion as a way of packaging socially important information, evolutionary anthropologists Finkel, Swartwout
and Sosis (2010) refer to *Elementary Forms* only through Durkheim's
concept of effervescence as applied to effects of ritual, both positive
(e.g., dance and chanting) and negative (e.g., scarification and genital
mutilation). Religion, in their view, serves the developmental process.
In a broader view, Durkheim is pigeonholed as a functionalist, and his
championing of the group is out of kilter with the current accent on
the individual agent (Gamble and Porr 2005; Meskell 1999) – proof,
if it was needed, that the debate Durkheim initiated continues into the
sources of morality that underpin human sociality.

But it does seem premature to consign Durkheim to the history
of anthropology, the fate meted out to Tylor, Pitt-Rivers, Frazer and
other nineteenth-century giants. Judging retrospectively, the conclusion must be that archaeology never worked through Durkheim's
agenda. When archaeologists did consider religion, they turned for
understanding to the bricolage of Frazer's *Golden Bough*, inspired by
classical texts and ethnographic borrowings, or much later to the
compartmentalization of systems theory that separated religious be-

haviour from other areas such as the economy, trade and crafts (Clark 1957; Clarke 1968; Renfrew 1972). Little attention was given to the social basis of religion, which instead was treated as a separate and, from a Palaeolithic perspective, unique attribute of an evolving humanity. The discovery for the Palaeolithic was the extension of ritual and ceremony to species other than ourselves, *Homo sapiens*. Neanderthals had religious rituals, as we have seen, as did some of the earliest examples of anatomically modern humans, 160,000 years ago from Herto in Ethopia (Clark et al. 2003). Complex mortuary practices are claimed for much older hominins at Atapuerca, Sima de la Huesos (c. 400,000 years old), involving a grave-good hand axe nicknamed Excalibur (Carbonell et al. 2003) and based on post-mortem treatment (Andrews and Fernandez Jalvo 1997) of the corpses. Further evidence of nutritional cannibalism, from Atapuerca, and dated to 800,000 years ago, has also been presented (Pettitt 2011: 47).

These are fascinating insights into the complexity of hominin behaviour. However, they continue the evidence-based approach to the study of ritual, and by inference religion, that has dominated the subject. The need for a convincing proxy has stunted the study of Palaeolithic religion, so much so that Pettitt's (2011) valuable compendium of human burial in the Palaeolithic does not refer to religion at all, but only to society among chimpanzees. This failure to close the loop between society and religion underscores the continuing value of *Elementary Forms* in 2012, a century after its first publication. Durkheim's importance is to remind archaeologists of the absolute importance of social life in their Palaeolithic histories. Religious behaviour, as Durkheim argued, comes in many forms and has a social origin. It should never be seen as separate, and there is no reason to restrict its analysis to the genealogy of material symbols.

References

Aiello, L. and R. Dunbar. 1993. 'Neocortex Size, Group Size and the Evolution of Language', *Current Anthropology* 34: 184–93.

Allen, N.J. 1998. 'Effervescence and the Origins of Human Society', in N.J. Allen, W.S.F. Pickering and W. Watts Miller (eds), *On Durkheim's Elementary Forms of Religious Life*. London: Routledge, pp. 149–61.

Andrews, P. and Y. Fernandez Jalvo. 1997. 'Surface Modifications of the Sima de los Huesos Fossil Humans', *Journal of Human Evolution* 33: 191–218.

Bagehot, W. 2007 [1872]. *Physics and Politics: Or Thoughts on the Application of the Principles of 'Natural Selection' and 'Inheritance' to Political Society*. New York: Cosimo Classics.

Binford, L.R. 2001. *Constructing Frames of Reference: An Analytical Method for Archaeological Theory Building Using Ethnographic and Environmental Datasets*. Berkeley: University of California Press.

Bordes, F. 1972. *A Tale of Two Caves*. New York: Harper and Row

Boule, M. 1911. 'L'homme fossile de la Chapelle-aux-Saints', *Annales de Paléontologie* 6: 1–64.

———. 1912. 'L'homme fossile de la Chapelle-aux-Saints', *Annales de Paléontologie* 7: 65–208.

———. 1913. 'L'homme fossile de la Chapelle-aux-Saints', *Annales de Paléontologie* 8: 209–79.

Breuil, H. 1949. *Beyond the Bounds of History*. London: P.R. Gawthorn.

Carbonell, E., M. Mosquera, A. Ollé, X.P. Rodríguez, R. Sala, J.M. Vergès, J.L. Arsuaga and J. M. Bermúdez de Castro. 2003. 'Les premiers comportments funéraires auraient-ils pris place à Atapuerca, il y a 350,000 ans?' *L'Anthropologie* 107: 1–14.

Childe, V.G. 1929. *The Danube in Prehistory*. Oxford: Oxford University Press.

———. 1951. *Social Evolution*. London: Watts.

Clark, J.D., Y. Beyenne, G. WoldeGabriel, W.K. Hart, P. Renne, H. Gilbert, A. Defleur, G. Suwa, S. Katoh, K.R. Ludwig, J.-R. Boisserie, B. Asfaw, and T.D. White. 2003. 'Stratigraphic, Chronological and Behavioural Contexts of Pleistocene *Homo sapiens* from Middle Awash, Ethiopia', *Nature* 423: 747–52.

Clark, J.G.D. 1957. *Archaeology and Society*, 3rd ed. London: Methuen.

Clarke, D.L. 1968. *Analytical Archaeology*. London: Methuen.

Collard, I.F. and R.A. Foley. 2002. 'Latitudinal Patterns and Environmental Determinants of Recent Human Cultural Diversity: Do Humans Follow Biogeographical Rules?' *Evolutionary Ecology Research* 4: 371–83.

de Chardin, T. 1937. *Le phénomène spirituel*. Paris: Editions du Seuil.

de Waal, F. 2006. *Primates and Philosophers: How Morality Evolved*. Princeton, NJ: Princeton University Press.

Djindjian, F., J. Kozlowski and M. Otte. 1999. *Le Paléolithique supérieur en Europe*. Paris: Armand Colin.

Dunbar, R.I.M. 2003. 'The Social Brain: Mind, Language, and Society in Evolutionary Perspective', *Annual Review of Anthropology* 32: 163–81.

Dunbar, R., C. Gamble, and J.A.J. Gowlett (eds). 2010. *Social Brain and Distributed Mind*. Oxford: Oxford University Press, *Proceedings of the British Academy* 158.

Durkheim, E. 1915 [1912]. *The Elementary Forms of the Religious Life*, trans. J.W. Swain. London: George Allen and Unwin.

Finkel, D.N., P. Swartwout and R. Sosis. 2010. 'The Socio-religious Brain: A Developmental Model', in R. Dunbar, C. Gamble and J.A.J. Gowlett (eds), *Social Brain and Distributed Mind*. Oxford: Oxford University Press, *Proceedings of the British Academy* 158, pp. 283–307.

Foley, R.A. and M.A. Lahr. 2011. 'The Evolution of the Diversity of Culture', *Philosophical Transactions of the Royal Society of London B* 366: 1080–89.

Gamble, C.S. 1982. 'Interaction and Alliance in Palaeolithic Society', *Man* 17: 92–107.

———. 1999. *The Palaeolithic Societies of Europe.* Cambridge: Cambridge University Press.

———. 2007. *Origins and Revolutions: Human Identity in Earliest Prehistory.* New York: Cambridge University Press.

———. 2010. 'Technologies of Separation and the Evolution of Social Extension', in R. Dunbar, C. Gamble and J.A.J. Gowlett (eds), *Social Brain and Distributed Mind.* Oxford: Oxford University Press, *Proceedings of the British Academy* 158, pp. 17–42.

Gamble, C.S., J.A.J. Gowlett and R. Dunbar. 2011. 'The Social Brain and the Shape of the Palaeolithic', *Cambridge Archaeological Journal* 21: 115–35.

Gamble, C.S. and T. Moutsiou. 2011. The time revolution of 1859 and the stratification of the primeval mind. *Notes and Records of the Royal Society* 65: 43-63.

Gamble, C.S. and M. Porr (eds). 2005. *The Individual Hominid in Context: Archaeological Investigations of Lower and Middle Palaeolithic Landscapes, Locales and Artefacts.* London: Routledge.

Gargett, R. 1989. 'Grave Shortcomings: The Evidence for Neanderthal Burial', *Current Anthropology* 30: 157–90.

Gosden, C. 2010. 'The Death of the Mind', in L. Malafouris and C. Renfrew (eds), *The Cognitive Life of Things: Recasting the Boundaries of the Mind.* Cambridge: McDonald Institute for Archaeological Research, pp. 39–46.

Guthrie, D. 2005. *The Nature of Paleolithic Art.* Chicago: Chicago University Press.

Hammond, M. 1982. 'The Expulsion of the Neanderthals from Human Ancestry: Marcellin Boule and the Social Context of Scientific Research', *Social Studies of Science* 12: 1–36.

James, W. 2003. *The Ceremonial Animal: A New Portrait of Anthropology.* Oxford: Oxford University Press.

Kuper, A. 1988. *The Invention of Primitive Society.* London: Routledge.

Lakoff, G. and M. Johnson. 1980. *Metaphors We Live By.* Chicago: University of Chicago Press.

———. 1999. *Philosophy in the Flesh: The Embodied Mind and Its Challenge to Western Thought.* New York: Basic Books.

Lane-Fox, A. 1875. 'On the Principles of Classification Adopted in the Arrangement of His Anthropological Collection, Now Exhibited in the Bethnal Green Museum', *The Journal of the Anthropological Institute of Great Britain and Ireland* 4: 293–308.

Leroi-Gourhan, A. 1964. *Les religions de la préhistoire.* Paris: Quadrige Presses Universitaires de France.

Lévi-Strauss, C. 1967. *The Scope of Anthropology.* London: Jonathan Cape.

McNabb, J. 2007. *British Lower Palaeolithic: Stones in Contention.* London: Routledge.

Meskell, L. 1999. *Archaeologies of Social Life.* Oxford: Blackwells.

Miller, D. 2008. *The Comfort of Things.* London: Polity.

Murray, T. 1992. Tasmania and the Constitution of 'the Dawn of Humanity'. *Antiquity* 66: 730–43.

Pettitt, P.B. 2011. *The Palaeolithic Origins of Human Burial*. London: Routledge.

Renfrew, C. 1972. *The Emergence of Civilisation: The Cyclades and the Aegaen in the Third Millennium BC*. London: Methuen.

———. 2007. *Prehistory: Making of the Human Mind*. London: Weidenfeld and Nicolson.

Rightmire, P. 2004. 'Brain Size and Encephalization in Early to Mid-Pleistocene *Homo*', *American Journal of Physical Anthropology* 124: 109–23.

Runciman, W.G. 2009. *The Theory of Cultural and Natural Selection*. Cambridge: Cambridge University Press.

Sollas, W.J. 1911. *Ancient Hunters and Their Modern Representatives*. London: Macmillan.

Spencer, W.B. and F.J. Gillen. 1899. *Native Tribes of Central Australia*. London: Macmillan.

Tylor, E.B. 1865. *Researches into the Early History of Mankind and the Development of Civilization*. London: John Murray.

———. 1894. 'On the Tasmanians as Representatives of Palaeolithic Man', *Journal of the Anthropological Institute* 23: 141–52.

Ucko, P.J. and A. Rosenfeld. 1967. *Palaeolithic Cave Art*. London: Weidenfeld and Nicholson.

Wynn, T. and F.L. Coolidge. 2004. 'The Skilled Neanderthal Mind', *Journal of Human Evolution* 46: 467–87.

Chapter 7

DURKHEIM, ANTHROPOLOGY AND THE QUESTION OF THE CATEGORIES IN *LES FORMES ÉLÉMENTAIRES DE LA VIE RELIGIEUSE*

Susan Stedman Jones

Durkheim's *Les Formes Élémentaires de la vie Religieuse* (hereafter called *Les Formes*) has exerted and continues to exert a fascination and a profound influence on subsequent sociological and anthropological thought. His influence was explicitly acknowledged by the twentieth-century founders of anthropology as we know it today, Malinowsi and Radcliffe-Brown, and indeed, Durkheim has been identified with these two thinkers as one of the early proponents of functionalism and structural functionalism. Elsewhere, I have challenged the crude identification of Durkheim with the adherents of structural functionalism (Stedman Jones 2001): his views on structure and function are more complicated than this unitary designation would imply.

So in turn the question arises as to how well these seminal anthropologists understood Durkheim's project. This is part of the topic of this chapter, which begins by examining some of the responses to Durkheim's famous work. It then takes up the question of how well Durkheim's project for the sociology of knowledge in *Les Formes* has been understood, bringing the focus to the question of the categories. Durkheim, together with the whole Année Sociologique team, undoubtedly had a profound influence on both Malinowski and Radcliffe-Brown. His influence is clear in the development of Malinowski's functionalism, and Radcliffe-Brown's interpretation of the Andaman Islanders' ceremonies was clearly influenced by Durkheim's account of the moral power of society (Radcliffe-Brown 1922: 325): the social relations amongst the Andamans exemplify solidarity – a great Durkheimian theme (241).

Radcliffe-Brown was one of the first professional anthropologists who at 'an early age was converted to the Durkheimian view of sociology and after Durkheim's death was, with Marcel Mauss, the leading exponent of this tradition' (Kuper 1977: 2). He founded structural and sociological anthropology in the face of both ethnology and social evolutionism. Durkheim indicated for subsequent thought that social anthropology should focus on the living structured and functional social relations that lie at the heart of society; indeed, he was seminal in the development of this approach, in contradistinction to previous theories. Radcliffe-Brown's insistence on the empirical observability of structures thus is preceded by Durkheim. I suggest that for Durkheim, to grasp social structure empirically is to describe actual social relations, as forms of representation, in a concrete historical situation. This is the basis of his great interest in the ethnography of Spencer and Gillen, who revealed the living actuality of a Stone Age culture. This insistence on empirical observability formed the basis of Radcliffe-Brown's 'structural positivism', which nevertheless lacked the logic of representation that underpinned Durkheim's account. The former's position differed from that of the later French Durkheimians, especially Levi-Strauss, for whom structures were models built after empirical observation (5). We will see that a similar claim could be made for Durkheim's *Les Formes*, where the Australian totemic material is used to exemplify a particular theory about the sociology of knowledge. In this sense the theoretical model does not succeed the data but precedes it, for which Durkheim has been roundly critiqued, even by some of the authors in this volume.[1]

Is this the reason, one wonders, why the work in which Durkheim explicitly uses ethnographic material seems to have less methodological significance for the history of the discipline of anthropology than does his earlier work, *Les Règles de la Méthode Sociologique*, especially for Malinowski? The approaches to *Les Formes* are generally informed by each thinker's ethnographic interests. In particular Radcliffe-Brown's reading of totemism differs considerably from that of Durkheim, although he confirms Durkheim's general theory as to the social function of the totemic religion of Australia and its rites (Kuper 1977: 119). And Malinowski, among others, rightly questions Durkheim's use of the single model of the Arunta as the basis of his general theory of religion.

Despite their sustained engagement with the text, however, Malinowski and Radcliffe-Brown significantly neglect the central aspect of Durkheim's sociology of knowledge in *Les Formes*, that is, the question of the categories. As we will see, certain important misunderstandings of his philosophical language are compounded by a significant neglect of his view of philosophy and history. And I will show that that a particular view of philosophy and history is central to how and why Durkheim thought he could use the ethnographic material as he did. That those who have represented him and his thinking in anthropology and the social sciences more generally have misunderstood the philosophical and historical aspects of Durkheim's thinking compounds the view of Durkheim as an ahistorical positivist.

To begin, it is critical to understand the role philosophy played in Durkheim's life, especially as it was a core aspect of intellectual life in the early years of the Third Republic. Minister of Education and University Rector Louis Liard, who did much to promote Durkheim's career, was a philosopher and also a follower of Renouvier; Durkheim wrote in a theoretical language known to the intellectual elite at the time. This background in philosophy distinguishes him from the subsequent training of most anthropologists, particularly in England (although here Malinowski is an exception).[2] We may examine these theoretical problems by dipping into some of the early reviews of *Les Formes* by then contemporary anthropologists.

Some Early Reviews of *Les Formes*

Hartland's review of *Les Formes* in *Man* (1913), like most reviews, praises it for its distinct sociological argument and for Durkheim's identification of religion with society. So while some will disagree with specific arguments of Durkheim, most hold to his association of religion with society: this premise is, after all, the sine qua non of subsequent research on religion in anthropology. Hartland sees the book as a general synthesis of the work of the *Année Sociologique* over 'the last 15 years' (Hartland 1913: 91).

Although Hartland here acknowledges Durkheim's treatment of religion and the study of totemism, he declines to follow the detail of Durkheim's philosophical argument 'with which he brings the book to a close' (96). Durkheim however, introduces philosophical arguments also in the first section of the book. Hartland does not recognize that the extensive exploration of totemism, besides being an examination of the 'earliest' and 'simplest' religion, is also an exemplification of the social origin of categories. Durkheim's reading of the totemic material is an attempt to prove this sociology of knowledge; he thus approaches the material with an argument about this already in hand. Hartland, although he notes the arguments about 'concepts' in the book's conclusion and acknowledges that Durkheim has formulated a philosophy, does not recognize that Durkheim's hypothesis is formulated in terms of the categories. Indeed, Hartland does not mention the question of the categories at all.

The same is true for Malinowski's review in *Folklore* (1913). He greatly praises Durkheim as 'one of the most acute and brilliant living sociologists' (Malinowski 1913: 531) and notes the great importance of the 'savants' of the *Année Sociologique* team. Although Malinowski notes that *Les Formes* is a substantial contribution to philosophy, like Hartland he neglects Durkheim's identification of the sociology of knowledge with the categories, and he too fails to mention them. In common with others he questions the thesis of 'absolute primitiveness' ascribed to the Arunta (526).

The main argument of Malinowski's review, however, attacks Durkheim's account of religion and its relation to society by turning the 'objective' method of *Les Règles de la Méthode Sociologique* against *Les Formes* (530). Because Malinowski assumes that the rule to treat social facts as things means the exclusion of psychological explanations, he claims that Durkheim is inconsistent throughout *Les Formes* in so far as he uses psychological explanations in his account of the large gatherings that are the source of collective effervescence, for these require a modification of individual consciences (530). In consequence, Malinowski argues, the sacred and divine must be psychological and not sociological, and Durkheim has gone back on himself. The sacred cannot stem from society as a being for Malinowski, who criticizes Durkheim's metaphysical view of society, a 'logical subject which thinks' (527), as akin to Hegel's view of *Geist*. The sacred can only be collective in so far as it pertains to a crowd, and nothing more (531).

This critique presupposes what the *conscience collective* is, but above all it misunderstands Durkheim's holism, which must be able to incorporate both the concept of social being and the conscience collective within the logic of representation. It must be remembered that Durkheim explicitly rejects the 'realism and ontologism' (Durkheim 1987 [1895]: 34) that characterize Hegelianism and insists that social life consists 'entirely in representations' (34). His holism must connect to representation, which in turn proscribes reference to an ontological being. Malinowki is wrong in this comparison to Hegel. And further, Malinowski, like all subsequent commentators, ignores the *psychique*.

This is not a psychological term but rather a central tenet of both Durkheim's rationalism and his functionalism:

> The judicial, governmental, scientific, industrial functions [are] all in a word special functions belonging to the psychic order (*sont d'ordre psychique*), because they consist in systems of representations and actions. (Durkheim 1986 [1893]: 39)

We must look at his philosophical background to understand this curious term. Renouvier uses the term *psychique* to cover the scientific approach to the mind. The study of *psychique* phenomena is the study of conscious representations or consciences (Renouvier 1912b [1875]: 11). But for Durkheim, society is 'a sui generis elaboration of psychic facts' ('*une élaboration sui generis de faits psychiques*') (Durkheim 1987 [1895]: 134). This is not akin to Hegelian absolutism.

Malinowski identifies the objective method with Durkheim's use of 'thing' in *Les Règles* (1987 [1895]), but he has not understood what Durkheim meant by this admittedly strange statement: 'to consider social facts as things' (1987 [1895]: 60). He fails to ask why a thinker who repudiates the materiality of social facts – social facts are characterized by 'extreme immateriality' (120) – and reductionism (Durkheim 1974 [1898]) should use the phrase 'thing' to indicate objectivity. Durkheim clarifies his meaning in the preface to the second edition: it is not an ontological but a methodological claim. His aim was not to reduce the superior to inferior forms of being but to indicate a degree of reality for the social world equal to that ascribed to the external world. Social facts are not material things, but are things in the same 'title' or class as them (Durkheim 1987 [1895]: 35); a thing is that which is observed. 'To be a thing ... is all that is given to observation', he writes (69). Renouvier's logic of reality and science can explain this usage, for here 'thing' means 'all that manifests, all that appears' (Hamelin 1927: 45). It is thus central to a logic of appearance.

Durkheim insists that 'social life consists entirely in representations' (1987 [1895]: 34). Malinowski does not see that a 'thing' is connected to the representational nature of sociality, and this misunderstanding of Durkheim has continued right through the twentieth century. It is exacerbated by Lukes (1982), who wrongly held that representation is a post-1895 concept. Malinowski, like most, treats externality as literally outside of individual minds. But externality must be understood in terms of the logic of representation: Malinowki, like many others, neglects not only representation but also its logic, which is central to the understanding of this position of Durkheim. Without also grasping that categories exist at the root of judgement (Durkheim

1985 [1912]: 8), Malinowski cannot explain how they are also social things for Durkheim (441).

Social facts, Durkheim famously says, 'have this remarkable property of existing outside of (*au dehors de*) individual consciences' (1987 [1895]: 52). Of course a social fact as representation cannot be literally 'outside' conscience (Durkheim 1974 [1898]: 23). Durkheim uses the term outside (*hors de*) in an unusual way: when we are distracted, then psychic states that are nevertheless 'real' and active are outside (*hors de*) conscience (1974 [1898]: 21). In Renouvier's rationalism, the phrase 'outside' (*au dehors*) has a specific logical meaning: it indicates relations that are logically external. To treat a phenomenon '"*du dehors*" is to treat it as having external relations' (Hamelin 1927: 183), that is, with something other than itself. Critiques of Durkheim on this point – and there have been many – overlook the connection between the inner (*le dedans*) and the outer (*le dehors*). The inner is important throughout Durkheim's work – he even uses it to characterize science: '[A]s science advances we see the outside return to the inside' (1987 [1895]: 70). With the phrase *du dehors* Durkheim is challenging the assumption that all consciousness is private and subjective: he identifies external relations within the sphere of representation as the source of social knowledge. Religion, in so far as it brings people together in association, is a unique and significant source of these external relations, and in turn of representations. This does not mean that religion is not absorbed internally, but that its source is not internal per se.

Although these particular arguments are uniquely his, Malinowski's review can be regarded as an exemplar of the anthropological understanding of Durkheim's account in the early decades of the twentieth century. As has been noted, Radcliffe-Brown also neglects the question of the categories and their connection with representation. Goldenweisser's review (1975 [1915]) does raise the question of the categories, but like most, he misconstrues the theoretical language Durkheim uses to comment on their nature. When Goldenweisser doubts that Durkheim can prove that more than a fraction of the categories will be of social derivation, he cites deep 'psychic processes' of the individual mind as a point against Durkheim (225) But this critique overlooks Durkheim's account of the depths of psychic life, which are beyond the rational mind: 'The understanding is the culminating and thus most superficial part of conscience. ... This can be modified by external influences, such as education without the foundation (*assises*) of psychic life being reached' (Durkheim 1986 [1893]: 225n31). Goldenweisser also neglects the whole logic of representation that grounds Durkheim's account of both society and its categories.

Worsley (1956) offers an interesting evaluation of Durkheim's sociology of knowledge using ethnographic observations from Groote Eylandt material. On this basis he, like Goldenweisser and Radcliffe-Brown, questions the account of the totemic. But he goes further still, questioning the social basis of classification. In contrast to Durkheim, he claims that classification often has a basis in careful and accurate observation of nature (59). With this argument, he too ignores (and indeed almost inverts) the whole representational logic that is the theoretical backbone of Durkheim's work.

This glance at some anthropological reactions to *Les Formes* shows that Durkheim's philosophical language is misapprehended; this is the case for both Malinowski and Radcliffe-Brown. The paradox here is that these thinkers are those with whom Durkheim is identified, even though they also neglect his view of philosophy and history. As I will show, Durkheim's theoretical statements are central to the coherence of his argument. So exactly what is Durkheim's project in *Les Formes*? How do anthropology, philosophy and history coexist in this famous text?

The Project of *Les Formes* and the Question of the Categories

Les Formes is a work on the 'religious nature of man', based on a study of 'the most primitive and the most simple religion that is known' (Durkheim 1985 [1912]: 1). It is accompanied by an argument for the sociology of knowledge, which begins in the introduction. Serving as an outline here are sections of an earlier article, *Sociologie religieuse et théorie de la connaissance* (Durkheim 1909), originally published in a journal of philosophy, *Revue de Metaphysique et Morale*. Its arguments are marked by both philosophical sophistication and an ambition for an advanced sociology of knowledge. Durkheim's aim in *Les Formes* is for the sociological study of religion, grounded in his reading of the totemic material, to 'renew problems' that previously were only 'debated among philosophers' (Durkheim 1985 [1912]: 8). This is the question of 'the notions which dominate all of our intellectual life'; they are what 'philosophers since Aristotle have called categories of the understanding' (8).

In constructing his thematics as such, Durkheim not only puts together ethnography and philosophy, but seems to do so to present the former as the solution to the questions of the latter. His actual aim is, at the beginning anyway, more modest. This approach will 'renew' these philosophical questions (Durkheim 1985 [1912]: 8). Nevertheless, it must be asked: How well is the philosophical complexity of this earlier article, together with its sociological ambition, supported by ethnography in Durkheim's reading of the totemic material? Indeed, does not his own empirical and comparative method proscribe this approach? How can philosophy, which emerges comparatively late in history and society, be answered through the religious structures of societies that lack it? Can the question of the categories submit to the method of historical observation as Durkheim requires? These pressing questions, together with the logic of his theories of mind and judgement, deserve more attention than can be raised here (see also Stedman Jones 2012). But the marriage of these philosophical ambitions and their proposed ethnographic bases mark the logic of his argument throughout *Les Formes* and his attempt to ground it empirically in the structure of early societies and their religious practices.

It is a difficult book to read, which may contribute to the neglect of the question of the categories in the earlier history of anthropology. And this difficulty centres precisely around the analysis of the categories, made more complicated by Durkheim's manner of presenting their theoretical nature. This question is raised in the introduction, but only in the conclusion, some 600 pages later, are the arguments are directly resumed, and indeed in some cases new definitions of the categories are introduced. For example, in section iv of the conclusion we learn that categories 'envelop' all other concepts (Durkheim 1985 [1912]: 441).[3] And only in the conclusion is there a sustained analysis of the conceptual (433). Now, since categories are a special kind of concept for Durkheim (13, 441), one would have expected – given his normal rigour and clarity – that this analysis of the nature of concepts would have preceded rather than succeeded the ethnographic analysis of the text. Yet the analysis of the categories, appearing as it does at the beginning and end of a theory and an account of religion, looks instead like a pair of bookends. This ostensibly limited discussion is deceptive, however, for as we will see, the analysis runs throughout the text.

At the beginning of the book, Durkheim argues that the categories are 'essential notions which dominate all our intellectual life' (1985 [1912]: 8). They are 'the solid framework which encloses thought ... they are like the skeleton of thought'. They are 'inseparable from the normal functioning of the mind' (9). We cannot think without them, that is, we can only think about the world through a conceptual organization. And categories are the framework through which we do so. Thus we perceive objects only through spatial, temporal or numerable frames. And again, the categories provide this mental structure (9). In the conclusion he stresses their stability and impersonality (441), their ability to envelop all other concepts, and their capacity to express the fundamental condition of understanding between minds (441). They are 'the permanent framework of mental life' ('*les cadres permanents de la vie mentale*'); they express relations, which exist implicitly in '*les consciences individuelles*' (441). The latter are personal, but the idea of a class, that is, a total framework (*cadre*) requires the group, which provides impersonality. The idea of '*le tout*' is at the basis of classification (442). To add to the complexity of his sociological enterprise, Durkheim accepts the account of categories given by the a priorists as opposed to the empiricists (13). Thus the categories have a universality and a necessity (13). Indeed, Durkheim espouses a theory of a priority, understood as irreducibility (14). He maintains the irreducibility of reason to individual experience ('*L'irreducibilté de la raison à l'expérience individuelle*' [16]). This is central to his rationalism and to the related question of logic: 'the world has a logical aspect that reason eminently expresses' (13).

This account of the nature of the categories and the list of what is counted as a category are drawn from the philosophical tradition. His list (1985 [1912]: 8) draws on Aristotle, who together with scholasticism held 'genre' (genus) as a category. The categories of number and personality, on the other hand, come from Renouvier (1912a [1875]) and Hamelin (1925). However, Durkheim opposes the philosophical tradition in terms of explanation. From Aristotle to Kant, the philosophical tradition held that the categories had to be understood purely in terms of the mind, whether in terms of innate ideas or of the faculties of mind, particularly reason and understanding. But this premise is precisely what Durkheim questions. He rejects the doctrine of innateness (1969 [1903]: 4), and the explanation of reason 'as inherent in the nature of the human intelligence' (1985 [1912]: 14). He insists that the 'dialectical and ideological' method of philosophy must be replaced, arguing rather that the categories are 'a result of history' and a 'collective work' (1909: 188). Against 'recent disciples of Kant' for whom the categories 'preform' the real, for Durkheim they 'resume' it (187).

So the categories, whilst being 'wise instruments of thought (*pensée*)' (1985 [1912]: 27), are 'constructed with social elements' (1985 [1912]: 17). They are complex; because they are not first and unanalysable facts, it is not sufficient to 'interrogate our conscience'

(18). The categories change with time and place (25), so we must turn to history to understand the categories. 'A whole part of the history of humanity is summarised here' ('*Toute une partie de l'histoire de l'humanité y est résumé*') (25). Categories, made by 'human groups', are 'laboriously forged over the centuries' in 'which the best of their intellectual capital is accumulated' (25). A reference to labour and indeed struggle is clear in Durkheim's '*laborieusement forgés*' (25). So against the philosophical tradition, he offers a type of social constructionism and locates the categories not only within human action, labour and history, but also within social being (15) and the *conscience collective* (445ff).

The Structure of the Argument

Durkheim develops the stages of the sociology of knowledge throughout *Les Formes* (1985 [1912]) and the totemic and other materials exemplify this argument for his new science of man. The argument begins with an analysis of space and time (9ff), whose social character (12) is the basis for what follows. His second argument concerns 'genre' and class (Book II chapter 3 section 2). 'Genre' (genus) is, of course, a philosophical concept, yet, as will become clear, he reads the totemic material through this lens. (This raises an important question that I will return to.) He shows that social organization influences classification: 'they have taken as their framework , the very framework of society. It is the phratries which serve as genera and the clans as species' (145).

His third argument (Book II chapter 7 section 6) concerns the parallel development of logical and social evolution. Totemism reveals the origin of a 'curious trait' of human mentality that has played a considerable role in 'the history of thought' (1985 [1912]: 236). At issue is the historical emergence of scientific culture, characterized for Durkheim by the role 'distinctions' play in its thought patterns, as contrasted with the 'indistinctions' common to mythological thinking. Religion is the 'exceptionally powerful cause', which intervenes to transfigure the sensible through mental effervescence. Totemism shows the development of the idea of essence, and of a common principle of different beings, through the necessity for a name or an emblem. This great intellectual step – on the part of all social groups – leads to the first explanation of the world and becomes proof that logical understanding is a function of society. All explanation shares the same logic, for 'to explain is to connect things one to another'; it is to show functional relations between things. It is 'the mind' (*l'esprit*) and not 'sensation' that discovers these 'internal relations' between things (239).

The fourth stage (Book II chapter 8) concerns the idea of the soul (*l'âme*) and personality. These beliefs, central to all religions (1985 [1912]: 242), are nothing other than the totemic principle incarnated in each individual (251). Durkheim's fifth argument (Books II and III) concerns force and causality: causality depends upon force, which was developed earlier in the book and which was then seen to be located in the powers of rite (24). He develops a sociological account of the principle of causality based upon an analysis of the mimetic rites, the Intichiuma, of the Arunta (Book III chapter 3 section 3). This frame for his analysis of causality, the ritual action, is in effect 'a statement' (*enoncé*) and one of the most primitive statements ever made (367). Power is the key to the argument, for the causal relation implies 'the idea of efficacity, of productive power, of active force' (367). The sixth stage concerns the conceptual, as the base for the link between logic and religion (Conclusion). If society can be seen to have a role in the genesis of concepts, then it can be seen to have a role in the genesis of logical thought and thereby religion (433).

His seventh and final stage, in the very last section of the book, concerns categories and the conscience collective. Since categories – the hallmark of logical thought – are concepts, their social origin becomes clear. The stability and impersonality of categories is a clear sign of their nature as collective representations (1985 [1912]: 441) – they express the 'fundamental conditions of agreement between minds' and as such can only have been 'elaborated by society' (441). Here is the introduction to totality, which lies at the basis of all classification and is the abstract form of society (443). It is the '*classe supreme*': 'Impersonal reason is only another name given to collective thought (636). Classification requires self-consciousness (444).This is the conscience collective: as the highest form of 'psychic life', it alone can furnish the mind with the '*cadres*' that apply to the totality of beings as understood from within that collective (444).

The Logic of the Argument

What is central to Durkheim's sociological explanation of the categories? I have suggested above that, theoretically, it is an account of representation, which forms the bridge between society, the mind and religion (it was this link that Malinowski and others failed to discern).

He insists 'nothing exists except by representation' ('*rien n'existe que par la représentation*') (Durkheim 1985 [1912]: 349n55). We have seen that earlier in his thought, he maintained that 'Social life consists entirely in representations' (Durkheim 1987 [1895]: 34). And in *Les Formes* he says categories are 'essentially collective representations' (Durkheim 1985 [1912]: 15); indeed, they are 'preponderant representations' (Durkheim 1909: 187). They play a role in the representational logic of the social for him. But how is this construction to be understood?

I have argued that representation is not a reflection of things, but a critical and communicative mental power: a 'thing' (*chose*) indicates – is – reality in a representational world. This reference demonstrates Durkheim's debt to Renouvier (Stedman Jones 2001: 141ff.). Yet this word has affected the whole interpretation of his work and his account here in particular. I suggest, on the contrary, that representation is not simply a reflection of things; it is rather a dynamic force that relates to action. As Durkheim said in his first book, 'A representation is not ... an inert shadow projected on us by things, but a force which raises up around itself a whirlwind of organic and psychic phenomena' (1986 [1893]: 53). This account of the nature of representation, its power and its relation to action is crucial to understanding how religion is instrumental in the development of the categories of thought.

Further, it is through the logic of representation that he rejects empiricism (Durkheim 1985 [1912]: 239), together with its account of the categories (13). Nevertheless, his account is empirical, since he attempts to ground it in observed realities of ethnography, but it is not empiricist. Representation is central to Durkheim's critical rationalism: the terms of his logic of explanation show that it is neither empirical or sensory facts, nor a material base, nor the individual mind and its rational faculties, nor the supra-rational in divine reason that count as satisfactory explanations in epistemology. He focuses rather on the middle ground of collective representations, which must bear the full explanatory weight. The significance is that this is a communicative sphere, where the flow of communication passes from '*le dehors*' to '*le dedans*'. This idea of communication between '*consciences*' is central to how the sphere of social relations can affect the formation of the categories (Durkheim 1974 [1898]: 19).

However, an important question emerges. For Durkheim, the categories concern knowledge, whereas religion concerns belief and ritual. How can the latter establish former? That is, what is the relation between religion and knowledge, such that the study of religion will solve central questions within epistemology?

Religion and the Question of Knowledge

Durkheim insists that categories are born in and of religion; they are '*un produit de la pensée religieuse*' (1985 [1912]: 9). What is the significance of religion in relation to the categories? The conclusion of the book is that religion is social: 'religious representations are collective representations which express collective realities' ('*Les représentations religieuses sont des représentations collectives qui experiment des réalités collectives*) (9). So first, the logic of representation and its collective and social nature will serve as part of the theoretical answer to this question. Second, there must be a connection between knowledge and action, for religion concerns beliefs and rites. 'Rites are ways of acting which are only born in assembled groups and which are destined to evoke, maintain and recreate certain mental states of those groups' (9). Religion is epistemologically significant, not just for its representational nature but also because it exemplifies the significance of action, understood here as ritual.

So exactly how is he going to answer a profound philosophical question in terms of a primitive religion? The truth of religion, for Durkheim (unlike William James, for whom it is grounded in faith alone [1985 [1912]: 420]), is institutional and historical. Primitive religions, like more advanced forms of religion, are human institutions, and institutions have a basis in reality. At the base of all cults there are necessarily '*un nombre de représentations fondamentales et d'attitudes rituelles*' – a number of fundamental representations and ritual attitudes – that everywhere have the same 'objective signification' and fulfil the same functions. The study of these representations and attitudes will in turn reveal 'the most essential forms of thought and of religious practice' (7).

Durkheim, in contrast to James, held that the earlier, that is, the 'most primitive and the most simple' forms of religion (1985 [1912]: 3), are more telling (6). The rational (Cartesian) and historical method, in the explanation of religion, is to go back to the simplest form and show how it develops (3). In the place of a logical concept constructed by the mind alone, there must be a 'concrete reality' that only historical and ethnographic observation can reveal. So with philosophy there is also a human, historical truth. As with religion, the earlier and the later are linked.

To chart Durkheim's thoughts on how religion develops the mind, we must look back to his first book. There we must confront philosophical terms that were ignored by the earlier anthropological understandings of his project – and indeed, have been ignored by all commentators largely because of translation. Religion, Durkheim said, does something remarkable in *'la vie psychique'* (1986 [1893]: 275). He talks about 'the essential characteristics of psychic life' as being 'more free, more complex and more independent of the organs which support it' (286). Religion as 'that eminent form of the conscience collective absorbs all representative functions with the practical functions' (228). Again we must look to his philosophical background to understand this phrasing. Renouvier had developed the term 'representative function' (1912b [1875]: 101ff.) to indicate the functions of mind that allow us to represent things; as such, they make knowledge of a world possible. They are central to what Durkheim calls the 'representative life of societies' (1986 [1893]: 227).

Only by understanding these terms can we understand the significance of religion as a developmental force for the mind. In particular it is through the close historical association of these two functions of the mind, the practical and the representative, that we can grasp the transformative potential of ritual action for Durkheim. In this early historical stage, the practical functions can affect and develop the intellectual ones because they are more closely connected than later in history. Durkheim argues that the development of *'la vie psychique'* occurs precisely through 'greater sociability' (1986 [1893]: 284). And religion is central to sociability because it brings people together. We see the force of association in ritual action, for it provides the forum for the passionate pursuit of collective ends. So Durkheim argues that in an accomplished ceremony, the desired result of action is seen as realized (1985 [1912]: 371). Through ritual action the first terms of the causal relation are established, for it is in ritual that an association, common to all agents of the action, is established between that which precedes and that which follows. The before and the after, and the connection between them, form a conceptual stage prior to the logic of casual explanation 'X happened because of Y'. So ritual is central to his sociological explanation of causality.

Philosophy and History in *Les Formes*

On what grounds does Durkheim think that what is found in the religious ethnography of a primitive society can solve a problem of philosophy? This central question goes to the heart of his proposal for the science of man and indeed for the sociology of knowledge: how does an ancient primitive cult solve a notably tenacious philosophical problem formulated at a much later time and under quite different social and historical conditions? Is there not a different intellectual division of labour here? And is not his own comparative method being stretched too far?[4]

Yet there is this puzzle also: however much Durkheim challenges the philosophical tradition in terms of historical and sociological method, he accepts certain characterizations of the categories from it. He reads the ethnographic material through 'genre', for example, a category that was itself developed within the philosophical tradition beginning with Aristotle. The philosophers of Ancient Greece, Neoplatonists, the Stoics, Buddhist philosophers, the schoolmen of the Middle Ages, Kant in the eighteenth century and Hegel in the nineteenth were thinkers from very different types of societies, yet all were concerned with the question of categories.

It is important to recognize that although he disputes their logic of explanation, Durkheim retains the central significance of the categories for this philosophical tradition. Indeed, in keeping with all these philosophical traditions, he retains what one might call a deep sense of category: categories are central to questions of both knowledge (1985 [1912]: 8) and being (15). For Aristotle, the categories concern reality, or being; for Kant, they are part of the rational understanding that science requires. (We must remember that post-Kantian nineteenth-century thought viewed the categories as fundamental to knowledge and science.[5]) Durkheim develops these questions later in *Les Formes* (particularly in the conclusion), arguing for a universality and a rationality to human thought, despite his concern with historical explanation and his emphasis upon the diversity of systems of classification. He is ultimately concerned with the logical faculties of knowledge and how they are 'constituted in humanity' (1969 [1903]: 393). But how are these universals compatible with the historical and sociological method he espouses? He has opened a Pandora's box that goes to the heart of contemporary debates in the sociology of knowledge and particularly the sociology of science.

Durkheim has a historical vision of the religious forces that lead to the development of the categories. The case he makes for the study of religion can help us understand his claim for philosophy. Durkheim caused outrage in his day by putting Christianity back to back with the primitive cults of totemic society. It is important to recognize the uniqueness of this position. Despite the constant accusation of positivism held against his thought, here he is quite unlike the positivists who say there is no truth in religion. He also distances himself from the adherents of the 'advanced' religions – Christianity, for example – who would say not all religions are equal. Durkheim rather insists that there is a profound truth in all religion. All religions are logically comparable since they are all species of the same kind (genus) (*'espèce d'un meme genre'*) (1985 [1912]: 4). And 'a human institution cannot rest on error and falsehood ... if it is not based on the nature of things it could not have prevailed' (2). Primitive religions have a basis in reality that they express; both ancient cults and more advanced religions are constituted by belief and practices (*'croyance et pratiques'* [44]).

The core of his divergence from philosophy is this: he replaces a logical concept, 'a pure possibility constructed by the forces of mind alone', with a 'concrete reality which alone historical and ethnographic observation can reveal' (3). From this position he turns towards the future science of man based upon ethnography. In effect he will apply to philosophy the same method he applies to religion. Seeing both cases as dealing with human truth, he stresses the 'essentially human' nature of rites (363). Again, like William James, he claims there is truth in religious experience (420), but it is not the truth of the believers – rather, it is the human and historical truth of the institutions that underlie religious action. Thus our dealings with human institutions and later accounts of what is real and rational in philosophy are historically related to earlier thought processes and systems of cosmology.

To return to our central concluding question of how Durkheim can use the ethnography of an ancient society to address the problems of a historically and socially different time, I suggest first that part of the answer lies in Durkheim's view of philosophy. He does not treat it as a mere ideology or as folk narrative as Rawls (2004) suggests; instead it has great importance, which he underlines in the excluded section of the 1909 article. He is not simply reading ethnography or social fact to dismiss philosophy; he has a distinct view of the subject. In the discarded part of the 1909 piece, he repudiates the accusation (inspired by his stress on the importance of a positive science) that he is hostile to philosophy. On the contrary, he argues, 'it is inadmissible that metaphysical problems, even the most audacious, which have stirred the philosophers should be forgotten' and sociology will 'renew these efforts' (Durkheim 1909: 186). What he argues for is a philosophy not as a form of literature: it is *'les sciences de l'esprit'* – the sciences of the mind – that can satisfy the condition of positivity (186).

He argues thus for a philosophical science that accommodates representation, synthesis and both subject and object. 'Since the world exists for us in so far as it is represented, the study of the subject envelops that of the object.' The individual conscience synthesizes imperfectly: 'It is the collective conscience which is the real microcosm' (1909:

186). Only from the point of view of the collective mind (*l'esprit collective*) can 'the unity of things' be grasped. Whilst the unity of things is of philosophical concern, it is sociology that can answer this puzzle. Nevertheless, 'the study of the categories will become the supreme concern (*la piece maîtrise*) of philosophical speculation' (187). This important passage shows that Durkheim does not tout court reject philosophy in favour of the empirical. But he does specify support for a particular type of philosophy, that is, one that accommodates representation, synthesis, subject-object relations and the idea of the conscience collective. And of course it must also be a philosophy that can accommodate history and change; it must logically accommodate changefulness. Only this allowance, after all, will explain how he can claim in 1903 that there is a 'becoming' ('*devenir*') of the logical faculties and how he believes that he can account for the progress of the human mind (1969 [1903]: 393).

Conclusion: Rereading Durkheim's Synthesis of History and Philosophy through the Categories

Durkheim's aim, then, is to solve the philosophical problem of the categories with sociological methods based on the religion of totemic society. But why does Durkheim think the ethnography of a primitive society can even begin to solve the problems of philosophy? I have suggested that this question can only be answered by acknowledging his views of philosophy and history. To understand these links, we must examine two important passages that have been largely overlooked. In both cases, the translations into English do not help us understand what he is doing. This first, in *La Division*, gives us a snapshot of his account of the emergence of philosophy. We have looked at the concept of psychic life '*la vie psychique*' (1986 [1893]: 275), which is central to Durkheim's description of both culture and religion. It is, for example, central to his functionalism.[6] But most significantly in relation to the present question, he says, 'as societies become more vast ... a psychic life of a new sort appears' (285). And in *Les Formes*, he repudiates the reduction of '*la vie psychique*' to a physical base (1985 [1912]: 230n41).

I suggest that for Durkheim, philosophy emerges historically within the historical forms and functions of '*la vie psychique*'. We have seen that religion unites the two great functions of the mind, the representative and the practical. Philosophy appears only upon the separation of these functions: its historical appearance requires their distinction.

'The first is only dissociated from the second when philosophy appears. This is only possible when religion has lost a little of its empire' (1986 [1893]: 228). So it is within *'la vie representative'* that philosophy appears. Philosophy is a new way of representing things, which clashes (*'heurte'*) with public opinion.

Only thus can we begin to understand how Durkheim can bring ethnography and philosophy together. It is through the close association of these two functions – the representative and the practical – that the formation of early concepts is brought to bear. On this basis he can argue for the early religious formation of representations, which later historically develop into philosophical concepts. Clearly, religion is significant here precisely because it brings these functions together: ritual stimulates the practical functions, which in turn affect the representative functions. This is, theoretically at least, the reason for religion's significance in relation to the early formation of the categories. This formulation requires that we understand the concepts of the representative and the representative function, which has not been the case in the interpretation of Durkheim.

The second passage is found in his argument about philosophy in *Les Formes*. 'Logical life presupposes ... that there is a truth distinct from sensible appearance. History shows that it took centuries for the conception of truth, as distinct from sensible appearances, 'to develop' (1985 [1912]: 437). It was with the Greeks, in the occident, that the clear consciousness of the definition of truth appeared, which Plato translated into 'magnificent language'. The Greeks, and Plato in particular, were the first to philosophically express this *'sentiment obscure'* (437). For Durkheim, 'obscure' may be understood to mean unconscious: 'the obscure consciousness which is talked about is a consciousness which is partly unconscious' (*'la conscience obscure dont on parle n'est qu'un inconscience partielle'*) (1974 [1898]: 22). And indeed, just a few pages before this important passage in *Les Formes*, it is clear that Durkheim is dealing with the unconscious in relation to thought: 'the great things of the past ... have become so customary that we have become unconscious of them' (*'les grandes choses du passé ... sont entrée dans l'usage commun au point de nous devenir inconscientes'*) (1985 [1912]: 429). His reference to the unconscious in relation to thought – which again is part of his philosophical debt to Renouvier (Stedman Jones 2001) – is eradicated through translation into English.

These considerations clarify how he can put ethnography and philosophy together in his science of man. In this important passage, he is showing that the past exists unconsciously and affectively, and that these structures of mind get transmitted historically. What philosophy does, in the instance he cites here, is to rationally formulate and make explicit what is unconscious socially and historically. The validity of this account of philosophy as the rational and conscious expression of the unconscious and emotional cannot be debated here. But significantly, what this account does allow, in his terms, is the use of logical concepts drawn from later philosophy to read ethnographic material. This is clear in relation to genus or '*genre*', which Aristotle was the first to formulate.

Durkheim does not fill in any of the stages of this historical development of thought after its earliest moment. But it is within the development of this 'history of thought' – or the development of representation – that these massive changes occur, for clearly, Durkheim sees human consciousness as always representational (see 1974 [1898]). And they are affected by the social and historical relations of which they are an integral part. In the transactional and communicative exchange here, it is above all the growing complexity and differentiation of experience that counts. The categories themselves are complex for Durkheim, for whom they open a window into the processes of history (1985 [1912]: 18).

How interesting it would be, to know how Durkheim would explain the emergence of the concern with the categories on the part of Aristotle, or the schoolmen of the Middle Ages or indeed Kant! What is clear, however, is that the intellectual division of labour is a great factor in the growth of philosophy in Durkheim's view, and this concrete history has implications for the sociology of knowledge. In this reading of Durkheim there is no justification for a simple reflectionist explanation, whereby social structure leads directly and simply to ideas in a fashion parallel to a base-superstructure model. He is not repeating the sociological equivalent of this relationship; indeed, he goes out of his way to reject historical materialism here (1985 [1912]: 426). He does not thus argue for philosophy as a kind of ideology, or as a mere reflection of social structure. It has its own autonomous nature connected to the intellectual division of labour and the growth of abstraction (1986 [1893]: 228, 232). It is part of a new intellectual life that becomes more impersonal and universal: the categories gain autonomy from the social frameworks that originally formed them, and the classification of things begins to follow its own logic as distinct from social organization. 'It follows that things can no longer be held within the social frameworks where they primitively classified; they demand to be organised according to their own principles and thus logical organisation differentiates itself from social organisation and becomes autonomous' (1985 [1912]: 446).

There appears to have been only limited, if any, recognition of this statement and thus of its consequences for the understanding of his sociology of knowledge.

Philosophy, in translating a deeply felt yet unconscious human and historical truth, is therefore not creating but rather expressing the collective thought of humanity (1985 [1912]: 438). What philosophers term 'reason' is actually human thinking, which itself has a historical development: 'real and strictly human thought is not a primitive given but a product of history' (446). His historical vision of philosophy, alongside his statement that he is dealing with the 'history of thought' (236), tends to be overlooked by both ethnographic and sociological accounts. Yet these aspects of his work are central to his claims for the sociology of knowledge and the construction of religion in its early formation. This neglect may be associated with the mistranslation of '*la vie psychique*'. For Durkheim, the idea of the 'history of thought' is a developmental and interconnected view of the historical process, and totemism is an early but crucial stage. But his is not a Eurocentric account of the development of thought: the totemism of ancient societies is a force to be reckoned with as foundational to the historical and intellectual development of humanity.

Notes

An earlier version of this chapter was published in German as 'Durkheim, die britische Anthropologie ud die Kategorienfrage in den *Elementaren Formen des religiösen Lebens*' in *Émile Durkheim – Soziologie, Ethnologie, Philosophie*, Collection 'Theorie und Gesellschaft' (2013), Tanja Bogusz and Heike Delitz, eds. New York & Frankfurt am Main: Campus.

1. For the complexities of Durkheim's reading of the ethnography of Spencer and Gillen, see Watts Miller (2012a, 2012b, this volume).
2. See my *Durkheim Reconsidered* (Stedman Jones 2001) on how the misunderstanding of Durkheim's philosophical language has affected the comprehension of his thought.
3. Please note that I am providing my own translation of certain passages, for in some cases the original meaning is obscured. So here 'enveloper' is translated as 'contain' in the Fields translation (1995 [1912]: 441). Page numbers refer to the translated editions.
4. I make similar claims in my article in *L'Année Sociologique* (Stedman Jones 2012).
5. We see this, for example, in Lask (1911).
6. In the Halls translation, the reference to '*psychique*' is eradicated and replaced by 'psychological'.

References

Durkheim, E. 1909. 'Sociologie réligieuse et théorie de la connaissance', *Revue de Metaphysique et Morale* 17: 733–758. Section 3 (754–758) reprinted in *Karady,V Textes.* 3 vols. Paris: Les Éditions de Minuit, 1975: 1: 184–97.

———. 1969 [1903] 'De quelques formes primitives de classification' (with Marcel Mauss), *L'Année Sociologique* 6: 1–72. Reprinted in *Journal Sociologique*, ed. J. Duvignaud. Paris: Presses Universitaires de France 1969: 395–464. In English: *Primitive Classification*, trans. R. Needham. London: Routledge (1970).

———. 1974 [1898]. 'Représentations individuelles et représentations collectives'. *Revue de Metaphysique et de Morale* 6: 273–302. Reprinted in *Sociologie et Philosophie* Presses universitaires de France 4ᵗʰ ed. 1974: 12–50. In English: *Sociology and Philosophy*, trans. D.F. Pocock. New York: Free Press (1974), pp. 1–34.

———. 1985 [1912]. *Les Formes Élémentaires de la vie Religieuse* 7ᵗʰ ed. Paris: Presses Universitaires de France. In English: *The Elementary Forms of Religious Life*, trans. K. Fields. New York: Free Press (1995).

———. 1986 [1893]. *De la Division du Travail Social.* 11ᵗʰ ed. Paris: Presses Universitaires de France. In English: *The Division of Labour in Society*, trans. W.D. Halls. London: Macmillan (1984).

———. 1987 [1895]. *Les Règles de la Méthode Sociologique.* 23ʳᵈ ed. Paris: Presses Universitaire de France. In English: The Rules of Sociological Method. trans. W.D. Halls, intro. S. Lukes. London: Macmillan (1982).

Goldenweisser, A.A. 1975 [1915]. 'Émile Durkheim – *Les Formes élémentaires de la vie réligieuse. Le système totémique en Australie* 1912', in W.S.F. Pickering (ed.), *Durkheim on Religion.* London: Routledge and Kegan Paul, pp. 206–27.

Hamelin, O. 1927. *Le système de Renouvier.* Paris: Vrin.

Hartland, S. 1913. 'Review – Australia : totemism. *Les Formes Élémentaires de la vie Religieuse'*, *Man* 13(6), pp. 91–96.

Kuper, A. (ed.). 1977. *The Social Anthropology of Radcliffe-Brown.* London: Routledge and Kegan Paul.

Lask, E. 2002 [1911]. *La logique de la philosophie et la doctrine des catégories: étude sur la forme logique et sa souveraineté.* Paris: Vrin. (Originally published in Tubingen as *Die Logik de Philosophie und die Kategorienle.*)

Lukes, S. 1982. Introduction to *The Rules of Sociological Method*, trans. W.D. Halls. London: Macmillan pp. 1–27.

Malinowski, B. 1913. 'Review *Les formes élémentaires de la vie réligieuse'*, *Folklore* 24: 525–31.

Radcliffe-Brown, A.R. 1922. *The Andaman Islanders.* Cambridge: Cambridge University Press.

Rawls, A. 2004. *Epistemology and Practice.* Cambridge: Cambridge University Press.

Renouvier, C. 1912a [1875]. *Traité de Logique Générale et de Logique Formelle*, 2nd ed., 2 vols. Paris: Librairie Armand Colin.

————. 1912b [1875]. *Traité de Psychologie rationnelle*, 2nd ed., 2 vols. Paris: Librairie Armand Colin.

Stedman Jones, S. 2001. *Durkheim Reconsidered*. Cambridge: Polity Press.

————. 2012. *Forms of thought and forms of society : Durkheim and the question of the categories* in *Les formes élémentaires de la vie religieuse*. *L'Année sociologique* Vol. 62, no 2: 387–407.

Watts Miller, W. 2012a. *A Durkheimian Quest: Solidarity and the Sacred*. Oxford: Berghahn Books.

————. 2012b. 'Durkheim's Re-imagination of Australia: A Case Study of the Relation between Theory and "facts"', *Année Sociologique* Vol. 62, no 2: 329–49.

Worsley, P.M. 1956. 'Émile Durkheim's Theory of Knowledge', *The Sociological Review* 4: 47–62.

PART IV

Effervescence

Chapter 8

IS INDIVIDUAL TO COLLECTIVE AS FREUD IS TO DURKHEIM?

Sondra L. Hausner

In contemporary social theory circles, Durkheim is thought of as distinctly old-fashioned: he is not the universal hero revered in the pages of this volume. It is troubling to think that Durkheim has simply fallen out of fashion in anthropological thinking, or among students of method in religion, especially because these are the very fields whose current manifestations were arguably enabled by *Elementary Forms.* It appears that a Durkheimian approach to religion is simply *passé*; it would seem that my generation has failed to see the perfect logic in *Elementary Forms.* And yet in the last decade, we have a remarkable new translation of the text into English (1995 [1912]), by the sociologist Karen Fields. In *The Elementary Forms,* or as some translate it, *The Elemental Forms,* Fields finds a seemingly mystical element in the work of the man known as the father of sociology. With new material with which to interpret the classic text, Durkheim might emerge as a social scientist's corollary to the mystical historian we find in Eliade.

This chapter is in part, then, an attempt to clarify to my contemporaries what I would prefer to see as a misunderstanding between Durkheimians and, say, Weberians, who place history and process above all else and lament their seeming absence in *Elementary Forms.* Or, equally, between Durkheimians and Marxists, who insist, correctly, upon revealing not only the mechanisms but also the terms of production of social forms (and who interpret *Elementary Forms* as about religion and religion alone and therefore not of use in the analysis of other social processes). Durkheim can be critiqued for not tending to these elements sufficiently, but he does offer more than he is usually given credit for in the areas of social process and – critically for sociology – the dynamics between the individual and the collective that continue to lie at the heart of social investigation. Weberian and Marxist scholarly concerns need not be undermined by Durkheimian discussions of social life, which can precisely contribute to our understanding of the processes of production of social realities, although he is rarely heard in this way.

What element of Durkheim has struck the wrong chord in contemporary socio-analytic circles, and how might we reclaim him? Durkheim is classically critiqued as giving the individual short shrift despite his famous insistence that 'man is double'. Part of the point of *Elementary Forms* is to demonstrate how the individual can be subsumed by the collective of which he or she is a part, and for which he or she is partly responsible. This seeming eclipse or erasure of the individual has struck the discordant note: we moderns have spent a good five hundred years learning how to analyse the self – in the variable forms of the will, the agent, the person, the subject, the mind, the brain – and we do not want to give it up now. Do we not see the forebears of unrelenting structure (taken to its logical conclusion, perhaps, in Foucault) in Durkheim's strict and inflexible distinction between sacred and profane? Whence agency, and with it all those individualized freedoms we have struggled so hard to define and even produce, in our astonishing efforts to create the civilization of which only our species is capable? *Surely* we have evolved beyond the primitive collective.

It is true that Durkheim gives us tantalizingly little about how an individual (or a multitude of them) can produce a collective with an identity – and even a mind – of its own. If we remain true to the spirit, as it were, of *Elementary Forms*, the conclusion is clear: our societies, our worlds – not unlike our persons – are greater than the sum of our individual parts, and in this victory it would be easy to assume that the individual part goes unheard or unnoticed, or becomes irrelevant. But no social logician (let alone the father of them all) would deny that there is a process that needs to be articulated or revealed as the basis of this transformation. Durkheim was well aware of this logico-social requirement and concerned with what these steps might be. As a theoretical anticipator of structuralist thought so often critiqued as flat, unchanging or static, Durkheim is not known for the study of dynamic process. And yet in his model there must be a subtle explanation of just how it is that religions – collectives, social orders – actually work. Against the grain of critics who bemoan the absence of the person in Durkheim's work, I suggest that he does explain how individuals become part of a collective, and the collective part of them. He is, after all, as attentive to the logical as he is to the social: concerned as he is with scientific method, he could not make the claim for a social form that is not grounded in process.

Durkheim was a member of the French Republican movement at the turn of the twentieth century, which might be described by some (though not, perhaps, by him) as a secularist movement; in other accounts he was an atheist. But these seemingly non-religious identifications do not mean he was uninterested in religion: on the contrary, he wanted to understand it and also to affiliate with it (if not with Judaism per se), by virtue of being human. He saw the power of belief, and further, he saw the power in collective belief, and he used the combination of these two powers – that of the individual mind and that of the collective one – to produce his account of religion and its functions. He is less concerned with the origin of religious thought – which, he claims, is part and parcel of being human – than with its source of sustenance; that is, he is precisely interested in religiosity as a mode of being that must be produced and reproduced. And he wishes to account for its enduring ability to emerge as the strongest force in people's lives, such that it turns them from discrete or isolated individuals into communal and collective beings.

Indeed, the most frequent critique against Durkheim is that his collective beings have lost their individual selves. But this reading does him a disservice, insofar as *Elementary Forms* may also be read as an account of how individual beings come to be viably associated with a clan or a social world. Such a collective certainly has a function that the evolutionists have taken up: groups of the size Durkheim uses as his case study, namely the aboriginal Australian tribe to which he refers, are apparently an ideal social type: closely knit clans ensure that people are kept warm, fed and mutually sustained. But feeling identified with a group from the subject's own position is not the same as participating in it from an evolutionary or instrumental point of view, which is all that may be reasonably observed at that level. What people say they are may not necessarily reflect who they feel themselves to be. The issue here is the transformation of an individual self into a social being who identifies and believes him or herself to be a member of a particular group configuration: how does one come to feel a member of a social body that is larger than oneself? Where is the source of collective feeling? This puzzle is an understudied question, even in Durkheimian studies, and yet it is where both the heart of sociology and that hint of Durkheimian process lie.

Theoretical Lineages

Here I want to suggest that Freud, although working on a different problem in his own right, and with rather different methods, might move us towards an understanding of Durkheim's understudied individuals and the processes by which they become something other than their individual selves. This possibility might sound somewhat outlandish, but in this line of thinking, I follow the suggestion of none other than a strict Weberian, Talcott Parsons. Parsons became famous in the United States for developing a school of social theory that combined the work of Durkheim, Weber, Marx and Freud to understand social systems and their individual constituents in their entirety. Freud was Parsons's answer to the individual problem in *Elementary Forms*: a social system may be produced or held together by an ideology, but people have to believe in it for it to work. Even among Weberians, agency has to come from somewhere. Where better than from the collective ideology so well articulated by Durkheim?

Concretely, Parsons brought Durkheim and Freud into conversation by identifying the social system in the work of the former with the superego in the work of the latter. Both are structures perceived to be outside of oneself (what we might call 'exteriorized') and understood to be formed or constituted by a set of norms by which one *should* live. Durkheim's social system is the collective by which individuals identify and orient themselves in both daily life and ritual time. Freud's psychoanalytic superego leads or guides the ego ideal: it is the realm of moral or ethical conduct, the world of social normativity. In contemporary anthropological terms, we might think of the superego as the ground of belonging, or at least the desire to belong.

In a little essay called 'The Superego and the Theory of Social Systems' (written for the 1951 convention of the American Psychiatric Association and published as part of *Working Papers in the Theory of Action*), Parsons considers the ways individual personalities contribute to, respond to, inherit and reproduce their own structures. He elaborates specifically on a process he calls 'cathexis', which he defines as what an 'object means to the person emotionally'. The psychological process is as follows: a person creates or develops a relationship with an object that in his or her perception is reciprocated, because he or she has imputed emotion into that object. This activity – cathexis – is a way of both distinguishing between and establishing a relationship with that which is perceived to be outside of one's individual or cognizing self, and that which is perceived to be within it. It could be an actual object, inanimate (in which case all the *mana*, if you will, is perceived by the individual), or it could be another person, in which case an interpersonal social reality is also formed. Either way, it all begins with our perception or, in the words of Durkheim, 'society is in the minds of individuals' (in Parsons 1953: 15).

In the language of *Elementary Forms*, the totem, emblematic of the clan or the collective (and also the sacred or transcendent), has an active – and therefore manipulable – engagement with the individual who has the cathexis. Parsons is primarily interested in cathexis, or the emotional content of the object to the individual, as a way of explaining how the Durkheimian collective functions as socially normative or constraining – how, in other words, 'the psychological mechanisms of internalization' work, or 'the place of internalized moral values in the structure of personality' (1953: 15). Ultimately Parsons is concerned with 'the patterning of the behavior of a plurality of individuals' (13), as a good sociologist should be; like cognitivists today, he is interested in how the social structure is read back, or encoded into, the individual. The superego – the system of moral standards that constrains or shapes our behaviour – is acquired through identification: 'while identification cannot mean coming *to be the object*, it is ... dependent on *positive cathexis of the object*' (24; emphasis in the original). Here, it appears, is a clear psychoanalytic case for the creation of the totem, the base of all religious identification.

The rest of Parsons's essay is concerned with clarifying notions of culture, and establishing a tentative taxonomy of different aspects of the symbolic and expressive components of social life as mapped on to Freud's ego and id. Following Durkheim (in a line of reasoning that would later be taken to its finest theoretical conclusions by Parsons's student Clifford Geertz), Parsons argues that symbolic content has to be out in the world for it to be internalized: 'it would seem to be clear that *only* cultural symbol systems can be internalized' (1953: 23) – the data has to come from *some* tangible locale. Symbols have to exist in the common pool (and, we could add, have to be put there in the first instance) if they are (again) to be internalized and reproduced; analogously, some of them have to exist in the individual's cognitive set if he is to be a member of a particular collective, or be able to communicate with or correctly interpret other members. Otherwise cultural breakdown would result.

Parsons considers 'the convergence of the fundamental insights of Freud and Durkheim' a 'massive phenomenon' as far as 'the internalization of values' (1953: 15), or the ways in which the collective structure makes itself felt. A question of equal or greater concern that must also be asked of *Elementary Forms* is how something external to the individual can come about. In any event, the inverse of either question is implicated in the other: Durkheim's model implies that what is internal or interior to the self can and must be made external or exterior, and what is exterior or external to the self can and will be internalized. When Durkheim writes that '[t]he force of the collectivity is not wholly external; it does not move us entirely from outside', he is primarily interested in the movement inward: 'it must enter into us and become organized within us' (1995 [1912]: 211). But in fact he also implies that there is a cyclical dynamism at the heart of collective effervescence, a social process that arises when 'the emotions aroused are transferred to the symbol' (221): 'Nothing comes out of nothing' (226). Here is the movement outward, what Durkheim casually refers to as a 'well-known law that the feelings a thing arouses in us are spontaneously transmitted to the symbol that represents it' (221), contending further that '[t]he whole social world seems populated with forces that in reality exist only in our minds' (228).

The religious idea may come from without and need to be lodged within, but there is also evidence that, in the Durkheimian model, the individual mind is the active agent in the process, the place from which cognitive interactions between the collective that is external to the self and the cognition that is internal to the self begins. But I would not want to identify too specifically the origin of the process: more than any other, perhaps, it is a chicken-and-egg proposition. Although he titles his chapters 'Origins of these Beliefs' (1995 [1912]: chaps. 5–7), his discussion presents rather a cyclical view of society and its modes of cultural transmission. Beliefs both come from outside the individual mind and are situated within and emerge from it: 'Social life is only possible thanks to a vast symbolism' (233), he writes. The social constellation of individual minds is located both within and without personal cognition; the individual and the collective are mutually interdependent and co-penetrating. The very production of society – and with it, religion – requires both individual consciousness and the *conscience collective*, encoded in symbolic form.

Psychoanalysis: Projection

Although he was speaking to psychoanalysts and psychiatrists when he presented the paper, Parsons was neither a psychoanalyst nor a psychiatrist: 'personality', in his theory of social action, seems to stand for psychology very broadly. Freudian or psychoanalytic thought is more complex than social and cognitive scientists can casually lay claim to: Freud developed psychoanalysis as a therapeutic practice, not as a theoretical tool, and to appreciate its subtle mechanics in full at the level of a practitioner requires a concerted daily effort sustained over many years (quite apart from medical or psychiatric training). We would do well to remember this caveat. Freud, as a medical psychiatrist whose training was in neurology, would no doubt have been fascinated with how far we have come in the neural and cognitive sciences. It is extraordinary that his theoretical work is now primarily taught in the humanities.

Freud (1856–1939) was born two years before Durkheim (1858–1917), and outlived him by more than twenty. There are real differences between Freud's and Durkheim's projects and orientations, and these divergences should not be elided in explorations of the psychological process in the works of the two thinkers. Freud sees the raw individual as fundamentally opposed to the structure of culture, which tries rather to mould him and make him behave. Rather than work as a dynamic or friendly process as in Durkheim's rendering, whereby the 'clan ... awaken[s] in its members the idea of forces existing outside them' (1995 [1912]: 216), civilization is a tragedy for Freud – only a rare process could rightfully be called an 'awakening'. Culture keeps us trapped in ways of our own making, all the while denying our own impulses – and worse, religion fools us into thinking we might attain happiness after all. From *Civilization and Its Discontents*, we draw his famous quote: 'by drawing them into a mass delusion, religion succeeds in sparing many people an individual neurosis. But hardly anything more' (1963 [1930]: 32). In *Future of an Illusion*, religion is a product of helplessness in the face of 'crushing supremacy of nature', ultimately a collective 'delusion' (1962 [1928]: 227); Durkheim has avidly and explicitly argued against this position in his attempt to explain what he regards as a perennial and real phenomenon. Asceticism is no better for Freud: the acceptance of suffering in the name of transcendence is no advance over the attempt to avoid it, although he is prepared to consider this proposition (probably in respect to Schopenhauer).[1]

Neither this view (nor this tone) is at all Durkheimian. Durkheim defends religion and religious belief, primitive or modern, precisely against the charge that it is 'hallucinatory' (1995 [1912]: 65): 'It is unthinkable that systems of ideas like religions, which have held such a large place in history – the well to which peoples in all the ages have come to draw the energy they had to have in order to live – could be mere fabrics of illusion' (66). Durkheim was, in this sense (and at this stage), an upbeat optimist: we are complicit in our own constraints, because we believe in them. Certainly *Elementary Forms* takes a positive, even cheerful, view of the social process: 'In sum, joyful confidence, rather than terror or constraint, is at the root of totemism'; he resists the idea that fear or terror is that which inspires belief: '*primus in orbe deos fecit timor* [first in the world, fear created the gods] is in no way warranted by the facts' (225). It is not hard to see that the First World War separated the most seminal writing of the two thinkers in time, and even more so in mood. Freud's mature work is the confrontation of what horrors may ensue if humans – especially in their collective forms – are permitted to take their capacity for violence to its logical extreme. One can only feel relief that he did not live to see the Second World War.

Despite their differences in character, certain aspects of Freudian psychology are useful to the Durkheimian project. Freud writes about unconscious impulses, forces that are established so early in life that they form the pattern of our behaviours in any frame or set of circumstances. We create our own patterns, if you will, repeatedly acting out our earliest dramas because they are cognitively familiar to us. The frame does matter, however, as we know from Durkheim, and from Parsons, and from culture: preconscious (if we wish to call them that) impulses need objects to glom on to, attach to or identify with, or against which to rebel. One does not need to be a cognitive scientist to see that there is a point – or a point in time, or multiple points in time – when the patterned neurons of human consciousness translate into symbols: here, I suggest, is the arising of cognition, the moment when the individual mind comes into contact with the social world, or the set of representations held dear by a particular social configuration (see Stedman Jones, this volume). Such an encounter is not, of course, limited to a single moment: these interpersonal (individual-collective) symbolic or representational exchanges mark the whole of human history.

In Parsons's explanation, cathexis is an emotional relation to an object. An additional mechanism that may be instructive in our consideration of the relationship between the individual and his or her collective, or totem, is projection. Moving further into psychoanalytic terminology, projection is the cognitive mechanism whereby one gets rid of unacceptable feelings or impulses by attributing them to someone else. What we perceive in others is a reflection of ourselves: if it were not within our sphere of consciousness, it would not be possible to perceive it elsewhere. And sometimes we attribute to some external object or person some aspect that we precisely cannot abide in ourselves. In classical Freudian terminology, projection is a way of separating that which must be ejected outside of oneself as too distasteful to be acceptable to one's moral idea of oneself: if someone else has that negative quality, it need not be accepted within.

Interestingly, Durkheim uses the idea of projection explicitly, although not in the Freudian sense: 'Religious force is none other than the feeling that the collectivity inspires in its members, but projected outside the minds that experience them' (1995 [1912]: 230). What is projected in this instance is not something too horrific to be abided, but something that is too powerful to be contained in a singular individual. 'Because we feel the weight of them [forces], we have no choice but to locate them outside ourselves', he writes (214). Here we have a succinct statement of how what is external to the mind is interpreted within it, digested and sent back out again to create its own reality.

This construction is thus precisely compatible with psychoanalytic thinking, although it is not strictly Freudian. The idea that what is projected is necessarily negative is questioned by Freud's follower Melanie Klein, who argued that projection could also be a person's getting rid of something good. (Here is where the psychoanalysts could use the anthropologists, by the way: it should be no surprise that the unconscionable and the desirable could appear as two sides of the same coin.) Simply put, an aspect of existence or a force that is too powerful or overwhelming to be handled in everyday circumstances has to be excised, or set apart.[2] Here, in psychoanalytic terms, is the very kernel of Durkheim's notion of the sacred.

A totem is only one object, but for Durkheim it is the most significant object there is, the wellspring of all social relations and social codes. In identifying this object, and the relationships that arise in interaction with it (what Parsons calls 'the terms of inter-activity'), Durkheim has pinpointed the basis of both social relationships and cognitive processes. Totems mediate both directions of this relation: they are the object of an individual's cathexis, or projection of power, and the source of the identification of that power. Thus the collective finds its weight in Durkheimian theory precisely in relation to individual cognition, rather than in a trumping or dismantling of it.

While Parsons focuses on the internalization of the social order, Freud is equally looking at the externalization of the self. The superego, or the moral sphere as understood in Durkheimian terms, is the collective production of an external force by which people believe they are judged, or towards which they aspire. In the language of *Elementary Forms*, 'we cannot help but feel that this moral toning up has an external cause ... we readily conceive of it in the form of a moral power that, while immanent in us, also represents something in us that is other than ourselves' (213). In a sense Durkheim asks the same question as Freud, but from the perspective of the collective.

Surplus is the projection, therefore, of a lack: it is the psychological process whereby someone can make exterior what is actually interior. Society is greater than the sum of its individual parts precisely because individuals offer up or send outward some element of themselves to that which is known to be outside themselves and from which, ironically, they draw power back in. The surplus force, or the totem, is both the object and the product of collective cathexis; it is, by definition, a constellation that responds. Here, in nascent form, is our explanation of the way a system of symbols works, as later laid out in Geertz's famous rendering (1973), after Parsons, after Durkheim. To mix a few theoretical metaphors, then, the surplus here is the transcendent. And although this mathematical equation might not sit well with materialists (or, possibly, theologians), in fact we arrive at Durkheim's own answer as to how there can be a surplus value in collectivity. If not in the minds of individuals, where does the transcendent lie? That transcendence might begin in the mind is no insult: the sacred is no less real for being both the source and the product of cognition. On the contrary: if the attribution of sacredness and human cognitive development are one and the same process, we know they are equally integral to human experience.

Social Systems: Effervescence

Elementary Forms was published just before the First World War began, before the power of the collective in the form of state armies took on a frightening, violent quality on a global scale.[3] Durkheim reminds us throughout his text that the nature of the object – the totem – holds its power through an arbitrary but collectively agreed-upon designation: it is a 'symbolic representation' (1995 [1912]: 208) and, in *Elementary Forms* at least, has a neutral or even a positive value.[4] Significantly, the totem is the product of a psychological mechanism that has the power to create social worlds: in these terms, no one can accuse Durkheim of denying an individual the capacity for agency. His intention was rather to understand how social configurations can vary depending on the collective project of individual actors. Durkheim's argument suggests that a totem is an eminently variably symbol, and Freud would have to agree.

Internalization and externalization imply different scales in their movements in opposite directions: the collective will becomes the individual mind (or superego) in the first instance, and individual cognitive process becomes the collective totem (or sacred) in the second. But, as has already been proposed, the two processes necessarily form a dialectic, whereby an externalized or collective ethos (and here Durkheim combines a symbolic system with a moral order) is imprinted on the individual mind, which needs its object in order to cognize (whether that impulse derives from a yearning for parental love, in the Freudian rendering, or from plain old yearning, in the Buddhist rendering); and, equally and in the opposite direction, the individual mind's appropriation or interpretation of this system plays out in public and in concert with the actions and symbolic systems of other members of that collective. That is, more important than either of these processes in isolation – collective to individual or individual to collective – or the mechanism by which the whole rigmarole is set into motion, is that both sets of dynamics are kept afloat. Extraordinarily, it seems to balance out as an integrated system, regardless of the differences in scale implied in the two directions.

Both flows, if you will – the collective making its way into the cognitive frame of the individual, and the individual's psychological processes establishing the reality of the totem that represents the clan – are located in the psychic process that separates (and then determines the relations between) self and other, or 'ego and alter in the structure of the interactive system', as Parsons puts it (1953: 18). The totem is the other, a projection of that which is not the self, as well as the symbol of a collective that is by definition constituted by both self and other; it is collectively acknowledged as greater-than-all-of-us. The individual's projection of self onto other – which both creates a collective ('I am no longer just me but me in concert with someone else, or many other someone elses') and establishes the specific terms and codes by which members of that collective relate – is also that which gives the other transcendent power over the self. It is the powerful – or, put more forcefully, the overpowering – part of oneself that is projected, so it will automatically have power, and will necessarily be that aspect of oneself that one must engage.

Fin

It would be too simple to say Durkheim tends to the dynamics of the collective while Freud tends to the dynamics of the individual. In a sense, Freud is simply despondent about the collective's hold on the individual, while Durkheim simply wants it both ways: the social lies in the minds of individuals, but also outside them; man 'has no more imagined the world in his own image than he has imagined himself in the image of the world. He has done both at once' (1995 [1912]: 237). Freud's focus is on the inevitable fission of the human psyche; Durkheim's is on its necessary – and productive – convergence with others: in his words, 'social life has promoted that fusion' (238). The capacity of the social body to move as one is a terror for Freud; it is rather a thing of near wonder for Durkheim.

Collective effervescence is the event from which social life bubbles forth, complete with the cultural codes that determine mores, conventions, modes of conduct and ethical configurations. What of the revolutionary, the agent, the thinking, feeling subject, the individual? Is effervescence effectively its obliteration? Is the purpose of the collective actually to dull the individual or the thinking subject by heightening the false or misleading sensibility that one is able to get more from outside oneself than from within? Certainly effervescence and its opposite, contained daily life, are two poles (or two times, as Watts Miller calls them in this volume) that in their oscillation produce religion for Durkheim, and yet they also represent what Freud had to say about the effects of religion: at its best it keeps people from discovering their true nature as animals (which many would say is no bad thing).

What if, returning to our opening question, effervescence has something of the mystical or magical in its froth? Are we not, then, living precisely as something greater than animals? The human individual creates the collective: the unique quality of being human, evolutionists suggest, is the ability to superimpose layers of symbolic thought in ritual. Consciousness is an ability to see this layering – the capacity to be self-referential to deeper and deeper degrees – and ritual is its representation, laid bare for all to see. Mysticism in this rendering is a kind of timelessness, or synchronous view: a perspective from which one can see the entire stack of those layers and their compositions in one go, a cross section of symbolically constructed reality. In some philosophical schools, it might also be viewed as the ability or capacity to see how malleable or unmoored those symbolic mortar blocks are, and thereby the ability to be free of the emotions that attend them in the incorrect belief that they are fixed.

Freud notices and is somewhat able to explain what individual human minds do, at the level of the brain. Durkheim notices and is somewhat able to explain what collective human minds do, at the level of the ritual. The parallels become more pronounced when these perceptions of the structural relationship of part to whole are placed in tandem: we can see how they depend upon each other to function and indeed exist as human society, with all its tensions and ambivalences, its effervescent moments and its quotidian ones. In a final sense, though, there is a theoretical inversion here: anticipating a disagreement with Freud, Durkheim finds the root of religion in our unrestrained expression of ourselves and the effervescence that comes about when we allow it to. From our animal nature, ironically, comes collective mind, and in this transformation is all the beauty of society.

Notes

Earlier versions of this chapter were given at the workshop commemorating *Elementary Forms* in Oxford in July 2011, and at a conference entitled 'Individuality in Modern Religious Thought', organized by the Centre for Theology and Modern European Thought in Oxford in September 2011, for which I am grateful to my colleague Johannes Zachhuber for his generous invitation and a thought-provoking discussion, and to Mark Chapman for a helpful set of comments. Henry Kaminer, David Schab and Ann Syz have all helped school me in Freudian thought; I hope I have done their tutorials justice. All errors are my own.

1. My thanks to my colleague Kevin Hilliard for suggesting this intellectual genealogy.
2. Hanna Segal, Klein's analysee, takes this idea further, suggesting that the quality that is projected is the quality that is identified with, thereby becoming Freud's ego ideal.
3. My thanks to Agata Bielik-Robson for drawing my attention to the fearsome quality of the collective in the context of the Eastern Bloc.
4. See Watts Miller (this volume) for a discussion of the development of Durkheim's concept of the effervescent: it did not start off as an unequivocally positive force.

References

Durkheim, E. 1995 [1912]. *The Elementary Forms of Religious Life*, trans. K.E. Fields. New York: The Free Press.

Freud, S. 1962 [1928]. *The Future of an Illusion*. London: Hogarth Press and Institute of Psycho-Analysis.

———. 1963 [1930]. *Civilization and Its Discontents*. London: Hogarth Press and Institute of Psycho-Analysis.

Geertz, C. 1973. *The Interpretation of Cultures*. New York: Basic Books.

Parsons, T. 1953. 'The Superego and the Theory of Social Systems', in T. Parsons, R.F. Bales and E.A. Shils (eds), *Working Papers in the Theory of Action*. Glencoe, IL: The Free Press, pp. 13–29.

Chapter 9

COLLECTIVE REPRESENTATIONS, DISCOURSES OF POWER AND PERSONAL AGENCY

THREE INCOMMENSURATE HISTORIES OF A COLLABORATOR'S REBELLION IN THE COLONIAL SUDAN

Gerd Baumann

Durkheim's stepchild, the vacuously vague notion of 'collective representations', was and remains widely suspect as a blanket defence against Marxian 'ideological' influences on the social sciences, flagged up just when sociology wanted to establish itself as a non-dangerous academic discipline. This chapter starts from the same historical reading. Can this toothless notion, signifying nothing more than 'shared ideas', mean anything to people familiar with what we have become aware of since: the rediscovery of ideology, the different paths opened by the sociology of knowledge, the distinction between dominant versus demotic discourses, and the alleged power of discourse regardless of personal agency? If the orphaned notion is to be tested for any remaining analytic value, clearly it needs to be seen beside more power-conscious competitors. This essay proposes a minutely small ethnographic case study to test the result of combining the options.[1]

Collective representations, it is argued, make sense as one of three conceptual axes of social analysis. The combination, I submit, can be applied to any social event, be it a workaday interaction, a big historical turning point, or anything in between, like the present case study.

The conceptual triad works, I shall argue, for three deductive reasons. First, we need collective representations to account for agency; otherwise, agency would be seen as madness or meaningless. We know of thousands of failed prophetic or millenarian movements that failed precisely because they were insufficiently attuned to long-standing or even latent collective representations. However, and second, discourses of power too must rely on collective representations, for even the most brutal among them will run into trouble unless they can appeal to collective, or at least popular, representations to legitimize their inherent tendencies towards coercion. Well-known examples cover most totalitarian regimes as well as most discourses legitimizing colonial power. Yet, and third, alternative collective representations can, at times, establish alternative discourses of power. Though these cannot abolish coercive relations, they can transform popular, and even revolutionize pervasive, representations of legitimacy, as we know from all successful prophetic or revolutionary movements, from Jesus to the daily news. My example here, a prima facie hopeless and absurd anticolonial rebellion in the Sudan, failed. Yet it succeeded in rewriting the history of its failure via the classic discourse of anti-power: myth, and even competing myths that become rival collective representations. In the end, I shall argue that the conceptual triad works like a triple helix, with all three coils of conceptual molecules intertwined in constantly changing but distinguishable relational dynamics. Unfortunately, just like Durkheim before he distilled an idea, I must ask the reader for empirical patience. These data, like his, come from incommensurate sources and develop sometimes-crazy complexities, even when all data 'mean' the same. The disparate data I try to triangulate, however, are a discourse analyst's dream, when combined with an open eye for the other two dimensions.[2]

The data come from a god-forgotten corner of the Sudan (although geographically speaking, from its centre) and from a god-forgotten period of history: colonialism, seemingly triumphant but, in hindsight, on its last legs. The Sudan was the last bit of Africa that any colonial power wanted, and the peoples of the Sudan knew this well: 'On the Seventh Day of Creation, God made the Sudan, and then He laughed', chuckles a Sudanese proverb. The Sudan, to put it somewhat pointedly, was half a million square miles of desert in the Arabic-speaking North and West, and another half a million square miles of waterlogged swamplands in the Nilotic and equatorial South. Sandwiched between them was a tiny area, the size of Switzerland or Wales, known as the Nuba Mountains and inhabited by a vast variety of Nuba peoples scratching a living from their terraced hill farms and livestock while living cheek by jowl with fluctuating populations of Arabic-speaking Baggara cattle nomads and Humr camel nomads seeking a living on the plains in between the hills by seasonal transhumance and slave raiding. Interrelations between and among these groups were conflictual at best, and slave raids, cattle raids and vengeance killings pitted Baggara against Humr, either of these against the Nuba groups and often also Nuba groups against other Nuba groups. Pacification of the region was a sheer impossible task for the Anglo-Egyptian colonizers, and Nuba resistance especially was ardent and prolonged. Not even a semblance of the Pax Britannica could be achieved until 1939, when artillery and even aircraft bombings were used to defeat the last revolt, that of the Nuba of Lafofa (MacMichael 1934: 178). The aerial bombardment of the Lafofa Hills marked the end of forty years of resistance that witnessed no less than thirty distinct rebellions in different mountain communities (Ibrahim 1985).

The most famed of these rebellions was that of the Nuba of the Miri Hills, led by a chief named Fiki Ali. It began in 1915 and continued, on and off, for over five years. What makes it historic, as opposed to an episodic footnote in anti-colonial history, may be summarized in three points: First, its crucial timing spanned the First World War and its aftermath, a period when British imperial resources were stretched beyond their limits. Second, it ended with the British rulers of the Anglo-Egyptian Condominium of the Sudan having to strike a compromise so embarrassing that no British sources dare admit to it explicitly. Third, it is covered by the most disparate sources, ranging from official colonial intelligence reports to retrospective Miri and even British myths. This variety of sources renders Fiki Ali's rebellion an episode worthy of study when trying to sort out the interrelations among our three theoretical axes of analysis: personal agency, collective representations and discourses of power.

A Discourse of Power Perfected: 'Induced to Surrender' (How British Intelligence Defeated the Collaborator-Rebel without a Cause)

[August 8th, 1916:] Despatch by the Sirdar and Governor-General [of the Anglo-Egyptian Condominium of the Sudan] to War Office, [London,] on Military Operations in Darfur, together with a brief report on the services of the Egyptian Army and the Sudanese Administration since the outbreak of war in Europe:

In the Nuba Mountains, incipient dislike of any Government control was fanned into action by stories of Government's decline and a situation arose which demanded immediate attention. Immediately after the suppression of a band of fanatics who had collected at Jebel Gedir, Fiki Ali, the chief of the Miri group of hills, and the most powerful and hitherto loyal native of the district, gathered together his adherents and defied the Government to dislodge him. Troops arrived in time to prevent the rebellion spreading, and after short but difficult operations secured the capture, or surrender of all except the Chief and a small following. The latter were hunted from hill to hill for several months before Fiki Ali was induced to surrender himself and the district reverted to its normal state. (Wingate 1916: 6)

Thus proclaimeth the discourse of power, by the voice of the governor-general of the vast Anglo-Egyptian Condominium of the Sudan, in August 1916. The power of the discourse is evident: 'Government' spelled with a capital G, silly 'stories' that motivate mad 'fanatics', dutiful troops arriving just 'in time ... to secure capture or surrender' of the terrorists. The London addressees of the dispatch knew perfectly well that the Sudan, called an 'Anglo-Egyptian Condominium', was a British colony in all but name, but that the Nuba Mountains, sandwiched between the deserts of the Arabic-speaking and Muslim Northern and Western Sudan and the swamps of the Southern Sudan were one of many vast stretches of land that were claimed, but not governable, by the colonial power residing in the faraway capital Khartoum and the pathetic provincial garrisons of Talodi and Kadugli. Nonetheless, this discourse of power reassures the Imperial War Office, London, of its own importance, and it is happy, later in the same text, to parade its own might in terms of sheer numbers. The game of numbers, so aptly placed in 'the colonial imagination' by Appaduari (1993), is so impressive that one may almost miss the disastrous outcome dutifully reported:

Fiki Ali, the powerful Mek (or chief) of Jebel Miri in the Nuba Mountains province, assumed a hostile attitude towards the Government and his dissatisfaction constituted a menace to the peace of the whole of the province. In April 1915 the following force, under the command of Major M.J. Huddleston, the Desert Regiment, was rapidly concentrated at Kadugli:

1 squadron of Cavalry
1 Camel Maxim Section
3 companies of Camel Corps
1 company VIIth Battalion
1 and ½ companies XIth Sudanese.
A total of 46 officers and 1007 rank and file.

On April 20th and the two ensuing days, our troops attacked Jebel Tuluk and the surrounding hills, which were strongly held by Fiki Ali and his tribesmen. The attack was completely successful and the enemy was driven out of their stronghold, a large number of prisoners being captured. Fiki Ali, with his immediate following, succeeded in effecting his escape ... (Wingate 1916: 18)

Even if boasting with numbers plays a crucial role in 'the colonial imagination' (Appadurai 1993), this admission of defeat despite numbers still belongs to the discourse of power pure. It expresses coercive might in coercive language: not the next few days, but 'ensuing days', a hill not held, but 'strongly held' and an operation not successful but 'completely successful', if only one ignores the rebel himself escaping – not exactly what the mighty force of power could have intended. The escape and its aftermath will still entertain us for a while, but so far as discourse is concerned, it is seldom much more powerful than this. Here it dictates power pure, requiring no frills of any merely popular or collective representations except perhaps 'our troops' in double numbers against 'his tribesmen'. Given the local military resources at the time, this appears as a world war–sized mobilization against a tiny gang of naughty tribal rebels. What on earth was going on? Let us trace this top discourse of power to its discursive origin, namely, the monthly Sudan Intelligence Reports, aptly abbreviated SIR – provincial-level reports that show the discourse of power rather more uncertain of itself. To compensate for uncertainties, this lesser discourse of power has to fall back on collective representations to account for the personal agency of the rebel without a cause.

A Discourse of Power Stuck for Causes: 'Cattle Returned of Their Own Accord' (How Accounting for Agency Falls Back on Collective Representations)

Locally, the first signs of Fiki Ali's intentions had already appeared in March 1915, when SIR reported:

> The attitude of Fiki Ali, of the Miri hills, south-west of Kadugli, has been unsatisfactory for some time past. It is now reported that reliable evidence has been obtained of a plot, in which he was implicated, to attack the station at Kadugli. Apparently some assistance from the Miri Nubas of the Territorial Company had been promised him. Fiki Ali was in consequence summoned to Talodi, and was actually on the road when he suddenly returned to his hill and gave out that he and his people declined to meet the Government official. The Governor of the province, Captain R.S. Wilson, with one company 11th Sudanese, immediately marched to Kadugli to reason with him and bring him to his senses, but on the 29th March, Fiki Ali beat his war drum and proclaimed his intention of attacking the Government. ... It is estimated

that he can collect a thousand men, about half of whom are armed with rifles. (SIR 248 1915: 5)

This lower-level discourse of power starts off remarkably uncertain of itself in this first-ever written reference to Fiki Ali, the collaborator turned rebel without a cause. In a double passive construction, 'it is reported' (one may ask: by whom?) that 'evidence has been obtained' (again: by whom?) of 'a plot' (to what end – overthrow of the British Empire?). Yet the matter is easily rectified: the discourse of power inserts a sentence before ('attitude unsatisfactory for some time past') and an adjective in between ('reliable' evidence). The rest should speak for itself: there is a plot, however badly thought out, against our power, and so we go and arrest the plotter. But wait – the good Captain Wilson takes no more than a company of lightly armed riflemen to 'reason with' the rebel? This is made eminently plausible, however: the rebel is clearly irrational ('suddenly returned') and thus needs merely to be brought back 'to his senses'. Yet despite Captain Wilson's good offices, the native eccentric mutates straight into a Red Indian plucked from pages by the popular novelist Rider Haggard (whom Wilson and all his British peers are certain to have read) and 'beats his war drum', an instrument unknown in the Nuba Mountains. Irony to one side, what is happening here is quite interesting. The local-level discourse of power is initially uncertain of itself, so it mobilizes an older set of collective representations to depict an irrational native ruler who takes decisions impulsively rather than rationally. It then introduces the reasonable colonial captain, who tries to talk some sense into the fool, only then to witness the native reverting to savagery by beating his (imaginary) war drum.

The clichés may appear quaint by now, but they intimate an analytical argument nonetheless: discourses of power that are uncertain of themselves take recourse to collective representations that are popular, rather than powerful in the literal sense. But whatever power these collective representations may have had, they turn entirely symbolic in the face of a near-farcical defeat of the colonial power: though no longer physically coercive, they have become metaphorically persuasive. The trouble is that Major Huddleston's persuasion was insufficient to deter the former collaborator from continuing his rebellion, and even the physical might of over a thousand soldiers was powerless against the rebel, who kept raiding in the region for cattle and other booty after his escape. After the unsuccessful siege, it took three months to induce the rebel to surrender in a place, called Rahad, some 200 kilometres removed from his local power base in the Nuba Mountains. SIR reported: 'Fiki Ali, his brother Musa and servant Maru Wad were arrested by the Sub-Mamur of Rahad on the 27th of the month [April]' (SIR 251 1915: 6).

The journey from Rahad to Talodi, the then provincial capital, must have taken at least two weeks at this time of the rainy season. Yet slow as the journey must have been, the trial for treason was fast. SIR's report for August 1915, however, is such an exemplar of a discourse of power fooled by its own rules that I cannot resist the temptation to gloss it, as the quickest way of performing a discourse analysis. It is the discourse of power at its most innocent, or should one say sheepish:

As stated in last month's report, ex-Mek Fiki Ali was tried by the Mudir's Court for treason.	Although we never reported this, there is no need to read this, Sir: A chief we have already sacked was tried by the Governor's Court posing as native justice for the worst crime in a colony of which he is a subject, not a citizen.
He was found guilty and sentenced to be hanged and his property confiscated.	He was sentenced to the most dishonorable death, and we kept his horse and his rifle.
The sentence was confirmed. He was sent under a strong escort of 50 men to undergo his sentence at Kadugli.	No one can doubt that this is justice. We took extra efforts to stage his execution near his home, where it would be most humiliating.
Unfortunately he contrived to escape at Khororak, not far from Talodi, and to join the remnants of his gang at J[ebel] Tuluk. (SIR 253 1915: 4)	But he managed to get away with the help of some natives nearby, right under our noses, and although the terrorists are beaten, he is going to give us the same trouble we've already had at the immense cost I hope you have forgotten, Sir. (discourse analysis gloss, GB)

By this point, in August 1915, the Jebel Tuluk group was led by Fiki Ali's brothers Idris Almi and Tia Musa, who had undertaken their own raids and partisan operations even during Fiki Ali's detention and trial. We shall return to them later, when we explain the unfathomable compromises that the British authorities entered into to vindicate a factually fictitious discourse of power. The rebel's brother had escaped a massive onslaught by government troops on 26 June, just one day before Fiki Ali's arrest in faraway Rahad, but they now welcomed the return of their leader (SIR 251 1915: 6). Under his command, the newly united group waged a seemingly endless succession of further raids, usually aimed at Baggara cattle nomads and their tasty cattle (SIR 252 1915: 7; SIR 253 1915: 6; SIR 254 1915: 4).

The last reported raids, however, indicate a new twist in the story. They seem to have been directed particularly at collaborating headmen, among them a prominent villager of the village Miri Bara, a man called Hasan Kua. The British intelligence for SIR downplayed this as a matter of routine:

> About Sept 22nd, 20 of Fiki Ali's gang (probably accompanied by Fiki himself) prowled around the Malakia village at Kadugli and stole 9 cattle from the Fellata village at Kubba. Of these, 3 were eaten and 4 subsequently returned, as the object of the party was to get the cattle of a relation of Hasan Kua. The remaining 2 cattle returned of their own accord. (SIR 255 1915: 4)

Who needs to worry about a colonial rebellion when even the cows vote against it with their own instincts? Yet the culprit singled out here, Hasan Kua, will be of immediate interest later, as we try to look behind the discourse of power and the collective representations that it must rely upon when it knows itself to be weak. The discourse of power could not quite celebrate its victorious might without asking what on earth could have caused the collaborator to rebel. This was all the more urgent as Fiki Ali had for years been a pillar of British power in the Nuba Mountains.

Positivist Interlude: '... and Took Advantage of ...' (How Even a Discourse of Power Must Reveal Its Own Impotence)

Fiki Ali had assumed the British-granted title of Mek – paramount chief or 'king' – of the Miri Hills in July 1909, upon the death of his predecessor, his brother Hamid Abu Sakkina, 'Hamid the Knife' (SIR 180 1909: 3). Hamid had held the office since at least 1905 (SIR 127 1905: 3), and together with his close friend and traditional ally, Mek Rehal of Kadugli, had provided the most effective support for Anglo-Egyptian power over the wider region. The chief means of enforcing this power were so-called punitive patrols, which punished either the non-payment of tribute to the British or internecine raids by one hill community on another. Punitive patrols were the only response that the British could see to a spiralling series of misunderstandings between themselves and the Nuba communities. A SIR of 1908 had already stuck its finger into the wound:

> When we took over the country, the Nubas agreed to pay tribute, and with few exceptions are ready to do so now, but they regard tribute as

> payment to Government for protection against Arab raids, and refuse to
> give up raiding other Nuba hills or to surrender the prisoners or cattle
> taken, or to pay blood money for people killed. ... As things are at pres-
> ent, we have stopped the Arabs raiding for slaves, but by making the
> plains secure for the Nubas we have opened the way to their doing more
> raiding than ever. (SIR 165 1908: 31)

Participation as 'Friendlies' consisted of contingents of local warriors fighting for the colonial authorities under the direct command
of their own local chiefs. As early as February 1905, Hamid the Knife
was leading his young men, on the government side, in a punitive patrol against the Nuba of Shat (SIR 127 1905: 3), and again in December 1908 against the Nuba of Nyimang (SIR 173 1908: 16). When
Fiki Ali succeeded his brother in July 1909, he continued this policy
of cooperation. Thus, in April 1910, he joined a government punitive
patrol against the Nuba of Moro (SIR 188 1910: 6) and, within a
month, against those of Dagig (SIR 189 1910: 6).

Fiki Ali's collaborationist zeal, however, had gone even further than
this, for he overplayed his cards vis-à-vis the other regional chiefs. In
May 1914, when the Anglo-Egyptian army wished to recruit about
fifty Nuba men for a newly formed company of Nuba Territorials at
Kadugli, Fiki Ali alone provided thirty of these from among his own
subjects, choosing mostly former slaves (Historical Records n.d.: 4).
This was all the more remarkable as even the most senior collaborationist chief at the time, Mek Rehal of Kadugli, had 'made his men
swear they would not enlist in the company' (Historical Records n.d.:
5). Ironically, these Miri slave soldiers would assume a key role in the
suppression of Fiki Ali's revolt, and they are one of the reasons given
by the official intelligence of SIR. Clearly, the discourse of power was
in dire straits at the time.

It is nothing new, of course, that collaborators can mutate overnight into heroes of resistance. This usually happens immediately
upon the announcement of liberation from occupation. Fiki Ali's
rebellion, however, was a special case. His volte-face from an exceptionally cooperative ally to an exceptionally fierce rebel threatened
to become a huge embarrassment to the discourse of power. Faced
with such implausibility, even the discourse of power had to search for
causes to explain the inexplicable. The key passage is provided by the
SIR of April 1915 (details in Baumann 2012).

The convoluted official explanation, however, suggests also that
Fiki Ali 'took advantage of the substitution of taxes for tribute' (SIR
249 1915: 4). The brevity of the remark merits expansion, as it may
help us understand the widespread support that Fiki Ali received.

The people of the Miri Hills, like most of their neighbours in surrounding districts, had been obliged to pay tribute both to the Turco-Egyptian administration of the Sudan (officially ca 1820 to 1870) and to the Mahdist rulers (officially 1881 to 1898). Any tribute obligations, however, had been utterly fictitious: the Turco-Egyptian and Mahdist states alike simply collected their tribute surpluses by making raids for cattle and/or slaves. The Anglo-Egyptian administration, however, demanded peaceable payments in cattle or grain, handed over by the chiefs for each group in its entirety. By 1912, the administration was receiving 'all Nuba tribute, with one exception, in cash' (SIR 215 1912: 6). The spread of cash payments facilitated the introduction of direct and personal taxation, which was to replace collective tribute. The introduction of taxation, however, came at a time of serious economic crisis. Thus in July 1915, that is, four months after Fiki Ali began his rebellion, even SIR had to admit that:

> Trade is practically at a standstill. Grain has in some parts been selling at 7 and 8 piastres for the ardeb of 300 rotls, and there seems little prospect of the people now being able to pay their taxes, owing to the almost total absence of money. (SIR 252 1915: 7)

As we therefore turn from the British discourse of power to Miri collective representations, it is crucial to abandon any assumption of discursive symmetry. True, the British discourse of power had to explain why a collaborator would suddenly turn into a rebel, but all gaps in the explanation could be filled by popular collective representations such as the vain and irrational native potentate. The Miri, by contrast, had to mobilize alternative collective representations to endow Fiki Ali with unquestionable legitimacy and an unbroken consistency as their chief both before and after his decision to rebel.

Subaltern Collective Representations: 'Ages Ago, There Was a Day When...' (How a Discourse of Power Can Be Neutralized by Mythologizing Agency)

The Miri's traditions of Fiki Ali do not recognize a change of allegiance. Rather, Fiki Ali acted in the Miri's interest before the rebellion, and in the Miri's interest by means of his rebellion. The problem thus vanishes in an alternative interpretation of Miri history and chieftainship.

Until long after Fiki Ali's rebellion, government control over Miri people's affairs was limited to three domains of operation. These were the appointment of chiefs (Sheikh and Mek, later also Omda), the suppression of civil and particularly intertribal violence, and the imposition of tribute and later tax. The former, the recognition or imposition of local authorities, was so confused that nobody could ever know which chief was paramount over any other. The second, as we have seen, consisted in relabelling proven raiders into loyal Friendlies continuing their raids under a new, British flag. The third, as we have seen, was an economic disaster. Concurrently, the presence of the Anglo-Egyptian army was confined to Talodi, Dilling and Kadugli, and its capacity was fully taken up by punitive patrols despatched in cases of civil violence and refusals to pay tribute. Raids by Nuba groups on other Nuba groups, which had become a constant in the economic and value system of most communities, continued to present endless problems to administrative and military control. In Miri understandings, none of the three operative controls amounted to a negation of tribal independence. The imposition of chiefs, potentially the most awkward innovation, might have shaken Miri beliefs in their own independence. However, official appointments were often little more than the recognition of local faits accomplis, and succession was often left to local decisions based on genealogical rights and the personal aptitude of candidates.

In Miri, a recognizable chieftainship is likely to date only back to the time of the Mahdist insurgency, whose conquest of the Miri Hills lasted from around 1884 until its defeat in 1898 at the hands of Britain's 'Lord Kitchener of Khartoum'. This new office was likely established to rival the power of the pre-Muslim authorities known as rainpriests or *tabogek*. The first chief of all Miri, resident in Miri Bara, is named as Almi, the father of the subsequent chief or Mek Hamid Abu Sakkina (Hamid the Knife) and of his younger successor, Fiki Ali Almi. While the original appointment was most probably due to Mahdist intervention, the Miri Hills having been conquered during the 1880s, Miri oral tradition locates the advent of chiefly office in a mythical past that shows no trace of Turco-Egyptian or Mahdist penetration. The story of Almi is told in a number of variants, three of which I shall relate here verbatim:

> Our ancestor Jigarani was found in the forest by the daughter of the old rainpriest (*tabogek*). She led him to her house, and there he told her that he had come from the West. She gave him sesame seeds, but he had never seen any! He stayed in her house, and he made her pregnant. Later on, he became powerful, even more powerful than his father-in-law, the rainpriest. (Mohammed Kafi, rainpriest, Tugo ward, Miri Bara, November 1978)

> Some people say that Almi was found in a basket floating on the stream. This is wrong; he was found as a baby, lying on an ant-hill. When peo-

ple found him, they slaughtered a white ox for him, because they were afraid of him: he looked different from them. Almi is his Arabic name; in Miri he was called Modu, and his original name was Jugaras. He was taken into the house of the rainpriest, and when he grew up he married the rainpriest's daughter. He begat Masi, who then begat Fiki Ali. Masi had a brother called Hamid who became the first chief. He was called Hamid Abu Sakkina. (Hasaneen Jerad, Sindo ward, Miri Bara, February 1979)

One day, people went to the forest, and they found a huge animal that they had never seen before. Maybe it was a horse. They killed it. Then Almi came out of the bushes, and cried that he used to ride on the animal. How could they kill it? And how would he continue his journey? They took him to the village and put him in the rainpriest's house. He made the rainpriest's daughter pregnant and had to marry her. They produced a son who was called Modu the Sheikh. His two sons, Hamid and Fiki Ali, both wanted to succeed him as chief after his death. (Mohammed Haroon, farmer, Tugo ward, Miri Bara, March 1979)

The stories present a remarkable amalgam of what appear to be references to an earlier immigration of a Western population, the institution of rainpriests and more recent events, all of which combine in the familiar mould of the Myth of the Wise Stranger as it occurs in many parts of the Western Sudan (Holt 1963). Although this is not the place to attempt to disentangle its elements, it is clear that Miri oral tradition does not view chieftainship as a as an imposition by conquering powers, and that it understands Fiki Ali's tenure of office as a matter of local custom and consent. Anglo-Egyptian control through government-approved chiefs has thus been expunged from Miri myth. However, the new government's other assertions of power – the levying of tributes and later taxes, as well as the ban on inter-tribal raiding – were too effective and conspicuous to disappear into oblivion. Instead, both impositions were interpreted as agreements freely concluded between two willing and equal parties. 'The English', so one might paraphrase the refrain of the statements from villagers, 'came to rule us, but they needed us'.

To the Miri, the lost freedom to raid on their own was fully replaced by participation in government patrols, which they had engaged in since at least 1905, when Fiki Ali's predecessor realized that raiding on the 'good' side was all that was required to turn a breach of the peace into the maintenance of public order. Although looting was prohibited on these punitive patrols, well-behaved Friendlies could expect to be compensated for their troubles with cattle and forfeited property. Without much doubt, one may surmise that the many benefits of cooperation in what was seen as the governmental protection racket included the occasional taking of slaves.

This understanding also clearly removed any doubts as to Fiki Ali's allegiance. To the Miri, he was not a collaborator turned rebel, but the hero of an effectively independent community that, for its own benefit, allied itself to the government of the day so long as that government treated it as an equal.

Needless to say, certain grave difficulties attend my juxtaposition of British official sources and Miri renderings of a mythical story. Do not the Miri remember the 'real', the 'historical' Fiki Ali? The answer is no. They do not, and there are several reasons to stress this discursive asymmetry. The first is that I am not the only researcher unsettled by it. Ahmed Uthman Muhammad Ibrahim, who researched the Fiki Ali story around the same time I did, in the early 1980s, was unlucky, as 'much of ... the archive of Kadugli district [had] already been destroyed by white ants' (Ibrahim 1985: 16). He was lucky, however, to find an old man named Rahhal Hasan Yahia who had been 'a personal friend of faki "Ali Wad Wad Almi"', as he arabicized Fiki Ali Almi's name. Let us see, then, what the old friend remembered:

> His father was known to be a Ja'ali who settled in the Miri hills. [n. 9: Wad Almi literally means the son of water. One of the Miri traditions relates that Ali's father, unlike other human beings, originated from a pool of water, and not from human parents. He was collected and adopted by Kafe Miri, the elder son of the eponymous father of the tribe. Ali, who is actually Wad Almi's son and himself is called Wad Almi, is also entitled as 'faki', holy man (Rahhal's personal account).] Wad Almi, as Ali's father was known at Miri, married one of the mak Kafe Miri's daughters. The couple had a number of sons, Hamid Abu Sikkin, Ali (faki) ... and others. When mak Kafe died, he was succeeded by Hamid Abu Sikkin who was succeeded by faki Ali on his death. ... (Ibrahim 1985: 16)

The oral history that Ibrahim (1985) secured from a surviving friend of Fiki Ali's bears an uncanny resemblance to the seemingly mythical accounts I collected from Miri villagers who had never met the rebel in person. Ibrahim also found that 'the story of faki Ali as related by his tribe, Miri, is more mythical than historical', and he raises an intriguing hypothesis:

> His personality is sketched by the stories about him as being almost like a Greek God, who would sometimes come down to earth to interact with human beings and then elevate himself to the sacred world beyond the reach of mere mortals. However, these irrational stories were believed by that simple community. Millenarianism can do miracles in primitive societies and faki Ali was undoubtedly a determined millenarian, with many blind believers around him. (Ibrahim 1985: 16)

Admittedly, I see no evidence of Fiki Ali as a millenarian leader, although he was certainly among the first generation of part-time converts to Islam, a religion learned next to the Miri's own religion, which persisted until the 1980s. Yet Ibrahim is doubtless right that the rebel must have combined the authority of a charismatic discourse with the discourse of power granted him as a mek or 'king' of the Miri, recognized by the colonial authorities no less than by his own people. Given this much convergence between Ibrahim's (1985) analysis and my own, let me try to address our one remaining difference, the vision of 'primitive societies [believing] irrational stories' or of 'a simple community [made up of] many blind believers' (Ibrahim 1985: 16).

The Miri, in my unequivocal conclusion, are world champions at not remembering historical facts when they do not want to, and this amnesia is by no means limited to the case of Fiki Ali. British intelligence knew full well that Miri had been conquered by the Mahdist troops:

> Under the Dervish regime, most of the hills were attacked by the Dervish armies; some, as Jebel Nyima, beat off the attacks with heavy losses, and some were conquered by force, as Jebel Ghulfan, or by treachery, as Jebel Miri. (SIR 186 1910: Appendix A, later published as Sagar 1922)

The doyen of Nuba Mountains linguistics and historiography, the late Roland Stevenson, even found an oral history account of the fact:

> in the Miri range (south-west of Kadugli) the chiefs and elders, having been induced to come down [from their hills], were captured, and the then disorganized hills were attacked. I have been told by an old woman of Kafina (near the southern edge of Miri) that Mahmud's army stormed and burnt her village at dawn, carrying her and many other villagers off, with captives from other hills, to El Odaiya, where they were apportioned among the army leaders before being marched off to Omdurman; she, like so many others, remained there until able to return home after its fall [to the British under Kitchener] in 1898.

The mention of Mahmud is bound to refer to Madhmud Wad Ahmed, who, according to Holt (1958: 213), swept across Kordofan towards the end of 1896.

The facts seem indisputable and entirely consistent across all available sources, yet no single Miri person I ever spoke to knew anything about this, with one exception: the old *tabogek* of Miri Bara, a rain-priest in his late eighties in the late 1970s, who had been abducted to Omdurman as a toddler. His memories were vague, but the fact, though preserved in his honorary nickname, was to Miri villagers *tumma ma bilí* (literally, 'word of the past').

All questions about dating, chronology and even genealogies only ever received one reply: in Arabic, a long, drawn-out *kan zamaaaan!*; in Miri language (*timirii*), an equally elongated *e biliii*, both meaning 'ages ago'. Engaging with the past does not, among Miri villagers, produce chronologies or history as opposed to myth. Rather, it produces, in Miri language: '*tumma ma bilí*', translated into Arabic as '*kalaam min zamaan*' and sometimes even translated into the Arabic word '*tariikh*'. Yet *tumma ma bilí* is not what English speakers mean by 'history' or what Arabic speakers mean by *tariikh*. *Tumma ma bilí* encompasses any number of ways of speaking of past events, ranging from the interpretation of recent events one has witnessed, to descriptions of past events one has not witnessed, to narratives that most ethnologists will readily call 'myths'. The discourse of *tumma ma bilí* concerns things of old (*ema ma bilí*, usually *emabilí*), and within that discourse, relative age, dates and chronology are irrelevant, and indeed absent.

It is not uncommon, of course, for either oral history or myth to show the 'condensing effect' that seems to push together events separated by long periods of time. There is nothing 'primitive' about this. Portelli (2010) studied the phenomenon in the oral histories of turbulently industrialized people in Italy and the United States, which push events closer together to make sense by orienting them around one crisis point in time. Interestingly, for the rebel's case, Portelli relates this to literacy having taken over the task of precise timing, thus liberating oral history from the dictates of the historical clock. This was tricky with the Miri, as even in the late 1970s, only a handful of villagers were just semi-literate, though a few Miri-born labour migrants were functionally literate. Yet no Miri I know even knows of a written account of Fiki Ali. Pace Portelli, one might expect Ibrahim's written chronology to have influenced the time management of the oral traditions, yet the myths in the genre of *tumma ma bilí* may well survive intact by self-generating ongoing transformations. Portelli's analyses seem plausible enough for the four oral histories about Fiki Ali, which proceed in one fell swoop from an ancient foundation myth to the relatively recent personages of Fiki Ali and his father and brother. Yet *tumma ma bilí* not only compresses events in time but also expands them beyond any narrative logic. I think it is an ethnocentric half-truth that the lack of chronology is due to condensing events in time. Rather, time does not even enter into *tumma ma bilí*: this discourse is not anachronistic within time, but a-chronic, that is, essentially without time. To clarify the difference, consider this *tumma ma bilí* account of how the Miri Bara chiefly office went from Tamuiu and later Bandás of the clan Kadoómfa to Suleman Tia of the clan Kafík:

> Kadoómfa and Kabolo were the first clans to settle here. Kafík only came third. But Kadoómfa and Kabolo only produced women, and Kafík only produced men. So the older clans lost their power since women went to live with their husbands and their husbands' clans. So the office of

Tamuiu and Bandás went to Suleman Tia who is Kafík. (Mohammed Tia, rainpriest, Miri Bara, January 1979)

At first sight, the story may resemble a myth of great age. It in fact concerns the succession to chiefly office in 1967, that is, twelve years before the telling of the story. The teller knew full well that the succession was decided by a long process of consultation, that the original three clans had been joined by five others over countless generations, and that the time between Bandás's death and Suleman Tia's succession was decennia or even centuries too short for Bandás's clan to be reduced to women only. In fact, the teller was a man in his best years when Bandás was chief and an authoritative old man when Suleman Tia was elected as the new chief, thus transferring of legitimacy to the best man from a clan not legitimized by descent. The story thus not only 'telescopes' the time between the first settlement of clan Kafík and the chiefly election of twelve years ago; it also expands time infinitely to accommodate the disappearance of Kadoómfa men. The explanation, however, is in the discourse of *tumma ma bilí*, and in that discourse, time does not matter. *Bilí*, the past, is both timeless without (as in: 'once upon a time') and timeless within: it is not about sequences in time, but about logics regardless of time.

Subaltern collective representations that transcend chronological time can also transcend, by that mechanism alone, any memory of powerlessness and even guilt or shame in the face of past events. One could go so far as to call *tumma ma bilí* not merely a genre of collective representations, as I have done, but indeed a discourse of anti-power, or better, an anti-discourse to power if that power is assumed to have been illegitimate and imposed by brute outside forces alone. Many full-fledged anti-colonial revolutions, after all, were built upon similar myth-style transformations that stripped the world of its temporal nature, turning Mao into the heir of Confucius and Jesus into the heir of King David.

A Discourse of Power Disempowered: 'The Honour of an Englishman' (How Dysfunctional Power Turns Personal Agency into a Mutual Virtue)

Let me adduce, then, a third discourse of power: a discourse disempowered, which must mean a discourse entirely dependent on appealing to collective and/or popular representations. This account of the Fiki Ali story (history, myth or fiction), written by H.C. Jackson, formerly of the Sudan Political Service, paints the British myth of Fiki Ali as told to the nearly post-imperial British public of the mid 1950s.

British myth requires realistic settings, so Jackson provides a scenic backdrop to the story he wishes to unfold. In the ever-restless arena of Sudan, the Nuba are yet 'another turbulent tribe' (Jackson 1955: 170) but one 'possessing in full that independence and virility which are so often found in mountain tribes' (173). Nature itself made their habitat a landscape of defiance and awe: their hills were 'honey-combed with caves in which the Nuba found natural fortresses' (170), and were covered by a vegetation that despite its sparseness included 'several bushes of which the juice is extracted for poisoning arrows' (170). Living, as they were, in 'caves and natural fortifications where ease of defense was a temptation to defiance' (171), it was hardly sur-prising that they felt 'mistrustful of any form of Government' (171). Here it is clear that H.C. Jackson had read the same Sudan Intelli-gence Reports we have discussed in this chapter: the formulations are the same, down to the top Sir's 'dislike of any Government control' (Wingate 1916: 6). Yet the spirit would soon turn different. Admit-tedly, with their history of 'misery, insecurity and bloodshed' (Jackson 1955: 61), it was 'not to be expected that they would submit to the authority of a new Government without prolonged resistance' (173). This expectation of a quasi-innate defiance was wise, not least since it deflected attention from the questions of the legitimacy and efficiency of the government in power.

Just as the old official sources make little of Fiki Ali's previous co-operation with the 'new' government, so Jackson, too, observes a po-lite silence on the reasons for the rebellion. Somewhat laconically, he records that 'at the beginning of 1915, a patrol was dispatched against the Mek, or King, of Jebel Miri – one Fiki Ali who had defied the Government and taken up arms against it' (Jackson 1955: 175). The history of the rebellion is thus independent of the history of colonial administration; rather, it forms an integral and unavoidable part of the Nuba's collective nature of defiance.

History thus safely put to one side, and collective representations smuggled in on the other, the myth may be developed in the spirit of good sportsmanship. Jackson's tale recounts the siege at Jebel Tuluk and surrender of most of the rebels, and reports Fiki Ali's first escape, arrest and death sentence at Talodi. The rebel's second escape and subsequent pursuit build up to what in Jackson's account forms the climax of the rebellion: the negotiation that led to Fiki Ali's surrender. Described in colourful detail, this negotiation merits quotation at length:

> On the appointed day [the Acting Governor, Frank] Balfour and Major Conran, O.C. of a detachment of the XIth Sudanese, with a party of between ten and twenty mounted police, rode to the rendezvous, carrying before them the flags of Great Britain and Egypt, to emphasise the official nature of their visit. The meeting-place was in an open watercourse and here Balfour and Conran sat down on two deck-chairs to await developments; but at the last minute Fiki Ali and his followers became suspicious and feared treachery. ... Fiki Ali could not bring himself to believe that one British officer and one British official would dare to come with an escort of so few police into the middle of a hostile force. There must, he felt, be a catch somewhere.
>
> However, in order to reassure the rebels, the police escort was ordered to retire to a distance of a quarter of a mile, leaving Balfour and Conran alone, with a rifle pointing at them from behind every rock. Then, ostentatiously laying down his revolver, Conran went forward to where, half a mile ahead, Fiki Ali could be seen waiting to receive him; while Balfour ... made a similar gesture of goodwill and sat unarmed in his chair.
>
> The spectacle of one British officer putting his head into the lion's maw and another official sitting calmly in a deck-chair appealed to the Nuba's sense of the ludicrous. Fiki Ali agreed to negotiate with Balfour and, with 50 of his relatives, was induced to surrender. Soon a pile of arms was stacked in front of Balfour, and Fiki Ali was sent to Khartoum to receive whatever punishment the Government should inflict upon him. (Jackson 1955: 178–79)

No shortened quotation could do justice to this skilfully painted tableau: the encounter of two officers-and-gentlemen faced with, and disarming, the confirmed rebel would at one time have made for a civic mural. What is more, the mural retains its forceful morale: 'On recalling this episode I have often wondered at the amazing confidence put in the Englishman's word. ... The honour of an Englishman still counts for something when such an incident is possible' (Jackson 1955: 180). Whether reality availed itself of this possibility is doubtful. According to Balfour's own account, the sketched encounter took place but relied on a go-between who could not have been more carefully chosen: a certain 'Mohammed Shayeb, whose father was an Arab, and mother a Miri Nuba' (Balfour 1951: 12).

Though Jackson can be readily forgiven for making little of the prosaic figure of a go-between, his summary of Fiki Ali's personal fate nonetheless exceeds the bonds of mythological licence. The public is assured that 'as a matter of fact, after a short detention in Khartoum, Fiki Ali was allowed to go back to his home, where he proved a loyal servant of the Government' (Jackson 1955: 180). The matter is less one of fact than one of myth, a myth of fair winners and good losers, a myth of colonial warfare as a higher form of cricket. In Jackson's version Fiki Ali is both reprieved and reformed. His reprieve would appear to show the British as fair winners who bear no grudge against their adversaries; his reformation would indicate that the Nuba, however rebellious, are good losers who know when they are beaten. Indeed, Jackson makes both myths explicit. As to the former, it is known, of course, that 'the British have a great admiration for those, of whatever race or colour, who can "put up a good show" against them'. Witness only 'the Nigerian soccer team in bare feet challenging some of our prominent football clubs' (181).

Just as they are assured of their well-shod patrons' applause, so Fiki Ali too is forgiven with a smile of recognition: 'Even the most law-abiding amongst us cannot fail to be impressed by the enterprise and ingenuity shown by this mountain rebel' (Jackson 1955: 178). Such fairness is not reserved to the outstanding rebel, but generously granted to all: 'In spite of the trouble caused by the Nuba, most British officers and officials who had to deal with them liked them immensely, and admired them for their bravery and for their spirit of adventure often expressed in strange ways' (173).

The Nuba themselves, on the other hand. are worthy of such fair play, as they in turn are good losers. Thus, not only does Fiki Ali become a faithful subject of the government, but his followers too undergo a similar conversion, as witnessed by the rebels interned at Talodi. After their capture, they were ordered to re-thatch the government buildings and barracks at Talodi; on this occasion, one could watch

> with amusement the activities of one of Fiki Ali's cousins, who was foreman of a gang of rebels. Perched upon the roof of a house, he drove the labourers harder than Pharaoh ever worked the Israelites. ... But only a few weeks had passed since the foreman had cut up the body of a Nuba (fortunately dead) who was friendly to the Government, and sent the bits round to neighbouring villages. (Jackson 1955: 179–80)

Apart from abandoning such savage habits, the rebel and his men had learnt not to 'resent their sudden change of fortune', and 'threw themselves wholeheartedly into the task of re-thatching ... the barracks of the troops who had, a short time ago, been fighting against them, and who might in the near future be called upon to do so once more' (Jackson 1955: 170). Granted so much cricket spirit, the mythologist could be forgiven for hearing resounding echoes of Sir Henry Newbolt's classic poem celebrating the cricket spirit as applied to another field of honour, that of dying for one's country or empire.[3]

The historian's record, fortunately, may diverge from the rules of battlefield sportsmanship, and this defiance of mythological convention will lend a twist of its own to the results of the rebellion. Playing the positivist for one last moment, I feel safer now in following the discourse of power of SIR, not least because it speaks against itself.

Positivist Self-Ironies to Welcome Durkheim Back from Sudan: Collective Representations, Discourses of Power and Personal Agency

Two positivist versions relate where Fiki Ali spent the rest of his life and when he died, and for once they are compatible. Ibrahim states that he was 'allowed to go to Kadugli (approx. 1926)' but 'was then moved to Dalanj [Dilling in the Northern Nuba Mountains] to live as an internee of the district commissioner till he died in 1936' (Ibrahim 1985: 19). According to SIR, he was detained in Khartoum, Halfa and Omdurman for more than five years, and in July 1922 was transferred 'to Talodi where quarters have been assigned to him. He arrived in July, accompanied by his brother, Idris, who had been on a visit to Khartoum' (SIR 336 1922: 4). This brother Idris, however, had been second-in-command in the rebellion; it was he who had led the rebels during Fiki Ali's first detention and trial (SIR 253 1915: 4). It was not least through his efforts that Fiki Ali had been able, after his escape from trial, to rejoin a viable fighting band and hold out for another five months. Idris had shared his brother's exile at Khartoum, but was released in, or before, 1920. In April of the same year, the two hundred rebels who had been detained at Talodi since 1915 were also freed and repatriated (SIR 310 1920: 5). After a few assassinations (SIR 270 1916: 3) and a 'snake bite' aimed at a rival collaborator, a new incumbent was soon found and officially recognized as Mek in November 1920. It was none other than Idris Almi, brother of Fiki Ali Almi and formerly his comrade-in-arms and second-in-command of the Miri rebellion (SIR 316 1920: 4).

With even a positivist history offering such gifts of irony, it remains only to pull together some of the threads of this argument about collective representations placed in the good company of discourses of power, and the power of personal agency.

The analytic idea of collective representations appears, at first blush, to imply that it is societies or, if you are backward, cultures that provide the prime parameters of all meaningful agency or lack of it. In some ways, this is indisputable: the mother of any agency is social

classification, and classification in turn is the progeny of collective representations. Such collective representations are indeed, as Durkheim
does not tire of restating time and again, socially constructed. But
what does Durkheim actually mean when he speaks of society as the
bedrock, the font and creator of collective representations? It may
be worth glancing back at a little-known passage of *The Elementary
Forms of the Religious Life*: 'What society is it that has thus made the
basis of religion?' Durkheim tests his reader: 'Is it the real society,
such as it is and acts before our very eyes ...?' The answer is negative:
'society is not an empirical fact, definite and observable'; instead, it
is something 'in which [we] have never really lived. It is merely an
idea ...' (1971 [1915]: 420). Durkheim's theory of society as the basis
of religion and, a fortiori, of all less far-fetched collective representations, applies to an abstract essence of society, closer perhaps to what
nowadays we call sociability or sociality, and certainly far removed
from any society in the empirical sense, as in 'this society' or even 'that
culture'. To reduce Durkheim's theorem of social facts to any particular society, empirically observable and positivistically describable, is to
fall victim to misplaced concreteness. The same applies to the misunderstanding that collective representations are collective in the sense
of being empirically unanimous, shared without doubt, prevarication
or dissent by all the actors in any given society or culture. What is collective about collective representations is that they are social by their
nature, and precisely that social nature makes them negotiable in any
empirically given society.

At Durkheim's most exultant level of abstraction, there is nothing
much to discuss, for all categories, classifications and collective representations are socially constructed, much à la Berger and Luckmann
(1966), who are better Durkheimians than Durkheim ever was. We
can, however, go even further by asking 'Our' Emile (as well as Rousseau's, whom he admired) to agree that every anti-discourse of resistance and even the concept of personal agency itself are themselves
social constructions. Durkheim would certainly agree.

Yet let us observe his own caveat quoted above: his concept of 'society is not an empirical fact [but] merely an idea' (1971 [1915]: 420).
Neither Durkheim the philosopher nor Durkheim the ethnographer,
nor indeed Durkheim the Jewish intellectual in an anti-Semitic society, could ever conceive of an empirical society without dissidents
or rebels placing themselves outside the ruling and 'average' collective representations. True, dissidents may have to express their new
alternatives by means of the ruling old collective representations (as
Durkheim did when establishing sociology as a science within a then

scientistic Sorbonne). But it is also true that Durkheim's own power of agency could never be reduced to an echo or shadow of some 'average' collective representations. Durkheim's collective representations are neither tribally primitivist nor nationally totalitarian. In modern parlance, his collective representations are the foil upon which, and against which, we have to project our personal social agency.

At this less exalted and thus more interesting level of abstraction, collective representations are therefore not collective in any all-encompassing tribalist or totalitarian sense, but are instead influential, whether rendered so by the agency of elites claiming hegemony, by their sheer taken-for-granted popularity or by counter-elites composed of rethinkers, rebels or revolutionaries. This is not what Durkheim alluded to, with his 'average' member of society defining which representations are collective and which individual. All representations are social representations at the most abstract level; some or even many representations are popular, or at least pervasive, in one society or another, one context or another. Some representations can be found popular by, and even work pervasively on, almost everyone: gender, seniority, power, honour and shame, perhaps truth – not to mention the media. Yet even these are not doxa, but 'collective' merely in the sense of being popular or pervasive. What, then, of discourses of power?

Discourses of power – aka dominant discourses, hegemonic discourses, Master Narratives (call them what you will) – are created, perpetuated, refined and instrumentalized by sleeper cells of elites striving to be recognized as real elites, that is, precisely the dross who controlled Durkheim's 'average' members of society. Controls by discourses of power are much cheaper and less messy than running a police state, and they are far more effective too, in that they hold out the promise of silent and taken-for-granted consent from those whom they control. Discourses of power rely on empowering certain hegemonic or counter-hegemonic representations and discrediting other hegemonic or counter-hegemonic representations. The most successful discourses of power are those that the 'average' member of society can internalize into his or her very personhood: 'the faith', 'our nation', 'democracy', 'individuality' and 'agency' may be current examples, not to forget 'the economy', 'the terrorists' and (indistinguishably) 'the market'.

My argument, then, can be summarized as a set of interrelations within the conceptual triad. These interrelations form a triple helix in both routine and non-routine interactions. In routine interactions, one recognizes the obvious: discourses of power deploy craftily selected collective representations to control personal agency, and personal

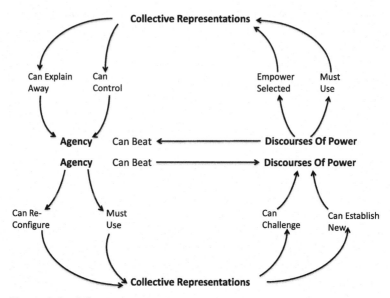

Figure 9.1. Collective representations.

agency must (re-)invent alternative collective representations to defy the powers that be. In non-routine constellations, personal agency can sometimes defeat ruling discourses of power, if it makes crafty use of pre-existing or alternative collective representation. In such cases genre does not matter, be it classified by contending parties as 'history', 'myth' or 'faction': however incommensurable the accounts may seem to be at first, one can glimpse the mutual mechanisms of social, cultural and incipient or long-lasting cognitive changes that are very much a Durkheimian trademark. Perhaps this helps to rehabilitate the prima facie blanket notion of 'collective representations' by differentiating its analytic ambit from its self-limitations.

Notes

We wish jointly to acknowledge gratitude to the bilingual journal *ERQ* (*Etnografia e ricerca qualitative/Ethnography and Qualitative Research*), its editor, Gianmarco Navarini, and its publisher, Il Mulino (Milan), for permitting this partial reprint from *ERQ* 2012(3). The complete ethnographic details can be found there, along with readers' comments, at www.mulino.it/edizioni

   1. The challenge of the title was formulated first by Prof. Thomas Fillitz at a European Association of Social Anthropologists (EASA) Summer School at the University of Vienna. The archival research was graciously

supported by the Sudan Archive at the University of Durham. Crown copyright of documents in the The National Archives, London, is granted by H.M. Permission. My especial thanks go to *ERQ*. As most relevant Sudanese archives were destroyed by termites or war (see Ibrahim 1985), I had sworn to myself that I would never publish this without including all the data that are still knowable. *ERQ*, its editor Prof. Gianmarco Navarini and *ERQ*'s excellent anonymous peer reviewers made this possible and better, and the fine rebel Fiki Ali would be proud of them.

2. I have largely limited the term discourse to verbal data, although I agree with Lutz and Abu-Lughod on a much wider definition (1990; see Baumann 1996). Laclau and Mouffe (2001) would want better, but the historical distance from the archival data and my argumentative purpose must determine theoretical choices. To test the notion of collective representations for its possible rest-value, I must prefer the ethnographic labyrinth of three incommensurate discourses to the labyrinths of epistemology, even at the price of sometimes playing positivist. All three discourses (indeed four, as I must include my own) revolve around alternative hegemonies, and in that sense I am a little more Gramscian than some post-Gramscians.

3. The poem moves by metaphor and metonymy from the cricket field of a public school to the battlefields of the empire and back again to the elite school as the mother of imperial manliness:

> VITAÏ LAMPADA
> There's a breathless hush in the Close to-night –
> Ten to make and the match to win –
> A bumpy pitch and a blinding light,
> An hour to play and the last man in.
> And it's not for the sake of a ribboned coat,
> Or the selfish hope of a season's fame,
> But his Captain's hand on his shoulder smote-
> "Play up! play up! and play the game!"
>
> The sand of the desert is sodden red, –
> Red with the wreck of a square that broke; –
> The Gatling's jammed and the Colonel dead,
> And the regiment blind with dust and smoke.
> The river of death has brimmed his banks,
> And England 's far, and Honour a name,
> But the voice of a schoolboy rallies the ranks:
> "Play up! play up! and play the game!"
> ...
> (Newbolt, Sir Henry 1940 [1892])

I owe this reference to my finest teacher, the enlightened post-Durkheimian Godfrey Lienhardt. It was published in 1892 and soon became school literature for most of the people we have met in this chapter or their successors: in spirit General Gordon who first claimed the Sudan and Lord Kitchener who 're'-conquered it in 1898; by chronology Governor-General Wingate who ruled it, the officers Balfour and Conran who dealt with Fiki Ali and wrote the SIR reports, as well as later sources such as Henderson.

References

Appadurai, A. 1993. 'Number in the Colonial Imagination', in C. Brecken-ridge and P. van der Veer (eds), *Orientalism and the Postcolonial Predicament: Perspectives on South Asia.* Pittsburgh: University of Pennsylvania Press, pp. 314–40.

Balfour, F.C.C. 1951. *Fiki Ali.* Unpublished typescript, Sudan Archive, University of Durham, Box 303/8.

Baumann, G. 1986. *National Integration and Local Integrity: The Miri of the Nuba Mountains in the Sudan.* Oxford: Clarendon Press.

———. 1996. *Contesting Culture: Discourses of Identity in Multi-Ethnic London.* Cambridge: Cambridge University Press.

———. 2012. 'Collective Representations, Discourses of Power, and Personal Agency: Three Incommensurate Histories of a Collaborator's Rebellion in the Colonial Sudan', *ERQ (Etnografia e ricerca qualitative/Ethnography and Qualitative Research)* 3: 393–422.

Berger, P. and T. Luckmann. 1966. *The Social Construction of Reality.* London: Anchor Books.

Durkheim, E. 1971 [1915]. *The Elementary Forms of the Religious Life,* trans. J.W. Swain. London: George Allen and Unwin.

Historical Records. n.d. *Historical Records Nuba Territorial Company.* Anonymous typescript, Sudan Archive, University of Durham, Box 106/5.

Holt, P.M. 1958. *The Mahdist State in the Sudan 1881–1898.* Oxford: Clarendon Press.

———. 1963. 'Funj Origins: A Critique and New Evidence', *Journal of African History* 4(1): 39–55.

Ibrahim, A.U.M. 1985. *The Dilemma of British Rule in the Nuba Mountains 1989–1947.* Khartoum: Graduate College Publications no. 15, University of Khartoum.

Jackson, H.C. 1955. *Behind the Modern Sudan.* London: Macmillan.

Laclau, E. and C. Mouffe. 2001 [1985]. *Hegemony and Socialist Strategy: Towards a Radical Democratic Politics.* London: Verso.

Lutz, C. and L. Abu-Lughod. 1990. *Language and the Politics of Emotion.* Cambridge: Cambridge University Press.

MacMichael, H.A. 1934. *The Anglo-Egyptian Sudan.* London: Faber and Faber.

Newbolt, H. 1940. *Selected Poems of Henry Newbolt.* London: Thomas Nelson.

Portelli, A. 2010. *They Say in Harlan County: An Oral History.* Oxford: Oxford University Press.

Sagar, J.W. 1922. 'Notes on the History, Religion and Customs of the Nuba', *Suda Notes and Records* 5: 137–56.

SIR (Sudan Intelligence Reports). Most of these are archived at the Public Record Office (PRO), London, under files of the War Office (WO) or the Foreign Office (FO). Transcripts of Crown copyright records in the Public Record Office appear by permission of the Controller of Her Majesty's Stationery Office.

127, February 1905: PRO: WO 106-227

165, April 1908: PRO: WO 106-231

173, December 1908: ibid.

180, July 1909: PRO: WO 160-232

186, January 1910: PRO: WO 160-234, also in: FO 371/1111 and in: FO 371/1361

188, March 1910: ibid.

189, April 1910: ibid.

215, June 1912: PRO: FO 371/1636

248, March 1915: PRO: FO 371-2349

249, April 1915: ibid.

251, June 1915: ibid.

252, July 1915: ibid.

253, August 1915: ibid.

254, September 1915: ibid.

255, October 1915: ibid.

270, January 1916: London, Whitehall Library, Ministry of Defence

310, May 1920: PRO: WO 33/997

316, November 1920: ibid.

336, July 1922: ibid.

Wingate, R. 1916. 'Despatch by the Sirdar and Governor-General to War Office on Military Operations in Darfur, Together with a Brief Report on the Services of the Egyptian Army and the Sudanese Administration since the Outbreak of War in Europe', 8 August 1916, here quoted from copy sent by Sir Anthony McMahon, Cairo, to Viscount Grey of Fallodon on 20 August 1916. London: Public Record Office, FO 371-2671, Political. Egypt (War). Files 12178-42685. 1916.

Chapter 10

ACTANTS AMASSING (AA)

BEYOND COLLECTIVE EFFERVESCENCE AND THE SOCIAL

Adam Yuet Chau

In this chapter I propose a critique of the anthropocentric and socio-centric perspective prevalent in Durkheim's *The Elementary Forms of Religious Life* and subsequent studies of ritual life. Drawing insights from Bruno Latour's actor network theory and Deleuze and Guattari's concept of assemblage (*agencement*), I present a multi-actant ethnography of a temple festival in northern Taiwan that gives a proper place and voice (i.e. *actancy*) to non-human actants.

Bruno Latour has launched a persistent attack on the Durkheimian fetishization of the social, which in his view has unnecessarily limited the scope of investigation and misled the so-called *social* sciences down a benighted path (2005, 2010). This article is a response to Latour's call to de-privilege Durkheimian sociologism and to revive a Tardean understanding of 'society' as composed of not just humans as social agents but a multitude of actants both human and non-human, sentient and non-sentient, organic and inorganic, material and non-material, representable and unrepresentable. I propose the notion of 'actants amassing' (AA) to characterize the convergence of a multitude of actants in the same time-space. Just as Durkheim built the edifice and artifice of 'Society' and 'the social' upon the analysis of communal ritual life, so from it a deconstruction of this edifice and artifice should also proceed. On the other hand, Durkheim's focus on intense social co-presence points to a critique of Maussian exchangism that I argue has corrupted anthropology as badly as Durkheim's sociologism has corrupted sociology. So I will first 'kill' the uncle and then 'kill' the nephew with what is left of the uncle – a 'patricidal' attempt that is entirely justified, given the prevalence of disciplinary patricide in anthropology.

From Collective Effervescence to 'Society'

In *The Elementary Forms of Religious Life*, Durkheim expounded on the role the convergence of a large number of people plays in generating intense sociality (Durkheim 1915 [1912]: 245–52). For most of the year, Australian aborigines disperse into separate family units in search of food, but at regular intervals they gather into a larger group and celebrate as members of a totemic clan. The dispersed state is characterized by 'very mediocre intensity'; it is 'uniform, languishing and dull.' On the other hand, when the group comes together, 'everything changes'. Here is the famous and most pivotal passage in the entire text:

> The very fact of the concentration acts as an exceptionally powerful stimulant. When they are once come together, a sort of electricity is formed by their collecting which quickly transports them to an extraordinary degree of exaltation.... [W]hen arrived at this state of exaltation, a man does not recognize himself any longer.... [E]verything is just as though he really were transported into a special world, entirely different from the one where he ordinarily lives, and into an environment filled with exceptionally intense forces that take hold of him and metamorphose him. (1915 [1912]: 246–47, 249–50)

Durkheim characterized this intense sociality as 'collective effervescence'. He then proceeded to argue that this intense group feeling becomes feeling *for* the group, which is the affective and cognitive basis of the idea of capital-S 'Society'. He argued that the aboriginals, after being enthralled by small-s 'society' (i.e., the ritual gathering), came to construct and worship capital-S 'Society' via the conduit of totems. Likewise, all human groups came to construct and worship 'Society' via the conduit of one form of religion or another.

However, one may argue that it was not early humans but Durkheim who confused the two separate aspects of 'society/Society', though this confusion was most likely a deliberate conceptual sleight of hand consisting of two steps. First, Durkheim made out 'Society' as the ensemble of individuals circumscribed within a given territory as a cognitive entity, as an abstract 'idea'. Second, and ingeniously, he converted this abstract idea into a concrete entity that he could then enshrine as the true Republican God (*la République française*), having substituted 'Australian Aboriginal totemic society' with '(then Third Republic) French society'. This conceptual conversion process can be summarized schematically as follows: concrete (Australian aboriginal totemic ritual) –> abstract ('Society' with capital 'S') –> concrete (*la République Française*).

The conceptual construction of Society was important for Durkheim's moral-political programme of constructing (French) Society (based on organic solidarity) and his professional programme of constructing sociology as a moral-academic discipline. But this construction had the fatal consequence of not only reifying Society and the social, but conceptually denigrating small-s society (such as ritual gathering) as ephemeral and therefore not worthy of serious investigation. In other words, collective effervescence and small-s society were only useful to Durkheim to the extent that they helped him (conceptually) generate something that they are not, namely, Society.

Small-s society (such as ritual gathering) was quickly and unceremoniously kicked out of the Durkheimian sociological conceptual universe, the same way that the concubine birth mother of an heir (a son, of course) in traditional China would be kicked out or banished from the household, never to see her son again, while her son grew up knowing only one mother, the legitimate wife of the father. Now the birth mother has come back, not so much to reclaim the son (who, having grown up to become a reputable scholar-official with morally orthodox views, is thus irretrievable) as to face off with the wife. One key purpose of this article is to restore dignity to the birth mother – small-s society.

Actants Amassing

For the purpose of this essay, I will use the expression actants amassing (AA) to designate the convergence and intense co-presence in one time-space (such as a 'totemic ritual' or temple festival) of diverse actants and all the associated activities, happenings and relationships. The word 'amassing' suggests the active state of being in the process of forming a mass. I am using 'mass' as an intransitive verb; it definitely does not mean 'crowd', since the actants doing the massing are so much more than just human beings. I have pilfered the term from architecture, where it was originally used to refer to the volume (massiveness) of built structures, to avoid using words with 'socio' as a root component. Even though I identify with Latour's de-Durkheimization project, I find his attempt to re-signify terms such as 'society' and 'the social' futile, if not misguided. By now these concepts are so entrenched, not only in the disciplines of sociology and anthropology but also in common discourse, that it is more advisable to invent new words and expressions or to invest theoretical value in existing words (e.g., massing) that do not carry the heavy baggage of received meanings. Latour's more recent invocation of the concept of 'composition' is potentially more appealing, though it has the unfortunate connotation of a little too much human agency (though such associations might have been intended) (see Latour 2010). Deleuze and Guattari's concept of 'assemblage' comes closest to what I have in mind. So AA has genealogical affinities with both Latour's actor network theory and Deleuze and Guattari's ruminations on 'assemblages', 'rhizomes', 'lines of flight', 'desiring-machines', and 'chaosmosis' (Deleuze and Guattari 1987 [1980]; Guattari 1995 [1992]).

AA refers not just to the convergence and co-presence of people but the co-presence within, and the convergence into, a certain time-space of people, animals, plants, bacteria and viruses, bodies, bodily and other fluids, spirits (gods, ghosts and ancestors), things, images, medias, acts, practices, concepts, knowledges (including, crucially, organizational know-hows), technologies, cosmologies, ontologies, works, theories, genealogies, competences, institutions, artefacts, machines, ritual-machines (Dean 1998), parts and wholes, couplings, articulations, potentialities, potions, worlds, worldings (Spivak), architectures, built and non/unbuilt environments, 'wind and water' (*fengshui*), heat (or lack thereof), sounds, smells, tastes, diseases, utterances, breaths, clashes, exuviae, wastes, *qi* (*chi*), vectors of forces, force fields, symbols, meanings, pysches, desires, affects, moods, ambiences, doings, undoings, innards, surfaces, splashings, enmeshings, embeddings, interweavings, slashings, hurts, channellings, suspensions, confusions, unfoldings, tendencies, efficacies, (actor-)networks and worknets (Latour), deployments of redistributed and recombined attributes (Latour), spheres (Sloterdijk 2011), folds (Deleuze 1988), lines of flight (Deleuze and Guattari 1987 [1980]), chaos (Guattari 1995 [1992]), orders of things (a nod to Foucault), possibilities, stoppages (Dakota Indian via Durkheim via Bergson via Lévi-Strauss via Alfred Gell; see Gell 1998: 248–50), vortexes, sinkholes, echoes, styles, frames, avidities (Tarde via Latour), monads (Leibniz via Tarde via Bergson via Deleuze via Latour), redundancies, profiles, shootings (of bullets as well as stars), and so on.

Compare this massing of actants with Durkheim's description of the Australian aboriginals' gathering, which seems to be made of humans and not much else (except perhaps the 'electricity' running through them that produces collective effervescence). Where were the kangaroos and other edible critters (or at least their meat), the bones and innards of these animals, the steaming blood splashed to the ground, the rocks, the trampled ground, the sand and dust, the drums and other ritual instruments, the bushes, the drugs, the fire, the ashes, the water, the snakes, the eagles, the bugs (mosquitoes, flies, moths, beetles, worms, spiders, etc.), the moisture in the air, the breeze, the sound waves, the paint applied to the bodies, the sweat, the latrines, the incantations, the drawings on the ground, the totems, the muscle cramps, the delirium, the fainting, the adrenaline, the sexual fluids, the fights, the knives, the sticks, the axes, the poisons? One cannot artificially disaggregate or isolate humans and their supposedly 'social' interactions from this 'compositional assemblage' and still make sense of what the whole thing is about.

AA, Not Exchanges or Transactions

Bronislow Malinowski's influential work *The Argonauts of the Western Pacific* (1984 [1922]) has long been recognized as a foundational text in the subfield of economic anthropology because of its detailed description of the kula ring, which refers to the large-scale, inter-island, inter-community exchange of shell armbands for shell necklaces amongst the islanders of Melanesia (the Trobrianders were one of many such communities) (ca 1910). Through these continuous, regulated exchanges, shell armbands flowed in one direction and shell necklaces in the opposite direction, forming a complete circle – hence the label 'kula ring' (see Figure 10.1).

Each community made elaborate preparations for its scheduled kula expeditions (making new canoes; readying the kula items; gathering other, non-kula exchange items; performing magic to ensure a favourable journey and exchanges, etc.). In the community receiving the kula expedition party, preparations for receiving the visitors were no less elaborate. Upon meeting up on the beach, the exchange parties performed greetings with their long-time kula partners, exchanged the kula as well as non-kula items, ate and made merry together. Then the expedition party was sent off to return to its home island. Dozens of islands, hundreds of communities and thousands of individuals were involved in this complex circulatory exchange network. Because of the ritualized and apparently non-utilitarian nature of the kula

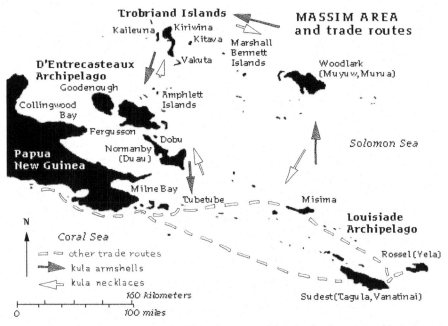

Figure 10.1. Massim area and trade routes showing the direction of kula ring cycles. Necklaces travel clockwise, armbands counter-clockwise. Source: http://www.art-pacific.com/artifacts/nuguinea/massim/trobkula.htm> (slightly modified from the original; used with permission)

items – the shell armbands and necklaces seem to have existed solely for the purpose of being exchanged (though some of these items did attain renown and could bolster the prestige of elite exchange partners) – generations of anthropologists have recognized the kula exchange as the ultimate case study of a 'gift economy', to be contrasted with the commodities economy.

Anthropology has subsequently made a fetish of 'gift exchange' as a form of social life, and reciprocity as a supreme social principle – particularly blameworthy is Marcel Mauss, whose *The Gift* (Mauss 2000 [1925]) drew upon Malinowski's kula ring case study. In its substantivist attempt to question and subvert formalist economicism, anthropology's gift exchange paradigm has inadvertently enshrined the worst and most central tenet of this very economism, which can be called 'exchangism' or 'transactionalism' (exemplified in the model 'A gives something to B and B reciprocates with something to A', A and B being social agents or groups of social agents or their near equivalents).

I posit that, in their rush to identify and analyse the logic behind rounds of 'prestations' and 'counter-prestations' in social life, anthropologists have neglected an even more fundamental aspect of these apparently merely 'social' practices: *massing*, defined as 'instituted co-presence' of not only social agents but many more actants. The kula partners do not so much exchange things *between* themselves (paradigmatically imagined as a pair of partners in a transaction) as mass *amongst* themselves, not just as a pair of exchange partners but as a large multitude of actants, together with their canoes, kula items, yams, and so forth. In fact, I will go as far as saying that the entire kula system existed simply to facilitate 'actants massing', and that unbeknownst to both the natives and the anthropologists, the apparent seriousness of the kula business was to ensure that the natives would continue to mass without fail.

This is on the surface a Durkheimian argument, though it substitutes 'actants massing' for his 'society': the real business of massing needs to be hidden behind some apparently sacred activity, be it engaging in kula exchanges, conducting worship, hosting temple festivals, attending football matches, conferencing, Olympicking, World-Fairing, tweeting on Twitter, experimenting with communal living (e.g., the annual Burning Man gathering in the Black Rock Desert of Nevada), joining riots (or protests or movements), battling (via war, hip hop or war re-enactment), gambling, engaging in torture (see Chau 2008), building a guided-transportation system (Latour 1996), finding cures for diseases, fighting climate change or 'composing a more realistic, liveable, breathable future' (Latour 2010). Freud was wrong in positing that libido lies at the bottom of all human desires and illusions; in fact libido's job is to ensure massing (again, defined not as merely interpersonal but 'inter-actant'). And Latour is wrong in characterizing the intergovernmental Copenhagen Climate Conference in 2009 as a 'non-event' simply because 'nothing happened' – after all, numerous actants were amassing in the 'vast pandemonium of the biggest diplomatic jamboree ever assembled' (Latour 2010), were they not? In other words, I hope to use this chapter to reinstate massing events (i.e., those in small-s society) to the seat of honour they deserve in anthropology, and in the process to expose the harm the duo of uncle and nephew has done to sociology and anthropology (to the extent that the two disciplines are still salvageable).

The core of the essay is a multi-perspectival, multi-actant ethnography showing the convergence into one time-space of more than two hundred specially fattened pigs (the heaviest weighing more than 900 kilograms), dozens of goats, a two-metre-long crocodile, a couple of ostriches, hundreds of chicken and fish, tens of thousands of bowls of snacks, hundreds of thousands of other food items, thousands of bottles of liquor and soft drinks, thousands of packets of cigarettes, hundreds of packets of betel nuts, thousands of tables and chairs, tens of thousands of people (including festival organizers and participants, vendors, craftsmen, truck drivers, ritual specialists, song-and-dance girls, martial artists, government officials, policemen, schoolchildren, volunteers, anthropologists and folklorists), hundreds of trucks, thousands of metres of electric wiring, thousands of integrated circuits, tons of fireworks and firecrackers, millions of ghosts, deities, ancestors, heavenly soldiers and more.

The time-space in question is the annual Righteous Martyrs Festival (*yiminjie*) celebrated among a cluster of semi-rural Hakka communities in northern Taiwan,[1] for which households of the particular community responsible for that year's festival compete to raise the biggest (heaviest) pigs as offerings to the spirits of 'forebears' who died defending their communities (the hosting responsibilities rotate among fifteen such communities, which are grouped together as village alliances). The biggest pigs are weighed and ranked, and the winning households honoured. All the pigs are slaughtered, elaborately decorated, fitted onto trucks, paraded through the streets, presented to the spirits and eventually partially eaten at household-centred banquets (where anyone can sit down and eat without invitation) and partially distributed (as slabs of fatty pork) to friends, relatives and associates as tokens of the spirits' blessing. The day of the offering presentation at the Righteous Martyrs Temple (*yiminmiao*) and accompanying festivities draw tens of thousands of visitors, who come to see and pass judgement on the offerings and enjoy a wide variety of entertainments (also presented as offerings to the spirits) such as folk operas, instrumental music ensembles, fireworks, and song-and-dance (and often striptease) shows performed by scantily dressed young women on fancy mobile stages with elaborate lighting and sound systems.

I will be presenting fragments of the 2009 festival from the 'perspectives' of various actants (though still a very tiny percentage of the total) that 'massed' on those hot, humid late summer days in Taiwan.[2] Because of space limits I will include the 'perspectives' of non-human actants only: one of the giant pig offerings, a crocodile that served as an companion offering, the giant alloy iron frame over which the giant pig's body was draped, a betel nut, a hungry ghost and the righteous martyrs. Of course humans feature prominently in their narra-

Figure 10.2. The display of decorated giant pig offerings in the temple square in front of the Righteous Martyrs Temple in Xinpu, Xinzhu County, Taiwan. Altogether, the top thirty ranked giant pigs have the honour of being displayed in front of the temple (on this occasion thirty-seven giant pigs were on display because of a few tied rankings among them). Photograph by Adam Yuet Chau

tives, but only as actants that are engaged with other actants, most of whom are not human.

The Giant Pig

I am a pig. A giant pig. I now weigh 1,531 Taiwanese *jin* (about 918 kilograms; 1 Taiwanese *jin* equals 0.6 kg). I have just been weighed this morning by the organizers of the giant pig offering competition – and may I say that I actually also *feel* my own weight? Have you ever felt the tensile tug of weighty matter inside yourself?

I don't have a name. I am not a pet. I belong to the category of giant pigs intended to be slaughtered and offered to the righteous martyrs' spirits at the temple festival tomorrow. I am about three years old, born and raised on a professional pig farm not too far from this village. When I was two, my present owners, Mr and Mrs Zhang, came to the farm, identified me as a potential prize-winning pig and signed a contract with the pig farmer who raised me, specifying how he would be compensated if I managed to win one of the top prizes.

About 200 households in the village-alliance community responsible for hosting the temple festival have contracted for a giant pig or raised their own, and some 60 households with the biggest pigs entered the competition. I came out ranking third in the competition! Mr and Mrs Zhang are very pleased to have certain knowledge that the righteous martyrs will bless and protect them for years to come. My pig farmer owner will get a huge bonus for helping them achieve this feat (on top of the agreed payment per kilogram). I am obviously very proud of this achievement, as I have spent three years eating and eating almost continuously so as to grow fatter and heavier and beat the other competition pigs, some of whom were raised side by side with me on the same farm. At first I drank milk from my mother's teats, fighting madly with my dozen or so piglet siblings. But soon my pig farmer owner began feeding me all kinds of delicious food, especially small fish called *qiudaoyu* (literally 'autumn knife fish' [*Cololabis saira*]) caught in the South China Sea and Japan Sea. I also drank a lot of milk and beer. Although I ate a lot of good food, I can't say my life was good, because as soon as I was chosen as a potential prize pig I was confined in a tight enclosure so I couldn't move around, which made me concentrate on growing fat and prevented the expenditure of precious energy. I eventually grew so big I could hardly stand. In the last year or so I ate lying down. And instead of letting me feed on my own, the pig farmer twice daily fed me highly nutritious liquid pig feed through a tube down my throat – up to 40 kilograms a day. (Some pig farmers resort to deviant means to make competition pigs heavier, like force-feeding them with iron sand right before the weigh-in.) Some animal rights activists have condemned this inhumane treatment of us competition pigs, but I say, 'Somebody has to sacrifice a little in order to become a sacrifice!'

I was transported by truck from the pig farm to the Zhangs' residence a few days ago. Because of my size and weight, lifting me on and off the truck proved a difficult operation (like weighing me, which was done by dragging me into an iron cage and lifting me up with a truck-lift). Many a prize pig gets injured this way, and an injured pig does not make a good offering, does it? Under an awning in front of their house, the Zhangs prepared a temporary sty made of sandbags and fine black sand. I settled in nicely for a few days, enjoying the best food of my life, which I ate from Mrs Zhang's own hand. There was cabbage, corn, fish, cuttlefish, rice gruel, beer and milk, as well as more industrial pig feed (perhaps laced with growth hormones) provided by the pig farmer. Feeding me at this late stage was important because I might still have managed to put on several kilograms that were needed to compensate for the kilograms lost in the stress and moving during transit. I have forgotten to mention how hot it is. Today the temperature peaked at 38 degrees Celsius. To keep me cool, the Zhangs installed two fans and two mist sprayers around me. Like all the other giant pigs, my accommodations are outside so that as many people as possible can see me: I am a proud display of the efforts of the household. The Zhangs' residence is by the road, so many passers-by have stopped to take a look at me, comment and chat with the family members. Before the weigh-in and the announcement of the prizes, countless people visited many of the households with competition pigs to guess which ones would rank the highest. I heard that bookies were setting up parties where people bet on the order of the three top-ranking pigs.

I don't know the Zhangs very well, since they didn't raise me for long themselves. In the past, all households raised their own pigs, including (and especially) competition pigs. The competition was really meant to demonstrate households' commitment to raising the biggest pigs and making the heaviest offerings. But the economic transition in Taiwan in the 1980s and 1990s left very few farming households, and it no longer makes sense to raise one's own pig. Raising a pig takes a lot of work and attention, and when households' members – especially the adult women, who are often the backbone of household-based petty capitalist businesses (see Gates 1996) – are all otherwise preoccupied making money in various ways (factory or clerical work, trade, business, home industries, etc.), there is no one left to feed the pig. Meanwhile, professional pig farming in Taiwan has become very sophisticated thanks to decades of efforts to industrialize pig farming (and to the agro-industrial policies and developments of both the Japanese colonial government [1895–1945] and the Nationalist government after 1949). So it was only natural that festival households began contracting pig raising to professional farmers, and that a system of correspondence between prize ranking and compensation and bonus evolved and eventually became standardized. There are even standardized prize pig contract forms for both parties to complete and sign. Taiwan used to export a lot of pork, especially to Japan, but in 1997 foot-and-mouth disease broke out and hit the pig farming industry hard. Pork exports ground to a halt almost overnight and never resumed. Professional pig farmers in the areas with giant pig competitions thus now have even more incentive to earn extra cash by engaging in competition pig raising.

Now it is past 11:00 P.M., and the auspicious moment for my slaughter – calculated by ritual specialists and announced beforehand to all households with competition pigs to slaughter (about two hundred pigs altogether) – has come. Some sixty people surround me: members of the Zhang household, the butcher and his teammates, curious passers-by (including many children), reporters and an anthropologist and his assistant. The butcher has a team of seven or eight people. Many items have been assembled in preparation for the slaughter: knives, buckets, a boiler with a big tank of constantly topped up boiling water, rice wine and salt (to be sprayed and spread on me later), and a metal frame for holding my skin up later for decoration.

The butcher produces a knife at least two feet long. His helpers flip me over onto my back and hold my feet up. I struggle, of course, but not too vigorously. The knife goes in at my neck and penetrates straight into my heart, so deep that only the handle of the knife is visible from outside. Then the knife is pulled out, and hot, steamy blood gushes out into the dirt. The butcher's helpers wash the blood away with buckets of hot water. I expel my last, hot breath.

Next the butcher and his helpers will cut me open, remove all my innards and my entire skeletal frame, and cut out most of the meat (which is cut into long strips to be cooked for tomorrow's banquet), leaving intact only my outer surface (i.e., my skin and an inch or so of thick subcutaneous fat). This process will take about an hour. They then will wipe rice wine and salt all over my remaining carcass to prevent it from rotting too quickly. After that, they will take a break from me to slaughter the crocodile (see below) that is the Zhangs' auxiliary offering (i.e., my companion offering) to the spirits. Having done so, they will spend the rest of the night (the next five to six hours until dawn) decorating me. By about 7:00 A.M. the next day they will have mounted me onto the specially decorated truck and moved me to the temple square of the Righteous Martyrs Temple alongside the other thirty-seven prize-winning giant pigs.

While my skin is displayed at the temple, the Zhangs' helpers will be busy cooking my meat and edible innards in preparation for the banquet the Zhangs will host in the evening. My 'skin' will return to the Zhang residence after about six hours (i.e., after the spirits have consumed the offerings), and at the right moment – close to midnight, after the hungry ghosts have also consumed their meals – the butcher and his helpers will carve my 'skin' into long, fatty strips that the Zhangs will distribute to friends, relatives and business associates. Because I am a blessed giant pig, receiving a piece of me will bring good fortune to the recipients. However, in recent years people are in-

Figure 10.3. The decoration of the giant pig offering. Mr Zhang is the man on the right standing by the ladder. The mouth of the young man with the kettle of boiling water atop the giant pig is stained red with betel nut juice. Photograph by Adam Yuet Chau

creasingly reluctant to receive such a large slab of fatty pork because they don't know what to do with it – the days of cooking with home-rendered lard are almost completely gone.

The Crocodile

I am a crocodile. I am now tied up by one of my hind legs to a post by the Zhangs' house, my mouth bound shut with industrial-strength adhesive tape. I am four years old and pretty big already (about two metres long, nose to tail-tip), though certainly not as big as the pig, whose slaughter I have just witnessed mere feet away from my nose. I was born and raised on a crocodile farm in southern Taiwan. In recent years, a few crocodile farms have sprung up in southern Taiwan to cater for the Taiwanese taste for exotic meat; also, our skin can be harvested to make bags and other accessories. I grew up with hundreds of other crocs. Most are slaughtered for their meat and skin before they are two years old, although some are allowed to live longer and grow bigger for pseudo 'nature tourism' purposes – some of these crocodile farms are open to tourists, who love to take pictures with big, bad crocs – and occasionally, unfortunately for me (despite the honour!),

Figure 10.4. The giant pig, elaborately decorated and mounted on the back of a special truck. Note the framed prize certificate issued by the county government, the framed picture of the owners of the pig with the pig before it was slaughtered, the incense stick and other offerings in front of the pig (including pink-coloured buns shaped like towers, cases of Taiwanese beer, a duck, a chicken and some of the pig's cooked internal organs). Photograph by Adam Yuet Chau

for sale to serve as offerings at temple festivals. Only now has a crocodile become an offering at this Righteous Martyrs Festival. In a way I should feel honoured and proud to be the first crocodile offering to the righteous martyrs. Mr and Mrs Zhang are certainly proud to have pulled off a major innovation – not only are they the *first* household to introduce crocodiles as offerings, but they are the *only* one that is doing it (there is always additional cachet for being the one and only). It is traditional practice at the Righteous Martyrs Festival to present a companion offering with the giant pig offering. The traditional companion piece is a goat, and there is even a competition to see which household's goat has the widest horn span (usually a dozen or so households include a goat in their repertoire of offerings). Some households have innovated recently, using ostriches as the companion offering (there are two ostriches this year). So the Zhangs' innovation is merely a variation on this conventionalized pattern.

The butcher commands his helpers to tie me up on a wooden board with my belly facing out. Then the board is propped against the wall of the Zhang residence. My moment has come. The butcher does not wait too long before slaughtering me because a lot of the onlookers are eager to see how he will do it (most of them have never seen a crocodile in real life, let alone the killing of one). The butcher claims to have slaughtered crocodiles before. Maybe he is bluffing. He takes out a smallish knife and tries to poke it into the middle of my chest, but it does not go in. He tries harder, using his fist to hammer on the hilt of the knife, but the knife still does not go in. People begin to laugh, and the butcher risks huge loss of face. He takes out a hammer and uses it to pound the knife in. Finally, it pierces my hard belly plaque. He then proceeds to cut through the belly plaque with a pair of scissors. A vertical slit a foot long opens up in the middle of my belly. Unlike the slaughter of the pig, no blood gushes out. Now comes the big moment: the butcher pokes his hand inside me and tears out my heart. He gives it to one of his young helpers, who holds it in his palm and parades around excitedly to show the curious crowd. My heart, no bigger than a prune, beats rhythmically in his hand. The crowd breaks into an excited wave of exclamations and commentaries, and many take out their cameras and mobile phones to take a picture of my heart. Then I am gutted. Tomorrow I will be decorated and displayed in a mini-aquarium next to the giant pig offering as a companion piece. The mini-aquarium is basically a shallow basin with water and water lilies, and I am made to perch on top of a rock looking ferociously alive. Many visitors get quite a fright upon first seeing me.

A Betel Nut

I am a betel nut, a preparation made from a fresh, shelled areca nut cut lengthwise and then laced with lime (calcium hydroxide paste) and wrapped in a single betel leaf. People chew me as a stimulant, similar to smoking and chewing tobacco, chewing *khat/qat* in some Middle Eastern and African countries or drinking coffee or tea. People chew me for a few minutes, mixing their saliva together with the lime and grinding the leaf and nut down into a wad of a blood-red colour (due to a chemical reaction). After all the taste and potency have been sucked out of the mixture, they spit out the blood-red pasty residue onto the ground. That's why many pavements and streets in Taiwan are stained with blood-red betel juice splatters in varying degrees of decomposition, from the freshly spat, bright-red wet ones to the sun-scorched greyish outlines of those of older vintage. Legend has it that some foreign visitors to Taiwan, unaware of this practice, saw these bloody splotches and thought the Taiwanese were working so hard they were vomiting blood.

Regular chewers chew several dozen nuts each day. I am in a box with twenty-nine other betel nuts like me (all neatly lined up), bought by the butcher who slaughtered the giant pig. The butcher and his teammates could have bought betel nuts from the scantily clad 'betel nut beauties' (*binlangxishi*) selling betel nuts from brightly lit, ornately decorated small glass booths along the roadside, but they prefer buy-ing larger quantities from professional betel nut preparers. Some men get a kick out of buying betel nuts from the sultry girls, who bring the nuts to their cars, allowing them to gawk at their generously exposed breasts and legs (the men are supposed to gawk at them; failure to do so might offend the girls) and engage in brief, 'spicy', flirty chit-chat. However, their betel nuts are more expensive, come in smaller packets and are not as good as those prepared by professionals. The profes-sional betel nut preparers and vendors tend to be family businesses that sell betel nuts in regular shops in towns and cities, and also along major roads because a lot of the customers are drivers; no sexy girls there.

I should be consumed within a few hours; otherwise I will go bad, given how hot the summer weather is here. I will last longer if you put me in the fridge, but most betel nut chewers prefer freshly prepared betel nuts; thus a regular chewer's daily life is punctuated by small trips to, or stops at, betel nut vendors. Do not look down on a small nut like me. According to some sources,[3] every year the Taiwanese spend more than 100 billion Taiwan dollars (about £2 billion) on betel nuts. About seventy thousand farming households are engaged in cultivat-ing and harvesting areca nuts in Taiwan, and the betel nut trade is crucial to the livelihoods of many hundreds of thousands of individu-als (farmers, transporters, wholesalers, preparers and vendors, 'betel nut beauties', and merchants, who import areca nuts from Thailand and other Southeast Asian countries when Taiwanese areca nuts are not in season). This is why the government cannot push very hard to eradicate this supposedly 'premodern', 'low-class' and surely carcinogenic practice (associated mostly with higher risk of oral cancer).

The Giant Iron Frame

I am a giant alloy iron (*baitie*) contraption specially made to hold and frame giant pig offerings. In the past, the pig offerings were put on simple vaulted wooden frames so the pigs lay horizontally, looking as they did when alive. People hauled these increasingly large pig offerings to the Righteous Martyrs Temple over many miles of rugged terrain. Once roads were built, people began to use tractor trucks to bring the giant pigs. The decorations on the giant pig offerings used to be relatively simple. Over time, people piled more and more elaborate decorations onto the pigs. Eventually professional giant pig decorators came onto the scene, providing large trucks and outfitting the pigs with ever fancier 'bling' (complete with modular 'gothic' towers and blinking neon lights). To exaggerate the size of the giant pigs, some genius in the 1970s invented me, a metal frame with a curved front

Figure 10.5. The mounting of the giant pig 'sur/face' onto the metal frame. Note the dead crocodile in the background. Photograph by Adam Yuet Chau

over which the entire surface of the pig can be draped, with the head at the bottom and tail at the top, spread taut across the curved surface of the front like a large round sail or canvas. Then the whole thing is mounted onto the back of the truck facing backwards, so that an unsuspecting spectator might mistake the size of the truck as the size of the giant pig. This invention was so successful that the design quickly spread to all the communities that held giant pig competitions. Nowadays, because of the combined weight of the giant pig and the metal frame, people have to use forklifts to mount the pigs on the trucks. I am owned by the butcher, who doubles as a professional giant pig mounter and decorator. Over the course of my career, I have already seen the inside of dozens of giant pigs as they were draped over me.

The Hungry Ghost

I am a hungry ghost. When I was alive, I was a fisherman off the coast of northern Taiwan. Our fishing boat capsized during a bad storm, and my shipmates and I all drowned. I never married and had no descendants, so I could not become an ancestor and receive regular offerings from my descendants. My spirit thus became a ghost. For more than two hundred years now I have roamed around hell, trying to grab whatever food I can lay hands on, such as the offerings laid out for other people's ancestors. Countless 'hungry ghosts' like me fight amongst ourselves for these leftovers. Many of us are in a kind of hell called 'flaming mouth', which means that whatever we put in our mouths immediately becomes a ball of flame. Even if we manage to grab some scraps of food, we remain always hungry – hence our name. The merciful Buddha has designed a ritual to relieve us of this condition so that we can actually eat the offerings, but this ritual is conducted too sporadically to benefit most of us.

We hungry ghosts are released from hell to roam the human world for the entire seventh lunar month each year. During this period, humans feed us with all kinds of offerings so that we do not bother them or cause them trouble. Households and businesses put out tables of offerings for us to eat. There are ducks, chicken, pork, beef jerky, instant noodles, crisps, candies, biscuits and cakes. Since we can feed only on the 'immaterial aspects' of the offerings through the rising smoke from lit incense sticks stuck into the offerings, after we are done feasting the humans take the food items back and eat them (we gulp up everything in a flash, but they can take their time over the next days and weeks to eat their share). Because people buy so much food during this month, supermarkets in Taiwan all have 'ghost month' sales at this time of year to compete for customers. Often members of a household or business choose their favourite food items to use as offerings. We hungry ghosts are not particular about what kinds of food are put out: we are grateful that people put out any offering at all. But it is true that we might cause trouble if we are not fed anything, so the Taiwanese call us 'good brothers' (*haoxiongdi*) and treat us well to make sure that we leave them alone.

I have mentioned the offering tables households and businesses put out for us, but these are small meals compared to the giant feasts that communities collectively lay out for us. On the fifteenth day of the seventh lunar month falls the Middle Prime (*zhongyuan*) Festival, when communities stage collective offerings to us, with rows and rows of food and dazzling shows such as folk operas and fireworks. The best part is the rituals conducted by Buddhist monks or Daoist priests (who are hired by the communities), which last for days and culminate in a 'feeding the hungry ghosts' finale on the night of the grand offering. In the case of the Righteous Martyrs Festival, this is the day when the giant pigs are displayed, and all the offerings are miraculously multiplied a millionfold by ritual magic. A feast it is indeed! Yum yum yum. But we pay a price to feast on this banquet: afterward we have to go back to hell to suffer for another year, until the next round of feasts. Such is the sorry existence of us hungry ghosts.

The Righteous Martyrs

We are the so-called righteous martyrs (*yimin*), the honourees of all this festive activity. We were young men who died defending our communities against other groups (especially in the many battles between us Hakka people and the aboriginals and Hokkien people) or who died fighting alongside Qing government troops against rebels. These battles and fights date to the eighteenth and nineteenth centuries, when thousands of us died without marrying or producing heirs, meaning that we have no descendants to burn incense for us or feed and clothe us on a regular basis. In that regard we are no different from the hungry ghost who spoke above. However, thanks to the initiative of some Hakka community leaders in the past, our bones were gathered and buried together, and a temple was built to honour us, ensuring that we would receive regular offerings and not go hungry like the hungry ghosts. The annual Righteous Martyrs Festival's purpose is to commemorate our bravery and contribution to our communities and make offerings to us (the giant pigs and the rest); but of course the hungry ghosts get to eat, too.

The Xinpu Righteous Martyrs Temple serves as the centre of the cult of righteous martyrs. In the past hundred years or so, the temple has spawned dozens of branch temples through the practice of 'incense division', where a new community wishing to establish its own temple brings fire and incense ashes from an older temple to its new temple. This is why many branch temples send representatives to their 'ancestral temple' to pay respects during the annual festival in our honour. These branch righteous martyrs temples have their own festivals and rotational hosting communities. Scholars studying the cult of righteous martyrs have mostly treated us as a subgenre of ghosts, but in recent years many Hakka community activists have contested this view, saying we are more like deities. Many deities in Chinese religious history have been ghosts first, so maybe we are in the process of being upgraded to godhood. Meanwhile, to appeal to younger people, some Hakka cultural workers have been engaging in efforts to 'cute-ify' us, even making smiling righteous martyr dolls.

AA and Apparatuses of Capture

Latour's actor network theory sees various actants as being connected in a dynamic, fragile web of suspension, moving through time in a permanent state of volatile heterogeneity. For Latour, institutions (universities, states, laboratories, companies, technological marvels, etc.) are no more real and enduring than the illusory moving images seen in a magic lantern. With this much I concur. But what forces compel these institutions and other seemingly real things to pull themselves over the existential gaps in time? What forces propel elements of these institutions and other seemingly real things to fall off and join other entities/assemblages, contributing to their shape-shifting and even eventual disappearance? Latour has demonstrated some of these forces in his case studies (e.g., on the conceptualization and eventual non-realization of the guided-transport system Aramis, Agencement en Rames Automatisées de Modules Indépendants dans les Stations, in Paris in the 1970s and 1980s), although I think more conceptualization is needed to get at the mechanisms of 'composition' and what might be called the various compositions' inter-actantal *mises-en-cohérence*, conceptually and spatio-temporally.

A useful concept in this endeavour is 'apparatuses of capture', originally introduced by Deleuze and Guattari (1987 [1980]) but reworked by the ritual studies scholar Kenneth Dean in the context of analysing complex ritual networks and 'ritual machines' in south-eastern coastal China (Dean 1998: 45; also Dean and Zheng 2010). In explicating the exuberance of ritual performances on the Fujian coast (across the Taiwan Strait from Taiwan), Dean defines 'appara-tuses of capture' as 'the capture and temporary consolidation of so-cial, economic, political, and libidinal forces by cultural forms' (Dean 1998: 45). Yet we can expand the range of items and forces that are captured and consolidated beyond the 'social, economic, political and libidinal' and regard the formal agency as broader than merely 'cultural'. I see my task as explicating how certain 'compositional as-semblages' – here I am combining Latour's notion of 'composition' (Latour 2010) with Deleuze and Guattari's notion of 'assemblage' (Deleuze and Guattari 1987 [1980]) – come about and seemingly at-tain staying power. What are the compositional equivalents of the configuration of gravitational and other forces that keeps the plan-ets in their tracks? The answers are necessarily fluid, as they depend on which level of complexity the analysis enters, and along which plane and axis. As an anthropologist, I prefer to enter the thicket via 'compositional forms' that appear to be more or less put together by humans, while doing my best to foreground the agency (or rather *actancy*) of non-human actants.

These fragments of narratives are better at showing the various 'apparatuses of capture' and elements (and processes and mecha-nisms) of convergence than demonstrating how they cohere. Why do so many human and non-human actants converge into this particu-lar time-space every year? There will not be any Righteous Martyrs Festival if these actants suddenly stop converging. Something is com-pelling them to converge thus year after year. The composition sticks. Here is where Alfred Gell comes in. In *Art and Agency* (Gell 1998), Gell explicates the generative potentials of artistic forms, suggesting that artistic forms as a whole within a particular cultural setting, or works within the overall oeuvre of a particular artist, are transformations of one another; in other words, they somehow cohere. A cultural prin-ciple, once invented and tried and found useful (for all kinds of rea-sons, and not all conscious), may persist over time, whereby various elements get captured and consolidated and the web thickens and becomes increasingly sticky, so that more elements want to accrue in-stead of falling off. The composition asserts substantial 'gravitational pull' – until it does not.

The Righteous Martyrs Festival is informed by one primary cul-tural form, widely found in many other festival contexts in Taiwan and other Chinese worlds: hosting (Chau 2006). Hosting is one of the most important and fundamental cultural idioms in Chinese social life. It refers to the practice (or ensemble of practices) of inviting, feasting and sending off guests on important occasions. These guests can be humans, deities, ancestors or ghosts. It is through reciprocal hosting that a household asserts its place in the social universe. But hosting is not simply or primarily about exchanges and social interactions, though these are important elements. Rather, hosting is an idiom for producing and consuming the 'social heat' (or 'red hot sociality') attributable to a long-established 'festive regime' (Chau 2006, 2008). I have called hosting occasions instances of 'rites of convergence' (as opposed to van Gennep's and Victor Turner's 'rites of passage'; see Chau 2006), in which heterogeneous elements are thrown into one compositional assemblage over a specific duration.

The idiom of hosting is re-enacted repeatedly and in multiple forms at the Righteous Martyrs Festival: in the households that raise the giant pigs; at the Righteous Martyrs Temple; at the riverbank, where lamps symbolizing offerings are floated downstream; by the households whose turn it is to host and organize the festival; by the hosting community collectively; by the Buddhist priests; by the politicians; by the local government and through food and drink as well as magical formulas. The guests include deities (the entire hierarchy from the highest of the high, the Jade Emperor and the Buddha, down to the lowest of the low, the heavenly soldiers), ghosts, ancestors and pseudo-ancestors (or half-ancestor and half-ghost, i.e., the righteous martyrs), and humans.

But two other important cultural forms accompany and have been integrated into the hosting idiom: competition and rotation. The hosting households compete amongst themselves to see who can raise the biggest pig (and thus be more blessed by the deities and spirits), who can present the most elaborate and beautifully-decorated giant pig offerings, who will host the biggest banquet, and who has the largest network of friends and associates to whom to give pork slabs. The fifteen rotating hosting communities compete (serially, over fifteen-year cycles) to see which communities can put together the best, most 'red hot' temple festival. The politicians (admittedly a much more recent addition, or captured element, to the festival scene) compete to stage the most sincere and elaborate 'show' to garner the blessings of the spirits and/or to attract votes.

Rotation is a pervasive cultural form (or compositional principle) of the religious landscape in Taiwan and other parts of the Chinese world. In the case of the Righteous Martyrs Festival, we find a classic example of nested and fractalized (see Gell 1998) rotational arrangement. The festival's main annual organizing and hosting duties are rotated amongst fifteen communities (territorially defined clusters of villages); within each annual on-duty (*zhinian*) community, the main organizing and hosting responsibility is rotated amongst all the member villages, and within the chief hosting village, the roles of leading hosts (especially the chief and deputy incense-pot hosts, *luzhu*) are rotated amongst the most respected members of the village (though hosts are selected by divination, the role is still essentially rotational, as households that serve as leading hosts one year cannot be candidates in future rounds until all the prominent households have served in these roles).

The space of a chapter does not allow me to explore the many, many more cultural forms operating at the Righteous Martyrs Festival. I hope, however, that I have adequately demonstrated how looking at ritual events in terms of AA can serve not only as a good entry point for dismantling Durkheimian sociologism and Maussian exchangism but also as a productive way of revealing previously hidden or understudied connections and coherences between various actants, as well as the 'apparatuses of capture' and 'cultural forms' that bring them together and tumble forward along with them. Not being a philosopher, I will not, like Latour, advocate any utopian compositionism. Instead, I merely offer the giant pig display and the Righteous Martyrs Festival as a compositional assemblage, folding and unfolding, folding and unfolding, folding and unfolding...

Notes

I would like to thank David Gellner for having invited me to participate in the July 2011 event at Oxford commemorating the centenary of the publication of Emile Durkheim's *Elementary Forms of Religious Life*. I learned a great deal from the other participants. I also want to thank Sondra Hausner for her engaging comments and editorial help on an earlier draft of this chapter. I thank Carolyn Leigh at Art-Pacific.com for granting me permission to use the kula ring map from her website. I would also like to acknowledge the crucial help from the copyeditor, Jaime Taber. I have presented related materials at a few other venues over the past few years, and I thank the organizers and those colleagues who have contributed comments and suggestions. I want to thank especially the people at the Righteous Martyrs Festival in Xinpu (Hsinpu), Xinzhu (Hsinchu), Taiwan for contributing to my study (especially the organizers of the festival in the summer of 2009 and members of the prize pig households I spoke with). Special thanks are also due to Ye Jih-jia and Yen Ping-jing for assisting with my fieldwork during the festival. I am grateful for the insights and help I have received from Taiwanese scholars Chiu Yen-kuei, Julia Huang, Lin Wei-ping and others. Many of the conceptual inspirations have come from Gilles Deleuze and Félix Guattari, Bruno Latour, Kenneth Dean, Brian Massumi (Massumi 2002) and Alfred Gell. The tone of this chapter is deliberately playful and provocative, but the critique of Durkheimian sociologism and Maussian exchangism is a serious one. I have drawn portions of this piece from another article (Chau 2013), which should be seen as a companion piece.

1. Here I drawing on fieldwork I conducted in the summer of 2009. For earlier anthropological studies on giant pig festivals in Taiwan see Ahern (1981) and Weller (1987). For studies on the Hsinpu Righteous Martyrs Festival see Chiu (2000) and Lai (2001).

2. A kind of representational conceit is inevitable, as I make pigs, a crocodile, a betel nut, a giant alloy iron frame, and spirits (a hungry ghost and the righteous martyrs) 'speak' (or narrate) the way they do here – what Bruno Latour calls 'the privileges of prosopopoeia' (Latour 1996: x). This is partly inspired by how Latour (1996) makes Aramis speak its mind, even when it existed only as an idea, a project. Non-human actants usually do not 'speak' like this, but I have given them at least some kind of 'voice'. Having them 'speak' allows the forces of capture to emerge more clearly and 'naturalistically', however deceptively. To the extent that actants need no material reality – for example, Latour's Aramis (Latour 1996) is merely a conception and prototype rather than a real train system –immaterial 'things' such as ghosts and spirits can also be conceived of as actants. Please note that such multi-perspectival, multi-actant ethnographic representation is not anthropomorphism because I have not attempted to make non-humans act like humans (e.g., the pigs in George Orwell's *Animal Farm*). I prefer to call this representational strategy *ethnographic ventriloquism*.

3. See Chinese wiki entry on betel nuts in Taiwan: http://zh.wikipedia .org/wiki/%E6%AA%B3%E6%A6%94

References

Ahern, E.M. 1981. 'The Thai Ti Kong Festival', in E.M. Ahern and H. Gates (eds), *The Anthropology of Taiwanese Society*. Stanford, CA: Stanford University Press, pp. 397–425.

Chau, A.Y. 2006. *Miraculous Response: Doing Popular Religion in Contemporary China*. Stanford, CA: Stanford University Press.

———. 2008. 'The Sensorial Production of the Social', *Ethnos* 73(4) [special issue 'The Senses and the Social', ed. Elisabeth Hsu]: 485–504.

———. 2013. 'Actants Amassing (AA),' in N.J. Long and H.L. Moore (eds), *Sociality: New Directions*. New York and Oxford: Berghahn Books, pp. 133–55.

Chiu Yen-kuei (Qiu Yangui). 2000. 'Cong jidian yishi kan bei Taiwan yimin xinyang: yi Fangliao baozhongci dingchounian Hukou lianzhuang zhinian zhongyuan wei li' [The Righteous Martyrs Belief in Northern Taiwan through Offering Rituals: The Case of the Rotational Duty of the Hukou Village Alliance in 1997 during the Zhongyuan Festival for the Fangliao Baozhong Temple], in *Di si jie guoji kejiaxue yantaohui lunwenji: zongjiao yuyan yu yinyue ce* [A Collection of Articles from the Fourth International Hakka Studies Conference: The 'Religion, Language and Music' Volume]. Taipei: Institute of Ethnology, Academia Sinica, pp. 1–47.

Dean, K. 1998. *Lord of the Three in One: The Spread of a Cult in Southeast China.* Princeton, NJ: Princeton University Press.

Dean, K. and Zheng Zhenman. 2010. *Ritual Alliances of the Putian Plain. Volume One: Historical Introduction to the Return of the Gods.* Leiden: Brill.

Deleuze, G. 1988. *Le pli: Leibniz et le Baroque.* Paris: Les édition de minuit.

Deleuze, G. and F. Guattari. 1987 [1980]. *A Thousand Plateaus: Capitalism and Schizophrenia,* trans. B. Massumi. Minneapolis: University of Minnesota Press.

Durkheim, E. 1915 [1912]. *The Elementary Forms of the Religious Life,* trans. J.W. Swain. New York: The Free Press.

Gates, H. 1996. *China's Motor: A Thousand Years of Petty Capitalism.* Ithaca, NY: Cornell University Press.

Gell, A. 1998. *Art and Agency: An Anthropological Theory.* Oxford and New York: Clarendon Press.

Guattari, F. 1995 [1992]. *Chaosmosis: An Ethico-Aesthetic Paradigm,* trans. P. Bains and J. Pefanis. Bloomington and Indianapolis: Indiana University Press.

Lai Yu-Ling. 2001. 'Xinpu Fangliao yiminye xinyang yu difang shehui de fazhan: yi Yangmei diqu wei li' [The Righteous Martyrs Belief in Fangliao, Xinpu, and the Development of Local Society: The Case of the Yangmei Region]. Master's Thesis, Department Graduate Institute of History. Taiwan: National Chung-yang University.

Latour, B. 1996. *Aramis, or the Love of Technology,* trans. C. Cambridge, MA: Harvard University Press.

———. 2005. *Reassembling the Social: An Introduction to Actor-Network-Theory.* Oxford: Oxford University Press.

———. 2010. 'An Attempt at a "Compositionist Manifesto",' *New Literary History* 41(3). Retrieved 14 May 2012 from http://www.bruno-latour .fr/sites/default/files/120-NLH-GB.pdf

Malinowski, B. 1984 [1922]. *Argonauts of the Western Pacific: An Account of Native Enterprise and Adventure in the Archipelagoes of Melanesian New Guinea.* Prospect Heights, IL: Waveland Press.

Massumi, B. 2002. *Parables for the Virtual: Movement, Affect, Sensation.* Durham, NC: Duke University Press.

Mauss, M. 2000 [1925]. *The Gift: The Form and Function of Exchange in Archaic Societies,* trans. W.D. Halls. London: W. W. Norton & Company.

Sloterdijk, P. 2011 [1998]. *Bubbles: Spheres Volume I: Microspherology,* trans. W. Hoban. Cambridge, MA: MIT Press.

Weller, R.P. 1987. 'The Politics of Ritual Disguise: Repression and Response in Taiwanese Popular Religion.' *Modern China* 13(1): 17–39.

PART V

Fin

Chapter 11

THE CREATION AND PROBLEMATIC ACHIEVEMENT OF *LES FORMES ÉLÉMENTAIRES*

W. Watts Miller

Introduction

It is possible to distinguish two basic approaches to Durkheim. Interest in his present-day relevance might be described as concern with a 'living' Durkheim. Interest in his life, work and times might be described as concern with the 'historical' Durkheim. One of the distinction's complications is how successive waves of interpretation – in the 1930s, 1950s, 1970s and so on – join the past, to become part of a complex history of 'Durkheim after Durkheim' in different countries, at different periods and on different issues. Another point, however, is that fresh explorations of his ideas and their relevance require anchorage in continuing investigations of his work. So an attempt is made here to trace the story of his creation of *Les Formes élémentaires*, and to suggest ways in which it is a problematic achievement. The questions it raises are precisely the reason for its power, a hundred years on, to challenge and stimulate.[1]

The Creation of a Work

Durkheim launched a new journal, the *Année sociologique*, with an essay that set out his core theory of the evolution of social and religious life (1898a). But this was soon threatened by shock news from Australia, which came in a pioneering ethnography by Baldwin Spencer and Francis Gillen (1899). In forcing him to rethink things, it sparked off a creative process that gradually brought together various developing ideas in a whole new landscape. It took him over five years to come up with a draft of the eventual work, in a lecture-course begun in 1906 on religion and its origins (1907). It took almost another five years to produce a final manuscript, essentially complete in 1911 and with the publisher early in 1912.[2] In the draft and again the eventual work, a key project is to dig around in the early and elementary but with the aim of unearthing the continuing and elemental. So in asking about a work that in terms of its own aims might be understood as *The Elemental Forms*, a key question is what, in the end, it identifies as universals of social and religious life. But given Durkheim's hopes in how to discover these, this question is bound up with his story of the early and elementary itself.

'In the Beginning'

Durkheim's thesis on the division of labour (1893) posits religion and society as originally fused together in worlds based on the clan, and his paradigmatic case of these worlds is ancient Israel. The essay that launched his new journal comes with the same essential picture, but with two significant changes. The religion that in the beginning permeates clan-based social worlds is now identified as totemism, and his paradigmatic case of these worlds has now become Australia. The significance of the changes is that they so closely link his theory with the ethnography not only of totemism, but totemism in Australia.

His thesis has a single brief mention of a study of Australia and says nothing about totemism. In a revision that is often unnoticed, a later edition inserts a reference to totemism (1902b: 273) while also quietly deleting passages setting out an earlier story of the first stages of religion. On the contrary, as very publicly announced in his new flagship journal, the first religion is totemism. Why had he become so attracted to this view of religion's origins?

In the essay launching his journal, the reference he approvingly cites again and again as a source of ethnographic information is James Frazer's *Totemism* (1887). This debt is something else that often goes unnoticed, overshadowed by Durkheim's subsequent, more famous disagreements with Frazer. Yet it helps to explain these disagreements, in helping to explain why Durkheim was so attracted to the view that totemism is the earliest religion. According to his future adversary's old ethnographic manual, totemism is 'both a religion and a social system', and although it is impossible to say with certainty, 'the evidence points strongly to the conclusion that the two sides were originally inseparable' (Frazer 1887: 3).

The situation was transformed, however, by Spencer and Gillen's *The Native Tribes of Central Australia.* Based on fieldwork among a people they called the Arunta, it was published in London in 1899, where its impact was immediate. Part of the reason was the patronage of Frazer, who organized its launch at a meeting of the Anthropological Institute to spread word of its significance.[3] Another reason was the impressive nature of Spencer and Gillen's research itself. Commentators remarked on the detail of their reports, on their access to sacred, hitherto unobserved ceremonies and on how they were 'fully initiated members of the Arunta'.[4] This perception was not altogether accurate. Nor did they really know the language of the Arunta, or live among them in a way that would nowadays count as participant observation. It remains the case that their fieldwork was seen as pioneering in the context of the time.

It is also only in the context of the time that it is possible to understand the importance of their news from Australia. Frazer explained, at the book's launch, how it changed his entire approach thanks to its 'momentous discoveries' (1899: 286). Indeed, it was with his blessing that his old theory of how totemism originally combined 'both a religious and a social aspect' was quoted, only to be rejected in a paper by Spencer (1899: 275). The work itself explains that the unit of ordinary everyday life among the Arunta is not the so-called 'clan', a term abandoned as misleading (Spencer and Gillen 1899: 59), but the group that, along with its other roles, is centrally involved in the regulation of marriage, in which 'the question of totem has nothing to do with the matter' (1899: 116). A general conclusion is that the Arunta represent an early way of life in which totemism is a magico-religious rather than a social affair. In the beginning, these two aspects are separate.

But the work's impact was perhaps best summarized by an independent eminent reviewer, Sidney Hartland (1899: 238): it turned previous ideas of totemism 'topsy-turvy', and 'we shall have enough ado to reconstruct the theory so as to make it fit the newly discovered facts'. This was the shock news from Australia, which then made its way from London to Paris. Durkheim's initial public response to Spencer and Gillen's ethnography came in a grudging review in which, unlike Frazer, he remained determined to hang on to an old theory. But he ended with the remark that their work was 'rich in materials' (1900a: 336). The years that followed involved a long effort to go through their material and reconstruct his theory.

Re-explorations

Spencer and Gillen followed up their study of 1899 with another in 1904. Taken together, the two studies constitute overwhelmingly the main ethnographic reference in *The Elemental Forms*. In various essays, Durkheim had tried various ways to tackle their news from Australia. But it was his lecture-course of 1906/1907 that for the first time came with the landscape characteristic of the eventual work. Moreover, instead of assuming the route to this was straight and direct, it can be seen as involving three different possibilities. Although his essay of 1902 on totemism suggests a project on religion, his essay of 1903 on primitive classification – co-authored with Mauss – suggests a project on basic forms of thought, and his essay of 1905 on matrimonial organization in Australia suggests a project on elementary structures of kinship.

The essay on totemism is still essentially defensive and repeatedly restates his old theory of how, in the beginning, religion and society were fused together in worlds of the clan. But it comes with the stirrings of two new ideas. One is towards recognition of a positive cult of joining together in communion, at the heart of religious life. The other is towards re-conceptualization of the sacred as an elemental 'force', 'energy' or 'power' (both *pouvoir* and *puissance*, so that it is in fact in a developing Durkheimian discourse of four interrelated terms).

His earlier essay on the definition of religious phenomena (1899a), far from distinguishing a positive from a negative cult, can seem preoccupied with the sacred as the set apart and forbidden. Indeed, in the essay on totemism, he himself confesses he had previously regarded it as a negative affair of taboos and was unaware of positive elements, but declares: 'from now on, this ignorance is at an end' (1902a: 116). What he especially had in mind was Spencer and Gillen's detailed material on the rite of the *intichiuma*, which his lecture-course then went on to develop into an account of 'the positive cult' (1907: 118–22).

His move towards an idea of the sacred as some sort of elemental 'force' is less obvious and more problematic. His earlier essay on the definition of religious phenomena had discussed the idea of 'extraordinarily intense forces' and 'energies', but only to block off and reject it as a key constitutive characteristic of religion (1899a: 19). The essay was instead preoccupied with the sacred as an affair of 'things' and, in the case of totemism, had identified the pre-eminently sacred thing as the totemic species itself. Now, his pre-eminently sacred thing has become the sacred symbolic object that Spencer and Gillen described as the *churinga*. At the same time, and without fanfare, he talks of the *churinga* as a container of 'guardian forces' or, again, as a focus of 'mysterious forces' (1902a: 93, 118). But this is not to assert a clear-cut belief in them: the Arunta have only a 'confused representation' of these 'religious forces' (1902a: 87). A problem that he fails to mention but that can help to explain the confused representations is the difficulty of finding any report of belief in such forces in Spencer and Gillen. The question, in other words, is how Durkheim himself came up with the idea, since it does not come from his ethnographic source.

An answer can be found in a much discussed article published in the wake of Spencer and Gillen by the Oxford anthropologist Robert Marett in 1900, which argued that the way to make sense of early religion was through the notion of an elemental force or power. A subsequent article unearthed Spencer and Gillen's report of a particular evil force called *arungquiltha* to link it with the ethnographically well-documented Melanesian idea of a general force called *mana* (Marett 1904: 60–61). In turn, an influential paper converted *mana* into an anthropological term for a whole type of belief in a whole range of societies (Marett 1908). Meanwhile, Durkheim's nephew had also linked *arungquiltha* with *mana* (Mauss 1904: 326, 368–69). From this and other evidence it is apparent that Marett and Mauss were heading in the same direction, towards *mana* as a comparative term for belief in a vast protean force, energy or power. Their work's joint impact on the anthropology of the time is the context of Durkheim's own use of *mana* in this way in the lectures of 1906/1907 and again in *The Elemental Forms* itself.

Another development involves the changing fortunes of effervescence, but together with interest in two times rather than merely two worlds of the sacred and profane. Thus the idea of effervescence has a long yet chequered Durkheimian history. The idea can be traced back to 1890, but what seems so far the first occasion of Durkheim's use of the actual term is in a lecture of 1896, which describes a pathological 'state of unruliness, effervescence and manic agitation' (1928: 297). Both the idea and the term are used in unambiguously negative ways in other texts of the period as well (for example, 1897: 408, 422). In a different case, already noted, Durkheim actively ruled out effervescence as a key constitutive characteristic of religion (1899a: 19). This was also when he first came across, but did not take up and develop, clear-cut cases of two times of the sacred and profane (1899b: 309;

1900b: 336) – a lesson, then, that it is a mistake just to hail the first
sighting of a particular idea. It is also necessary to track the career of
a number of ideas and chart how they begin to join together in a new
theoretical whole.

In the case of effervescence, a switch towards a positive, central
theoretical interest in it is signalled in an obscure, minor review.
Durkheim comments on the French Revolution to emphasize how
the 'effervescence and collective enthusiasm' of such a 'creative era'
necessarily took on 'a religious character' (1905b: 382). This is about
mould-breaking, momentous times, rather than an established calendar's regularly recurring, periodic times. But these two aspects of
effervescence were becoming interwoven in Durkheimian theory. Momentous times are embedded in collective memory through recall in
rites of a calendar's periodic times.

In an essay on the collective representation of time, Mauss's close
colleague, Henri Hubert, had just explored the nature and structure
of calendars in detail (Hubert: 1905). This is also one of the concerns
in an essay on seasonal variations among the Eskimo by Mauss himself (1906). For his part, Durkheim had some years ago encountered,
but not exploited, well-documented cases of alternating times of the
sacred and profane. The intellectual context had now changed, however, thanks to the collaborative work of his group as a whole. In his
nephew's essay, the idea of two times of the sacred and profane at
last surfaces as a theoretically central Durkheimian interest. Summer among the Eskimo is a time of individualistic dispersal and the
ordinary mundane business of life, while winter is a time of non-stop
religion and 'a season when the society, densely concentrated, is in a
continuous state of effervescence' (Mauss 1906: 125). The idea re-
appears in the lecture-course that Durkheim began the same year,
where it is applied to Australia and incorporated within a new overall
theoretical landscape. However, there are particular reasons why the
idea of two times of the sacred and profane is a key to understanding
his creation of *The Elemental Forms*.

First, it is a way of tackling an internally generated paradox within
his developing theory itself. His universal dualism of the sacred and
profane was originally announced in his essay on the definition of
religious phenomena (1899a: 19). Yet he went on to conceptualize
the sacred as an energy with the power to spread everywhere and per-
meate everything. How is it possible to hold on to his dualism, then, if
the sacred can spread everywhere and leave nothing profane? What
is involved is 'a sort of contradiction' (1912: 454). The idea of two
times rather than merely two worlds of the sacred and profane is a key

to this, since it locates the source of the sacred's energy in special effervescent times while erecting barriers to its spread everywhere and complete permeation of everything in routine times.

But also and not least, the idea is a way of tackling the externally generated problem of Spencer and Gillen's news from Australia. It makes it possible to concede that the totemic group might lack importance in ordinary times yet also to assert that it remains the centre of socio-religious life thanks to its pre-eminent role in the great communal rites, social renewal and effervescence of special times.

Writing Up

In writing up *Les Formes*, Durkheim kept to the same basic plan he had laid down in his lecture-course of 1906/1907. This constitutes a draft of the final text and, after an introduction, goes over in outline but in the same order the material of what became Book I, Book II and Book III's two opening chapters on a negative cult and on sacrifice as a rite of the positive cult. It then has a brief conclusion, concerned with a modern crisis and what is 'eternal' in religion (1907: 122).

An obvious type of change in writing up is that Durkheim added, after the account of sacrifice, a mass of further material on rites and also expanded the overall conclusion. Another type of change involves an extensive elaboration of the draft's interest in elemental forms of thought, such as the basic general notion of a 'force' and the idea of causality (1907: 93). But instead of creating a separate part of the work on this interest, he interwove sections on it within accounts of religious life itself, such as Book II's chapter on the soul and Book III's chapters on rites. Finally, and distinct from these types of change, he made innumerable revisions to material already outlined in his draft. Indeed, it is a formidable task to check through all of them, and variations with far-reaching significance can be easy to miss.

In the case of Book III's expansion, the draft had ended with an account of sacrifice but also with a contrast between ritual's 'physical' and 'moral' efficacy: 'The profound moral efficacy of the rite determines belief in its physical efficacy, which is illusory' (1907: 122). The work transfers this remark to the new chapter that follows, on what is discussed as the mimetic rite: 'The moral efficacy of the rite, which is real, has driven belief in its physical efficacy, which is imaginary' (1912: 513). But the remark's relocation also prepares the way for the rite that is next on the agenda and how it is very different. Variously discussed as a representative, commemorative and dramatic rite, it is singled out as of 'exceptional importance' (1912: 542). This is because it involves little or no belief in an imagined physical efficacy, and is instead understood by the faithful themselves in essentially social and moral terms. There is no notion of such a ritual in the draft: it is a new, theoretically crucial piece of evidence for Durkheim's own understanding of religion as a social affair, introduced in writing up the work itself.

In the case of elemental forms of thought, both the draft and the work draw on Durkheim and Mauss's essay of 1903 and its concern with both universalities of thought and an evolution from 'primitive' to 'modern' styles of thought. This concern, outlined in the centrepiece of the draft, keeps pride of place in the centrepiece of the work. Moreover, in both the draft and the work, but in contrast with the essay of 1903, it is the creative energy of effervescent times that helps to give birth to the whole realm of logical and conceptual thought. Another development, not in the draft but in the work, builds on the earlier essay's set of distinctions between primitive and modern styles of thought by adding a further dimension. Modern thought is 'nuanced', while primitive thought 'seeks extremes': 'when it makes links, it sees a total identity; when it makes distinctions, it sees a total opposition' (1912: 342). But all along, in the essay, in the draft of the eventual work and in the work itself, Durkheim insists on universalities of every style of thought. Indeed – and perhaps to underline opposition to the idea of a 'pre-logical' primitive mentality in a then just-published book by Lucien Lévy-Bruhl (1910) – the work is especially emphatic in its denial of a 'gulf' between modern and primitive ways of thinking. On the contrary, 'our logic was born from their logic' and 'they are made with the same essential elements' (Durkheim 1912: 340–42).

Bound up with these questions of universality, a concern already noted is with the elemental notion of a 'force', 'energy' or 'power'. The idea is highlighted in the centrepiece of the draft and again in the centrepiece of the work. An account of its different manifestations is then interwoven into Book III's chapters on rites. This begins with time, understood in terms of periodic upsurges of energy in rhythms of social life and rites of its renewal. It next deals with causality, understood in terms of forces at work in the necessary connections of an underlying logic of things. It then moves on to creativity, in the section on art in the chapter on a rite of 'exceptional importance'. Creativity might not be a conventional philosophical category, yet is fundamental to Durkheim's concern with society's creation and re-creation through effervescent energies, which include what he describes, in his discussion of art, as the creative energies of a 'surplus' (1912: 545). In sum, although the draft prepares the ground, a significantly new development in the work explores expressions of the same many-sided power in time, causality and creativity.

As for the other changes, three, each with far-reaching implications, will be mentioned here. In the draft and again in the work, the account of the soul comes with a major theoretical statement of the relationship between the individual and society, and also concerns a 'dualism' or 'duality' of human nature. Thus in both the draft and the work, Durkheim goes on from an account of the 'totemic principle' or mana to identify the soul as this impersonal, collective power incarnated in each individual. Or rather, as in the draft, the soul is this power incarnated in individuals and 'individualizing itself' in them (1907: 106). The remark, though very brief and not altogether clear, could be seen as the basis of a longer, repeated, explicit argument in the work. It insists on a simultaneous emergence and individualization of collective forces, in the process of internalization on which their existence depends (1912: 356, 382). This position implies the impossibility of forces that are purely collective in nature, but also the mistake of picturing the collective as prior to the individual in the sense that it is prior in time. So a further implication is that the argument requires a search for other ways to claim a priority of the collective. Alternatively, it means dropping the claim, but this might not seem very Durkheimian.

The next two points can be discussed together. The draft repeats Durkheim's long-running view, going back to his thesis on the division of labour, that religion, with its gods, 'symbolically expresses' society (1907: 99). But the conclusion incorporates the similarly long-running view, traceable to his thesis, that 'it is not a necessity of human life' to represent society in this way (1907: 122). The work, though often also just talking of religion as an 'expression' of society, comes with a new, radically different argument. Perhaps it arose while writing up, from thinking through implications of an idea of effervescence that had become central. In any case, its thrust is that the tumultuous energies creating the sacred simultaneously create society and in the process transfigure it. Here the sacred is still seen as an expression of the social, but now the reason is that it expresses society since involved in creating it. Or rather, it is a symbolic expression of society since society is made possible by the creative and transfigurative energies of effervescence. So, in contrast with the draft's belief in a sociology that keeps the way open to a world of enlightenment, does the work's new argument commit it to a sociology of an inevitable mystification?

Although many passages suggest Durkheim's continuing attachment to a sociology of enlightenment, an issue is not just the author's intentions but the work's arguments themselves. Or rather, it is partly a problem of how to interpret its discourse of 'transfiguration', and if this is always about forces of mystification or, alternatively, its underlying, essential concern is with energies of society's renewal and transformation. In turn, this involves interpretation of the 'society' at stake and attention to the work's conclusion. It emphasizes the importance for social life of representations of actual social relations in which these are not only schematized but are accorded a higher value, so that, indeed, there is a 'double' idealization (1912: 603). What also seems involved, in the work's move to a conclusion, is a move away from preoccupation with the sacred towards concern with the ideal. A crucial argument is that 'a society can neither create nor recreate itself without, in the same action, creating an ideal' (1912: 603). Perhaps this is a key to a revised version, in the work, of the draft's hope in the possibility of moving towards a world of enlightenment. Much still needs to be done to tackle the arguments that point instead to the social world's inevitable mystification.

A Problematic Achievement

A way to begin, in exploring the achievement of a work intended above all as a work of science, is to explore the relation in it between theory and 'facts'. A way to continue, given its basic method and aims, is to address a set of issues through an underlying, thematic problem of trying to distinguish, from the 'elementary', what might in the end be understood as the 'elemental'. A way to conclude, in acknowledging the work's range of interests, is to keep in sight its concern with action for reform in a present-day time of crisis and 'moral mediocrity' (1912: 610).

Theory and 'Facts'

Studies of the 'historical' Durkheim have tended to focus on his arguments with other theorists, and to pay less attention to ethnographies that formed a key part of overall debates. His essays of 1902, 1903 and 1905 drew extensively on Spencer and Gillen, prompting Spencer to comment: 'Sometime I must certainly have a go at Durkheim. ... He does not I think deliberately distort things in order to make them fit in with any theory of his own. He simply does not understand matters' (Spencer, letter of 1906, in Mulvaney and Calaby 1985: 394). However, he never had his 'go at Durkheim', or at least never seems to have responded publicly to *The Elemental Forms*. In an update of the earlier study of the Arunta (Spencer 1927), he says nothing about Durkheim or his theories and instead targets a rival ethnographer, Carl Strehlow.

In 1907, just after Durkheim finished the draft of his eventual work, Strehlow started to publish a series of studies of the people made anthropologically famous as the Arunta (Strehlow 1907–11). But he re-described them as the Aranda, in a set of detailed attacks on Spencer and Gillen, and was attacked in turn in what became a bitter dispute.[5.] As to how Durkheim himself handled the situation, a basic pattern is that his eventual work draws on or disregards Strehlow's ethnography in line with the new theory he had already begun to create in the draft. Originally sparked off by the challenge of Spencer and Gillen, the theory had by now acquired its own internal momentum. In selecting examples of what is at stake, I will concentrate on Book II's search for mana in Australia and Book III's discovery of a rite of 'exceptional importance'.

On checking through Durkheim's references to ethnographic sources, it emerges that many are accurate enough, many are erroneous and many are seriously misleading – or at least it might be thought misleading to cite a reference as if it reports what it does not report. This is what happens when he builds up his case for an Australian notion of a force like mana. For example, a reference supposed to describe such a force describes nothing of the kind and simply says that food restrictions 'seem to be done away with in the instance of very old men; they may eat anything, but this only when they are really very old and their hair is turning white' (Spencer and Gillen 1904: 167–168). Durkheim may have been both convinced and sincere in inferring from such material an underlying notion of a force that in his view makes sense of what is described. But he gives readers the impression of solid ethnographic 'facts', instead of explaining to them, as in these cases, that he is only making inferences from the available material.

In other cases, however, he makes clearer to readers what he is doing, as when he makes perhaps his boldest inference of all about a notion of a vast force. Located in the work's centrepiece, it suggests that the extraordinary collective effervescent energy of special times is what gives rise to 'the religious idea' (1912: 313). The inference, then, is that it is impossible for such explosions of energy to take place without also generating the notion of a vast power itself. And it is a fair enough inference to draw from the 'scenes of the wildest excitement' reported by Spencer and Gillen (1904: 237). Although Durkheim is

sometimes accused of wild exaggeration in his description of effervescence, perhaps it is because his critics have not read what he read. On
occasion, he touches up what Spencer and Gillen in fact say, but he
also, on occasion, tones it down. On the whole, however, he is quite
faithful to their account of such scenes.

At the same time, it is worth noticing something else about this star
case of effervescence, situated at the centre of the work. It is based
on Spencer and Gillen's account of the ceremony among the Warra-
munga that is also the basis of Book III's key case of a rite understood
by the faithful themselves in essentially social and moral terms. As the
ethnographers report, the rite is concerned with the great ancestral
snake, Wollunqua, and they suggest that the real, underlying motive
is to control and placate the snake. But they emphasize it is their own
interpretation of the purpose of the ceremonies: 'the natives have no
very definite idea in regard to this, merely saying that it pleases the
Wollunqua when they are performed and displeases him when they
are not' (Spencer and Gillen 1904: 227–28). In other words, the ethnographers have no hard evidence of the rite as anything other than
as described in detail in their account, namely, a way to enact, recall
and bring to life a sacred history. The way is in turn open to Durkheim
to insist:

> Here, then, is a whole set of ceremonies that are solely intended to
> arouse certain ideas and sentiments, to connect the present with the
> past and the individual with the collectivity. In fact, not only can they
> serve no other ends but the faithful themselves ask nothing more from
> them. (1912: 541)

Yet like other rites – at least in terms of Durkheim's own theory, if
not Spencer and Gillen's ethnography – the ceremony is presumably
still shot through with religious belief in a vast force, energy or power,
for it is precisely the rite that, in the work's centrepiece, gives birth to
the religious idea. But what might now be discussed as sacred drama,
thanks to its enactment of sacred myth, can still be seen as special.
It is at core an existentialist rite, in that it is less a means of effecting
particular practical concerns than an effort to reflect on a whole hu-
man-divine relationship. Its enactment of myth is of what Durkheim
describes as 'an ethic and a cosmology at the same time as a history',
and the point is not only to bring myth to life but to keep it alive in new
enactments that 'revitalize the most essential elements of the collective consciousness' (1912: 536).

The rite is also special because, reappearing in Book III as sacred
drama, it is his paradigmatic case of art and introduces his sketch of
an entire general theory of aesthetics. But the same rite, in its first

appearance in the centrepiece, is his paradigmatic case of effervescence and introduces his sketch of a general theory of symbolism. So although the centrepiece's account implicitly includes art, it is incomplete without bringing art in explicitly, which finally happens over two hundred pages later. An issue at stake here – and elsewhere in the work – is Durkheim's simultaneous reinterpretation and reorganization of his main ethnographic source's material. In each of their two studies, Spencer and Gillen not only conclude with a long chapter on the art and aesthetic achievements of Australian peoples, but also weave symbolism and art together in their accounts of particular sacred ceremonies and particular sacred objects with key roles in these rites. In contrast, Durkheim reorganizes symbolism and art within a structure that can suggest their radical separation, potentially encouraging readers to focus on religious life as if it is only a symbolism, when it is also, ineliminably, an aesthetics. Or as he himself eventually puts this, 'there is a poetry inherent in all religion' (1912: 546). Put another way, the energies of collective creative effervescence fuse together the power of assembly, the power of symbolism and the power of art.

Durkheim is commonly depicted as a dogmatic thinker who imposed a pre-existing theory on the facts and so had no need to visit Australia or anywhere else. But this picture itself lacks sensitivity to facts. Durkheim had little choice other than to re-explore Australia. Spencer and Gillen's ethnography, with its sensational impact in London, threatened the theory he had just set out in his new flagship journal of French social science. Indeed, a gap of well over five years separates the appearance of their first study in 1899 from the first known version of *The Elemental Forms* in 1906/1907. This was a time of experimentation, when he tried out various responses involving various projects, which could have resulted in three major works. But what counts – and as at last happens in the draft – is the coming together of a set of developing ideas in a whole new theoretical vision. In the process of writing up, this vision acquired an internal momentum of its own amounting to an intellectual effervescence. It is nonetheless abundantly evident that the need to revisit Spencer and Gillen's Australia was a major stimulus and driving force in the creation of this new theoretical vision.

It also emerges that Durkheim's representation of their Australia is not always particularly accurate or reliable. But in terms of the bigger picture, it is necessary to evaluate his active search through their material to find a way to keep together the aspects of the social and the religious they had separated, which in turn meant putting together and developing a new theoretical landscape. This had far-reaching implications across a range of issues and gave rise to a work of the creative scientific imagination that transformed Spencer and Gillen's Australia and left behind the old Durkheimian Australia.

The Individual, the Collective and
the Duality of Human Nature

Shortly after his new book came out, Durkheim presented a paper to a meeting of philosophers on the 'duality' of human nature (1913). The following year he published what became a famous article, on the 'dualism' of human nature and its social conditions (1914). His use of these terms has been examined in detail by Giovanni Paoletti (2012). To clarify what is at stake, and drawing on Paoletti,[6] it might help to make a number of suggestions. The first is to talk of Durkheim's concern with a 'dualism' as concern with a *belief* that human nature is double. However, he not only saw this belief as more or less universal, but maintained it is universal because it has a basis in the *fact* that human nature is in some way double. So the next suggestion is to distinguish two ways in which this might be the case, by talking of one as a 'substantivist' and the other as a 'relational' doubleness. In the substantivist version, there are two beings or two entities that in a sense are only contingently co-present, since a possibility is that one could exist independent of the other. In the relational version, there are two elements or sets of elements that are inseparably bound up with one another, not only in every human world but in any vision of a human world. A final suggestion is to talk of relational doubleness as a 'duality'. As already emphasized, Durkheim continued to develop his ideas, and these developments include his ideas on how a universal dualistic belief has a basis in the reality of some sort of doubleness. But he increasingly tended towards a relational doubleness – that is, a duality – of human nature, in concerns focused on understanding the elements of this duality.

A crucial development, in writing up his new book, was the argument in which the very existence of collective forces depends on a simultaneous process of their internalization and individualization (1912: 382). His question, then, is what might operate in the collective's internalization as the 'factor of individuation', and his answer is that 'it is the body that plays this role' (1912: 386). However, one possible objection to this apparent attempt to correlate embodiedness and individuation is that embodiedness is an important source of collective life; another is that society is an important source of individuation. Moreover, both objections can be raised in terms of his own sociology itself.

In the work's centrepiece, the energy of collective effervescence is characterized as a 'bodily and mental' high (1912: 310). In a discussion that elaborates on this and explains how social life is made possible 'only thanks to a vast symbolism', the symbol is characterized as a 'material intermediary' between the individual's world of sense-data and society's realm of conceptual thought (1912: 330–31). Thus, at the core of the work, embodiedness is an artery and vital channel of collective life. In turn, society is a key factor of individuation, at least according to Durkheim himself in his thesis on the division of labour and he cites its re-edition of 1911 in re-endorsing it on this issue in his new book (1912: 390). Moreover, his duality of human nature requires analysis in terms not only of the individual and collective but also a set of interrelated dimensions and perspectives. Indeed, in the case of what still seems his major concern with the dimension of the individual and collective, from one viewpoint it is a duality of society itself, while from another it is a duality of the personality. From both viewpoints, even so, it is a duality of a set of dimensions. At the same time this involves the issue of whether or not they stack up and align with one another.

Durkheim's argument about god as society draws on a theological discourse to talk of a power that is simultaneously immanent and transcendent: it is both a deep-rooted presence within the lives of individuals, and over and beyond everyone. This aligns the individual with the immanent and the collective with the transcendent, from a viewpoint in which the duality of a one-and-manifold power is society, religiously expressed as god. But from another viewpoint it is a duality of the personality, religiously expressed as the soul. In Durkheim's Australia, the soul is '*mana* individualized' (1912: 378), and introduces a complex discussion of the relation between the individual, the person and the personality. This involves, among other things, an alignment of the individual with what is different and particular about each personality, and an alignment of the person with what is shared and impersonal, not least the realm of conceptual thought (1912: 387–90). In sum so far, and whether as a duality of society or of the personality, it aligns the dimensions of the individual-particular-immanent vis-à-vis those of the collective-impersonal-transcendent. However, what might be seen as his paradigmatic case of relational doubleness is the duality of the sacred and profane.

A long-running Durkheimian effort looks for a way to appreciate the importance of the individual while nonetheless emphasizing, and in a sense prioritizing, the collective. On the one hand, then, his new argument about a simultaneous formation and individualization of collective forces more or less rules out a priority of the collective in time. On the other, he remained attached to socio-historical explanation and opposed Kantian appeals to a realm of the a priori that is empirically inexplicable but necessary to postulate. So although he remarks at one point that the collective is prior in a 'logical' sense (1912: 382), developing this point further risks coming too close for comfort to doctrines of the a priori that he rejected as mystical. In any case, the issue was now bound up with his commitment to human nature's relational doubleness. And a general challenge in working with a duality is how it can make sense to single out one of a set of inseparably interrelated components as somehow more important or fundamental and as having a priority.

Perhaps the Durkheimian key to this problem is that a priority clearly seems built into his paradigmatic duality of the sacred and profane, which can transfer, through alignment, to his duality of the individual and collective and its associated dimensions. Yet the sacred, in his own account, is a power that can criss-cross these dimensions, as, for instance, in his many Australian examples of sacralization of the body and bodily parts. Nor is it altogether satisfactory, in his concern with a modern cult of the person, to maintain it does not also sacralize individuals. No doubt the 'cult' must draw on a collective ideal of the force of reason and on a collective ethic of everyone's status as a person. But a basic point of this ideal and ethic is to invest individuals with respect as centres of autonomous thought and action.

Even so, a basic point of my own discussion is to indicate how working with a Durkheimian duality generates various particular questions as well as more general challenges. These include exploring the duality, at least to ask if and why it can assign priority to one of its elements, even or especially in the case of the sacred vis-à-vis the profane. But it is also essential to tackle the puzzle of a distinction that concentrates the sacred in special times and limits its impact on society in everyday times.

Varieties of Religious Life and a Paradox of the Sacred

Even if the scenes of frenzy in Durkheimian Australia constitute an elementary form of effervescence, a mistake is to assume they must also constitute its elemental form. More generally, even if the landscape of Durkheimian Australia constitutes an elementary form of social and religious life, a mistake is to assume it must also constitute its elemental form. Indeed, this is why it is important to recall his distinction in which primitive thought seeks extremes, while modern thought is nuanced. Applied to his own sociology, it requires an approach that disentangles the universal from varieties of religious life according to a variety of dimensions, such as the more collective versus the more individualistic, or the more emotive versus the more rational, or the more concrete versus the more abstract.

A more concrete style of religion tends to revolve around ritual, art and symbolism. A more abstract style tends to revolve around bare, naked belief. It is the first, more 'Catholic' style that might seem his work's star case of religion, as against the second and more 'Protestant'. The same applies to his concern with a modern secular religion, in which the work's star case is the French Revolution, complete with its new altars, rites, festivals and symbols (1912: 306). This contrasts with an earlier essay's concern with a modern secular cult of the person, in which he describes ritual and symbolism as 'superficial' and a mere 'external apparatus' of religion (1898b: 270). Even so, strands of the earlier essay's 'Protestantism' also run through the subsequent work. The centrepiece leads on from ritual and symbolism to culminate in a focus on conceptual thought. The next chapter, on the soul, culminates with a focus on the person that is again concerned with conceptual thought. Indeed, it comes with approving references to Kant, an exemplar of 'Protestantism', in a story of development towards a society of autonomous persons – the Durkheimian version of Kant's ideal of a kingdom of ends[7] – and of how 'we are all the more a person the more we are liberated from the senses, and the more we are capable of thinking and acting through concepts' (Durkheim 1912: 389).

But in a Durkheimian search for elemental forms of social and religious life, it is especially important to distinguish these from varieties of effervescence and different timescapes of the sacred and profane. Thus some cases of effervescence might be more emotive as well as more concrete in their use of ritual, art and symbolism, while some might be more intellectual in their excitement with abstract ideas. However, it also possible to draw on his distinction between different forms of the cult, some of which are more positive in their whole sense of elan, while some are more negative in an uplift through abstinence, pain, suffering and in general what he discusses as asceticism. He sees this as a characteristic of rites of initiation, which subject individuals to trials that qualify them as full participants in a society's realm of sacred life. But he also discusses a 'systematic asceticism' that is not for everyone or part of a standard religious career but instead is

practised by monks, hermits and other holy people who 'acquire a special sanctity through fasts, vigils, retreat and silence, in sum, through
privations' (1912: 445). This permanent, unflagging asceticism is a
form of permanent, intense communion with the divine. So it not only
contrasts with a lay world's breaks from the sacred in mundane times,
but also highlights the puzzle of why there is a lay, mundane world at
all, constituting a Durkheimian elemental form of social life yet somehow escaping the full-time grip of the vast power he sees religiously
expressed as god.

Whatever the theological explanations, his project entails a search
for the underlying social logic of what seems a contradiction. Yet does
he ever make clear a solution? Very generally, he is concerned with
an ebb and flow of social life's energies that rule out both a permanent state of monotony and a permanent state of effervescence. A
more specific clue is that it is especially the everyday business of work
that is interrupted and suspended during sacred times, since 'work is
the pre-eminent form of profane activity' (1912: 438). Another clue,
however, lies in the account of full-time specialized asceticism and
its full-time devotion to the divine. 'It is necessary that an elite sets
the goal too high, so that the crowd does not set it too low' (1912:
452). Rereading these clues in line with the work's overall theory, it
is possible to suggest and make explicit at least one of the keys to a
paradox of the sacred and its social understanding. Life in ordinary
times would aim too low, without the idealism of effervescent times
that sets sights so high.

To create a vision of a social world, there is a need to fence off
this activity and protect idealism from ordinary workaday life, with
its inevitable compromises. But things also go the other way, in that
there is a need to get on with mundane business, complete with its
compromises, and to protect it from an idealism that 'sets the goal too
high'. Yet without an impact on ordinary life, idealism, like the sacred,
would be good for nothing. To influence and spread to ordinary times,
idealism, like the sacred, requires the energies generated in special
times. Everyday rituals and everyday symbols – as well as the everyday
school of hard knocks – might do their bit. But everyday uplift is above
all based on the moments of inspiration and idealism in collective,
creative, effervescent times.

Transfiguration and Transparence

In the work's centrepiece, Durkheim cites the French Revolution as a
time of creative effervescence that not only generated a new secular

religion but also constitutes an actual case in which 'society and its essential ideas became the object of a genuine cult, directly and without transfiguration of any sort' (1912: 306). The message, in other words, is that it is not mere utopianism to envisage a world with enlightened understanding of itself, since history already provides an example of movement towards this ideal. Yet later on, in Book III's account of a rite that has exceptional importance since understood by the faithful themselves in social and moral terms, the discussion of art nonetheless comes with the notion of a 'surplus'.

> Although, as we have shown, religious thought is altogether different from a system of fictions, the realities with which it corresponds can acquire religious expression only if the imagination transfigures them. ... Because the intellectual forces that go into making it are intense and tumultuous, the task that just consists in expressing the real with the help of appropriate symbols is not enough to occupy them. A surplus remains generally available. (1912: 544–545)

In one reading, an elemental form of social life is its transfiguration through creative yet mystifying energies. In another, the underlying commitment is to the possibility of a world of transparence, developing an enlightened understanding of itself with the help of science and a bare, naked, rational discourse. Taking both readings together, the passage is a critical moment in the work's ambivalence between two sociologies, a sociology of transfiguration and a sociology of transparence.

A way out of the impasse is through a radical rethink involving exploration of an epistemological pluralism that gives up on privileging conceptual thought as the one and only path to enlightenment. In effect, it is to ask how it might be that transfiguration is also transparence. At stake here is not just the sacred as god, but the sacred as poetry and the role of art, in particular the existential rite of drama. At core, it is about thinking through the symbolic-aesthetic rather than only the conceptual, in a style of discourse that is thick-textured and concrete rather than thin-textured and abstract. But this is precisely why it can be both a powerful and illuminating way to reflect on the human situation and, in the process, on socially transformative ideals.

Moreover, a reason why it is important to ask how the transfigurative, transformative power of art might be a force for transparence is that art is an essential part of a wider public culture. This in turn is an essential part of any route to enlightenment, as against a reliance on science on its own. In Durkheim's overall work, it is possible to identify a set of three forms of enlightenment. Indeed, these can be found jostling together in a single page of his thesis on the division of labour (1893: 53 [1902b: 14–15]). In what I suggest calling esoteric enlightenment, the increasing specialization of science entails an increasingly secret knowledge confined to experts and inaccessible to the laity. A Durkheimian commitment, however, is to the active public role of science – not least, his new sociology – so that, in what might be called expert-led enlightenment, 'intelligence guided by science' is the way ahead. But in what might be called civic enlightenment, the overall processes going on in modern life itself entail that 'the field of consciousness, whether individual or social, becomes greater and clearer'.

In *The Elemental Forms*, the French Revolution is cast as a form of civic enlightenment in a vision of society's own effort to free itself from mystification and achieve social understanding that is part of public culture. Elsewhere in the work it is expert-led enlightenment that can seem to come to the fore. A striking example is the insistence in the conclusion that religion must increasingly submit to the critique of science, a 'rival power' with ever growing importance and indeed 'without it being possible to assign a limit to its future influence' (1912: 616). But in the end, the advance of this power depends on civic enlightenment, given an argument that applies across the board to include science as a specialized, esoteric knowledge. The argument, made in the centrepiece, then repeated in the conclusion, is essentially that the flourishing of science depends on the respect in which it is held in public opinion (1912: 298, 626). True, the idea of a public culture is not discussed explicitly, yet it is difficult, for example, to envisage religion's submission to the critique of science without an appreciation of science that is part of wider public culture's developing civic enlightenment. On the other hand, this can be taken as implicit in the argument, and also as an instance of how *The Elemental Forms* in many ways amounts to a work in progress, generating a range of issues requiring further exploration and even, in some cases, a radical rethink.

Conclusion: The Project of Durkheimian Social Science

In line with long-running Durkheimian concerns, the conclusion to *The Elemental Forms* worries about a present-day crisis and period of moral mediocrity in which idealism has fallen on hard times. Papering over the crisis with a bit of ritual and symbolism is not a solution. Greater forces are at work, and Durkheim once more recalls the French Revolution to look to another moment of collective creative effervescence for a renewal of social and moral life through a renewed upsurge of idealism (1912: 610–11). Yet in acknowledging that the Revolution's hopes had turned sour, he is vague about the explanation and why history might not just repeat itself. But an explanation can be found in a lecture-course of around 1905 and the time of the draft of his eventual work: 'Revolutionary effervescence was immensely creative of new ideas, but the Revolution did not know how to create organs that can give these life, institutions that can actualize them' (1938, vol. 2: 169).

In turn, this passage can be read as involving the campaign throughout his career for social and moral reform through the organization of a new web of intermediate occupational groups. He summarized the campaign in his preface to *The Division of Labour*'s edition of 1902, republished in 1911, the year he completed *The Elemental Forms*. This is a reason for reading the two together on what they say about a modern crisis and looking for a route out of it. Another reason is that Durkheim himself was preparing to draw these interests together, on the evidence of a manuscript that he was writing at his death in 1917 and that introduced the project of a new great work on *Ethics* (1920). It is centrally concerned with ideals, but also plans to bring in his material on organization through a new web of intermediate groups. In any case, there is a basic lesson in trying to draw his interests together ourselves, and in reflecting on the current, far-reaching contemporary crisis, which is not simply an economic but a social and moral crisis. Hopes for reform are likely once again to turn sour, without a web of new intermediate groups that can articulate the diffused, disorganized forces of public opinion and give them an effective, democratic voice. But the impetus for such reform depends on the pressures generated, in the crisis, by the energies of a new upsurge of idealism.

Durkheim's project for a social science, far from retreating to the stance of a spectator, is committed to participation in public debate on understanding a crisis and on the practical 'art' of charting a route to reform. This long-held view is forcibly expressed in the manuscript, at the end of his life, on *Ethics*:

> There is no science worthy of the name that is not ultimately a way to art: otherwise it would be a mere game, an intellectual amusement, erudition pure and simple. (1920: 317)

On the other hand, he was similarly adamant that science must stay true to itself to fulfil its public role. So it seems appropriate to conclude with some general thoughts on what this means in the case of the work he entitled *Les Formes élémentaires de la vie religieuse: le système totémique en Australie.*

Although Durkheim aimed to uncover continuing elemental forms of religious and social life, my own impression is that he became involved in the anthropology of Australia not just as a means to this end but as absorbing in itself. An example is his effort to crack the 'mathematics' and underlying 'logic' of highly complex kinship structures in his intellectually formidable essay on matrimonial organization in Australia (1905a). But a basic point, which I have tried to bring out, is that the simultaneously problematic and creative achievement of *The Elemental Forms* is inconceivable without his detailed engagement with the anthropology of Australia, in an attempt to defend old ideas that instead transformed them into a new theoretical landscape. This is also why, as suggested, the final version of *The Elemental Forms* is still, in a way, a work in progress. He himself continued to develop it, as evidenced by the recently rediscovered notes of the inaugural lecture that he gave in 1913 as the first Chair of Sociology in France, and that introduced his course on sociology and pragmatism (Durkheim 2012; Baciocchi and Fabiani 2012). In a sense the work's very character as an ongoing enquiry is at the bottom of its commemoration, and grounds our discussion a hundred years on.

Notes

1. This essay draws on a book (Watts Miller 2012), while also trying to clarify and develop some of its material.
2. Explaining why a study of 1911 could not be discussed, Durkheim says *Les Formes* was being finalized (1912: 130, n. 1). He gave the manuscript to Félix Alcan and signed a contract with him on 7 February 1912 (Borlandi 2012: 284).
3. On Frazer's influence, see the biography of Spencer by D.J. Mulvaney and J.H. Calaby (1985: 178–180, 185–186). On Spencer and Gillen's impact on the whole course of theoretical debate on totemism, see Frederico Rosa (2003).
4. See, for example, the anonymous reviews of Spencer and Gillen, both in 1899, in *Journal of the Anthropological Institute* n.s. 1: 330–332 and in *Notes and Queries* 9: 338–39.
5. See Mulvaney and Calaby (1985: 378–96).
6. I would like to thank Sondra Hausner for her critical but invaluable comments on an earlier draft of this section.
7. See Watts Miller (1996). Although Durkheim rejected Kantian doctrines of the a priori, he was sympathetic with Kantian ethics. It is misleading to picture him as a general opponent of Kantianism.

References

Baciocchi, S. and J.-L. Fabiani. 2012. 'Durkheim's Lost Argument (1895–1955): Critical Moves on Method and Truth', *Durkheimian Studies* 18: 19–40.

Borlandi, M. 2012. 'Présentation', in *Émile Durkheim: Les Formes élémentaires de la vie religieuse un siècle après*, edited by M. Borlandi, *L'Annee sociologique* 62 (2), pp. 283–88.

Durkheim, E. 1893. *De la Division du travail social*. Paris: Alcan (thesis, published commercially the same year with the subtitle *étude sur l'organisation des sociétés supérieures*).

———. 1897. *Le Suicide: étude de sociologie*. Paris: Alcan.

———. 1898a. 'La Prohibition de l'inceste et ses origines', *L'Année sociologique* 1: 1–70.

———. 1898b. 'L'Individualisme et les intellectuels', in Durkheim 1970, pp. 261–78.

———. 1899a. 'De la Définition des phénomènes religieux', *L'Année sociologique* 2: 1–28.

———. 1899b. Review of A. Hagelstange, *Süddeutsches Bauernleben im Mittelalter*, *L'Année sociologique* 2: 306–9.

———. 1900a. Review of B. Spencer and F. Gillen, *The Native Tribes of Central Australia*, *L'Année sociologique* 3: 330–36.

———. 1900b. Review of F. Boas, *The Social Organization and the Secret Societies of the Kwakiutl Indians*, *L'Année sociologique* 3: 336–40.

———. 1902a. 'Sur le totémisme', *L'Année sociologique* 5: 82–121.

———. 1902b. *De la Division du travail social*, 2nd ed. Paris: Alcan.

———. 1905a. 'Sur l'organisation matrimoniale des sociétés australiennes', *L'Année sociologique* 8: 118–47.

———. 1905b. Review of M. Pellison, *La Sécularisation de la morale au XVIIIe siècle*, *L'Année sociologique* 8: 381–82.

———. 1907. 'La religion: les origines', in Durkheim 1975, vol. 2: 65–122.

———. 1911. *De la Division du travail social*, 3rd ed. Paris: Alcan.

———. 1912. *Les Formes élémentaires de la vie religieuse: le système totémique en Australie*. Paris: Alcan.

———. 1913. 'Le Problème religieux et la dualité de la nature humaine', in Durkheim 1975, vol. 1: 23–59.

———. 1914. 'Le Dualisme de la nature humaine et ses conditions sociales', in Durkheim 1970, pp. 314–32.

———. 1920. 'Introduction à la morale', in Durkheim 1975, vol. 2: 313–31.

———. 1928. *Le Socialisme*, edited by M. Mauss. Paris: Alcan.

———. 1938. *L'Évolution pédagogique en France*, 2 vols, edited by M. Halbwachs. Paris: Alcan.

———. 1970. *La Science sociale et l'action*, edited by J.-C. Filloux. Paris: Presses Universitaires de France.

———. 1975. *Textes*, 3 vols, edited by V. Karady. Paris: Minuit.

———. 2012. 'Leçon inaugurale: Pragmatisme et Sociologie' (Inaugural Lecture: Pragmatism and Sociology, 1913), edited and translated by S. Baciocchi, J.-L. Fabiani and W. Watts Miller, *Durkheimian Studies* 18: 41–58.

Durkheim, E. and M. Mauss. 1903. 'De quelques formes primitives de classification: contribution à l'étude des représentations collectives', *L'Année sociologique* 6: 1–72.

Frazer, J. 1887. *Totemism*. Edinburgh: Adam & Charles Black.

———. 1899. 'Observations on Central Australian Totemism', *Journal of the Anthropological Institute* n.s. 1: 281–86.

Hartland, S. 1899. Review of B. Spencer and J. Gillen, *The Native Tribes of Central Australia*, *Folk-Lore* 10: 233–39.

Hubert, H. 1905. 'Étude sommaire de la représentation du temps dans la magie et la religion', *Annuaire de l'Ecole Pratique des Hautes Etudes, Section des Sciences Religieuses:* 1–39.

Lévy-Bruhl, L. 1910. *Les Fonctions mentales dans les sociétés inférieures*. Paris: Alcan.

Marett, R. 1900. 'Pre-animistic Religion', in Marett 1909, pp. 1–32.

———. 1904. 'From Spell to Prayer', in Marett 1909, pp. 33–84.

———. 1908. 'The Conception of *Mana*', in Marett 1909, pp. 115–41.

———. 1909. *The Threshold of Religion*. London: Methuen.

Mauss, M. 1904. 'L'Origine des pouvoirs magiques dans les sociétés australiennes', in Mauss 1969, vol. 2: 319–69.

———. 1906. 'Essai sur les variations saisonnières des sociétés eskimo', *L'Année sociologique* 9: 39–132.

———. 1969. *Œuvres*, 3 vols, edited by V. Karady. Paris: Minuit.

Mulvaney, D.J. and J.H. Calaby. 1985. *'So Much That Is New': Baldwin Spencer 1860–1929, A Biography*. Melbourne: University of Melbourne Press.

Paoletti, G. 2012. 'Durkheim's "Dualism of Human Nature": Personal Identity and Social Links', trans. A. Zhok and W. Watts Miller, *Durkheimian Studies* 18: 61–80.

Rosa, F. 2003. *L'Âge d'or du totémisme: histoire d'un débat anthropologique (1887–1929)*. Paris: CNRS Editions.

Spencer, B. 1899. 'Some Remarks on Totemism as applied to Australian Tribes', *Journal of the Anthropological Institute* n.s. 1: 275–80.

———. 1927. *The Arunta*, 2 vols. London: Macmillan.

Spencer, B. and F.J. Gillen. 1899. *The Native Tribes of Central Australia*. London: Macmillan.

———. 1904. *The Northern Tribes of Central Australia*. London: Macmillan.

Strehlow, C. 1907–1911. *Die Aranda- und Loritja-Stämme in Zentral-Australien*. Frankfurt am Main: Baer.

Watts Miller, W. 1996. *Durkheim, Morals and Modernity*. London: UCL Press.

———. 2012. *A Durkheimian Quest: Solidarity and the Sacred*. New York and Oxford: Berghahn Books.

CONTRIBUTORS

After studying classics and medicine, **N.J. Allen** qualified in social anthropology at Oxford, undertaking fieldwork in Nepal. He lectured at Durham and, from 1976 to 2001, at Oxford, where he became Reader in the Social Anthropology of South Asia. He has published on the Himalayas, kinship theory, the Durkheimian school and Indo-European cultural comparativism. The last three of these interests are represented in his *Categories and Classifications* (Berghahn, 2000); since retirement, still in Oxford, he has continued to concentrate on them.

Gerd Baumann (b. 1953) worked in and on the Sudan (*National Integration and Local Integrity*, OUP 1986) and then turned to studying multiculturalisms in practice (*Contesting Culture*, CUP 1993) and theory (*The Multicultural Riddle*, Routledge 1999). Since then, he has done fieldwork with rice farmers in the Guayanas and worked on (not for) the BBC World Service. He works at the University of Amsterdam and the Amsterdam Institute of Social Science Research.

Adam Yuet Chau is University Lecturer in the Anthropology of Modern China at the University of Cambridge. He received his Ph.D. in anthropology from Stanford University in 2001. He has researched the politics of religious revival in contemporary rural China and is interested in the conceptualization of religious practices both in today's China and historically. He is the author of *Miraculous Response: Doing Popular Religion in Contemporary China* (Stanford University Press, 2006) and editor of *Religion in Contemporary China: Revitalization and Innovation* (Routledge, 2011). He has also published articles in *Minsu quyi, Asian Anthropology, Modern China, Ethnology, Ethnos, Visual Studies, Past and Present, Religion* and the *Journal of Chinese Religions.*

Louise Child is Lecturer in the Department of Religious Studies and Theology at Cardiff University, U.K. Her thesis and first book, *Tantric Buddhism and Altered States of Consciousness* (Ashgate, 2007), explored ways in which the ideas of Durkheim and Jung could illuminate the study of visionary experiences and the consort relationship in tantric Buddhist ritual and biography. She is currently interested in tensions between portrayals of psychology and the sacred in contemporary western serial drama and film, and has published articles exploring a number of themes in this context, including possession trance, dreaming and ritual initiation.

Karen E. Fields, an independent scholar, holds degrees from Harvard University, Brandeis University and the Sorbonne. She is the author of many articles and three published books: *Revival and Rebellion in Colonial Central Africa* (PUP, 1985), about millennarianism; *Lemon Swamp and Other Places: A Carolina Memoir* (with Mamie Garvin Fields, Free Press, 1982), about life in the twentieth-century South and a retranslation of Emile Durkheim's masterpiece, *The Elementary Forms of Religious Life* (Free Press, 1995). Her fourth book, *Racecraft: The Soul of Inequality in American Life* (Verso, 2012), written with Barbara J. Fields, applies Durkheim's account of totemic clans to the phenomena Americans shorthand as 'race'.

Clive Gamble is Professor in the Faculty of Humanities, University of Southampton, where he is a member of its Centre for the Archaeology of Human Origins, which he founded in 2001. His recent projects include the British Academy's Centenary Project *From Lucy to Language: the Archaeology of the Social Brain* (2004–2011), which brought together archaeologists and psychologists to study when hominin brains became human minds. His recent research has examined the evolution of material culture; *Origins and Revolutions* was published in 2007. He is currently President of the Royal Anthropological Institute.

Sondra L. Hausner is Oxford's first University Lecturer in the Study of Religion. An anthropologist by training, she teaches social and cultural theories of religion in the Faculty of Theology and Religion at the University of Oxford. Her ethnographic work focuses on Himalayan and South Asian religions; she won the Joseph W. Elder Prize in the Social Sciences from the American Institute of Indian Studies for her Durkheim-inspired monograph *Wandering with Sadhus: Ascetics in the Hindu Himalayas* (IUP, 2007). She is Fellow and Tutor in the Study of Religion at St. Peter's College and a member of the British Centre for Durkheimian Studies.

Ji Zhe received his Ph.D. in sociology from École des Hautes Études en Sciences Sociales (Paris) in 2007. He is currently Assistant Professor at the Institut National des Langues et Civilisations Orientales, and Associated Research Fellow at the Groupe Sociétés, Religions, Laïcités in France. Chinese translator of *The Elementary Forms of the Religious Life* and other Durkheimian sociological works, he is also the author of articles on Buddhism, Confucianism, youth religiosity and sociological theory of religion in various academic journals and collections.

Paul Richards is a British anthropologist. He is Emeritus Professor of Wageningen University, The Netherlands, and adjunct Professor of the School of Environmental Studies at Njala University, Sierra Leone. He contributes an anthropological perspective to two large interdisciplinary research projects in West Africa, one focused on African rice and the other on the Gola forest in Liberia and Sierra Leone. His major publications include the books *Coping with Hunger* (Allen & Unwin, 1986) and *Fighting for the Rain Forest* (James Currey, 1996). In progress is a book (*The Emotions at War*) applying a neo-Durkheimian theory of ritual agency to patterns and processes of wartime atrocity in Sierra Leone.

Susan Stedman Jones received her first degree in philosophy and then studied postgraduate anthropology, both at University College, London. She completed a Ph.D. in philosophy (*From Kant to Durkheim*). Formerly Convenor of the Philosophy of Social Sciences course at Goldsmiths College, London University, she now pursues independent research, dividing her time between London and Paris. She is a member of the British Centre for Durkheimian Studies, Institute of Social and Cultural Anthropology, University of Oxford, and is on the editorial board of *Durkheimian Studies/Études Durkheimiennes.*

W. Watts Miller is editor of the journal *Durkheimian Studies* and a member of the British Centre for Durkheimian Studies, Oxford. His extensive writings on Durkheim include, most recently, *A Durkheimian Quest: Solidarity and the Sacred* (Berghahn 2012). His various translations of Durkheimian texts include, most recently, the newly discovered notes of the inaugural lecture of 1913 as the first Chair of Sociology in France (Durkheim 2012). He is also one of the international team collaborating, under the direction of Massimo Borlandi, on a critical edition of Durkheim's *Complete Works.*

INDEX

Lightning Source UK Ltd.
Milton Keynes UK
UKOW05f2057201116

288101UK00002B/21/P